MW00891030

Library of Congress Control Number: 2012910726
ISBN: Hardcover   978-1-4771-2883-1
               Softcover   978-1-4771-2882-4
               Ebook   978-1-4771-2884-8

This book was printed in the United States of America.

To order additional copies of this book, contact:

Xlibris Corporation
1-888-795-4274
www.Xlibris.com
Orders@Xlibris.com
116523

RUNNING WITH
GOD ACROSS
AMERICA

JEFF GRABOSKY

RUNNING WITH
GOD ACROSS
AMERICA

Reviews

Jeff Grabosky ran 3,700 miles across America to clear his head, put his life back together, and pray for the intentions of others. Along the way, he confronted a long and lonesome highway and his own rocky emotional terrain. This book is 'Zen and the Art of Motorcycle Maintenance' for believing Christians.
-Brett M. Decker, Editorial Page Editor, Washington Times

Jeff Grabosky is living proof that we can do all things through Christ who strengthens us (Phil 4:13). Powered by prayer, Jeff ran from despair to hope . . . and then A-Cross the entire country. His miraculous journey will inspire you to pray and believe that God-sized works can indeed be accomplished through us (1 Cor 3:6). As a lifetime Catholic runner, I felt called to meet Jeff when I discovered his route passed nearby in Illinois. Our meeting has God's fingerprints all over it. A high-five for Jeff's redemptive running (Heb 12:1-2)!
-Dr. Patrick Castle, LIFE Group president, National LIFE Runners coach http://liferunners.org

Can you imagine running across an entire continent, for the most part alone (along with 80 pounds of gear in a well-worn baby stroller)? Well you don't have to do it of course—or even just imagine it. You can experience this amazing physical and spiritual odyssey in the comfort of your easy chair by reading Jeff Grabosky's *Running with God across America*. As you can tell from his title though, Jeff was never really alone. Read this book to learn why he did it, how he did it, who he met, who he prayed for and with, and to learn how you too can be inspired to go that extra mile for God.
-Kevin Vost, Psy.D., author of Catholic books including *Memorize the Faith!* & *Three Irish Saints*

CONTENTS

PART I

Introduction

PART II

The Run

Dedication

To my father, Jerry
my late mother, Valerie
my sister, Kristina
and my brother, David

I am so blessed to be a part of a family
that has always believed in me

PART I

Introduction

CHAPTER ONE

You can only come to the morning through the shadows.

J. R. R. Tolkien

Nights were the worst. Each time the sun went down, a part of me hoped I would not be around when it came back up the following morning. I had never felt so lost and hopeless. The feeling of despair sank deeper with each passing moment, making it impossible to think I could ever be happy again.

Everything seemed to be working against me. On one particular December night in Chicago, I was even depressed about my height. I tried my best to stretch out my lanky, six-foot-three-inch body. It was no surprise that I was unable to get comfortable. My only escape from life was in my dreams, but I could not even manage to fall asleep. I cursed my height as I sat up to turn on the heat for a few minutes. It was useless. The numbing cold returned as soon as I removed the keys from the ignition and lay down again in the backseat of my Honda Civic. I curled up my legs and pulled my coat around me as tight as possible.

I had parked in a church parking lot for the night. I felt safe there. It was an effort to get as close to the Lord as possible. I felt abandoned in so many ways but held on to the hope that God would never leave my side. Everything I owned was in the car with me, but the only thing I truly possessed was a small amount of hope that things would get better. At that moment, I had a difficult time imagining how the situation could get any worse.

As I had done a hundred times already that night, I replayed in my mind how my life had fallen apart. It was difficult to think back to only a year earlier. I had married my girlfriend of three years and bought a house soon after the wedding. My parents and two siblings had all visited me in my new home. Working in auto insurance was not ideal, but my coworkers were awesome, and I earned a good living. My life was not perfect, but I was surrounded by those I loved. My outlook on life was very optimistic, and there were even plans of having kids one day. Life was good, and the future appeared bright.

I had always adored my wife and loved her very much. We met during my sophomore year at Notre Dame and instantly connected. We had a mutual love for sports, we made each other laugh, and we both played the saxophone. Both of us had been raised Catholic, but she had almost completely stopped going to Mass when I first met her. After we started dating, she began attending Mass with me each weekend. I loved how we talked about our faith together. I especially enjoyed seeing her become part of a local band after graduation. Our relationship was not without its flaws, and we certainly had our arguments, but we always worked things out. This led to our marriage in November of 2005.

By May, after only six months of marriage, I knew our relationship was in trouble. I saw the trouble began with alcohol. It was an issue our relationship faced before our marriage. At one point, my wife had given it up for a few weeks to prove to me she could go without it. However, it became a problem again and quickly progressed to drugs. I believed I was a coward because I stayed quiet on the issue too long. When I finally said something, it was too late. My wife abruptly stopped attending church. We became very distant from each other. The aching in my heart was ever present.

I was too ashamed to ask for outside help. Instead, I tried to be a better husband. I cleaned the house, mowed the lawn, cooked dinner, and did the laundry. I thought it would give us more time to be together. I told her I loved her every day. I even tried to show my support for her musical interests by attempting to help her book an event to play. Nothing worked. The distance between us continued to separate us from each other.

One night while sitting on the couch together, she told me she was thinking about a divorce. When I asked her if she would be open to marriage counseling, her response crushed me. She completely unloaded on me with statements that I imagined she had been holding in for some time. She told me that she was already in love with another man. I had suspected the person she was in love with, but to hear her say it broke my heart. She told me that she never took her faith or our wedding vows seriously. I stared blankly at my wife, wondering who I was talking to. I had no verbal response. I knew things were over by the look in her eyes. My calm demeanor fell apart when I nearly broke my hand as I punched a wall on my way out of the room.

For days, we avoided each other. I knew she wanted nothing to do with me. I did my best to make plans for how I could somehow save our marriage. There was no time to put those plans into place as I received a call only days later. It was a call no son ever wants to receive. My mother's liver was failing. She had been fighting cancer for five years, and her battle was about to come to an end. I flew home immediately to New Jersey to be with my family for her final days. I made it back there in time to pray with her. She said goodbye to each of us and told us she would be waiting for us in heaven.

I could not handle watching my mom slowly fade away in our living room over the final five days. I tried to see her in brief visits throughout day. I also tried to hold it together but would lose it as I drove around town, making all the preparations for her funeral. I secured her final resting place and made the arrangements for the wake. I could not stop the tears from streaming down my face as I picked out her casket. I was close to my mom, and it was excruciating to watch her die. I finally went into the living room one night and told her everything on my heart, even though I did not know if she could hear me. I told her how much I loved her and thanked her for being such a great example. I then gave her a kiss on the forehead and went upstairs to bed. I prayed that the Lord would take her so she could finally be in peace. Before I awoke on Sunday morning, she died as my dad finished praying the rosary with her one last time. I heard his slow, heavy footsteps coming up the stairs. I knew she was gone.

The following days were numbing. My siblings and I gave the eulogy. My wife came to the wake but was so cold to me and barely said hello. It made the day even more unbearable. I carried my mom's casket at the funeral and then finally said goodbye. On the night of the funeral, I talked to my wife over the phone. She told me that when I came home, she would be going through with the divorce.

I got on the plane the next day and headed back to our house. It was my hope she would have a change of heart, but that thought was far too optimistic. Within two weeks, there was a separation agreement drawn up, and I was out of the house. She told me I would be hearing from her lawyer about the divorce.

I could barely take care of myself. The feeling of sadness was so deep that it overwhelmed even my appetite. I often went the entire day without eating anything. I found a nearly finished apartment still under construction and put a deposit down on it. However, the landlord continued to tell me it would be ready the following week from the moment I met him—it never was ready to move in during the two months I waited. I had no energy to find another place and was worried about spending the money I had in case my wife came after me financially. As such, I spent the nights in my car. During the weekend, I would slide into the back row in church. I sat there, feeling incredibly lonely. I believed God was somewhere in my personal disaster. I prayed that I could see him anywhere within the troubles of my life. As hard as I tried, I did not see God in my life at the time. I held on to my faith for dear life as everything around me continued to come crashing down.

Eventually, some of my coworkers noticed I was in rough shape and let me stay on their couches while I figured things out. They were so kind to me during a time when my entire world was falling apart. Sometimes I was so ashamed of the situation that I would tell them I had a place to stay when I really did not. I was miserable and felt even worse for having such a bad attitude about life around such great people. This is how I ended up in my car for yet another cold night.

Since I could not sleep and was exhausted from repeating the recent events of my life in my mind, I decided to pray. I had so often asked God for things I thought I needed. It took a complete collapse of my life to bring me to the point of asking the Lord to place me where he wanted me to be. I meant it with all my heart. I desperately wanted to hear an answer to the prayer—I felt I had nothing else to live for but that answer.

CHAPTER TWO

Do not pray for easy lives. Pray to be stronger men.
Do not pray for tasks equal to your powers, pray for powers equal to
your task.

Phillips Brooks

I continued living through my daily battle while awaiting an answer to my prayer. I heard it loud and clear late in December when the landlord told me again that it would be much longer than he anticipated before the apartment would be completed. I told him I wanted my money back, and he obliged. I called my sister Kristina who was living in Alexandria, Virginia. She had a two-bedroom condo, and I asked if I could stay with her while I tried to piece my life back together. We had always been close, and she told me to move as soon as possible. After speaking with my employer, I was able to secure a transfer to an office in Alexandria. Things were coming together perfectly, and I felt as if the Lord's fingerprints were all over it.

I moved just after New Year's Day in 2007. I was so excited to see my sister after my long drive. It was priceless to be around family after the events of the previous few months. I was still very sad but already felt much better than at any moment since our mother had passed away. Kristina had a plan for me. She took me to sign up for a gym membership before driving me to the outskirts of Washington DC to go for a run.

I had been a runner in high school and had even run a marathon my senior year of college. However, my legs were very rusty. In the prior two years, I had run only a few times. I received a six-mile tour of DC on foot that day. My troubles were soon forgotten as I struggled for every step. At one point during the run, I prayed for strength because I did not think I would make it back to the car. I somehow finished the run and felt stronger for sticking it out during the times when my body wanted to quit. I thought that if I could get through the physical struggle of running, then perhaps I could also make it through the struggles of my life.

Instead of allowing the pain from running to act as a deterrent, I decided to embrace it. I ran through the heartache of the divorce. I ran through the difficulty of the annulment process. I did not run with music but rather prayed as I ran. Prayer was how I made it through both my runs and the frustrations of my life. I eventually tackled a marathon in 2008—something I had sworn to never do again after my first marathon four years earlier. I trained hard for it and raced with a purpose. The marathon was completed in memory of my mother, as I had raised money for cancer research during the months of training. Finishing that marathon changed my life. I did not race for myself but rather for my mother and anyone else who had to face cancer. The feeling was so powerful that upon crossing the finish line, my first thought was that I wanted to do more. The idea entered my mind that it would be awesome to run across America one day to bring attention to a cause. I knew it sounded crazy, but I simply filed it in my mind as something to consider in the future.

CHAPTER THREE

We must accept finite disappointment, but never lose infinite hope.
Martin Luther King Jr.

Ever since I first asked God to place me where I was needed, I had noticed yearnings in my heart to continue praying in that manner. The first prayer of that nature was a desperate cry for help in the middle of the night at a church parking lot. It was a catalyst for a stronger prayer life. I believed God had a plan for me, and I simply needed to follow the yearnings he placed in my heart. I desired to be close to the Lord and to follow his will. That is why I decided to change my life in the summer of 2008.

My job in the insurance business was going very well, and I loved my coworkers. However, I had entered the field to simply earn a living. During one of my weekend long runs, I felt a strong calling to leave my job. After more prayer and discernment, I followed my heart and resigned from my job to work as a camp counselor for the summer. Working with kids for two months was awesome, and I loved every minute of it. When the camp ended, the director told me that I should be a teacher or enter a field where I could work with children.

I made great friends at the camp and was sad to leave it behind. I was also nervous because I did not have another job lined up. Upon my arrival back in Virginia, I decided to start looking for a job as soon as I ran a race with my siblings. My brother Dave had moved to Alexandria over the summer, so the three of us were all together in one city. It was just two days after I returned home when Kristina, Dave, and I headed out to pick up our packets for the race. I had woken up that morning with a pain in my chest area but dismissed it as a phantom ache. However, when

I tried jogging across the street as we made our way to the packet pickup, I doubled over in pain. I knew something was not right.

My siblings took me to a nearby hospital, where I learned that my left lung had collapsed. The doctors cut into my side and reinflated my lung, but I had to stay overnight. I was upset I had to miss the race but was thankful to be in relatively good shape despite some lingering pain. I was not feeling great as I went for a follow-up visit a few days later. After taking an x-ray, I understood why I had not felt better. My lung had collapsed again. I was sent into surgery immediately, where they removed part of my lung and attached the rest of it to my chest cavity. I came out of surgery in a great deal of pain and spent the following week in intensive care as I recovered.

I received so many messages of encouragement and welcomed many visitors as well. My dad flew up from Florida, my sister and brother came to see me, and my former coworker Matt even showed up with pizza one day. I was happy to have so much support, but inside I was still trying to figure out my life. One of the nights in intensive care, my nurse asked me why I looked so sad. I told her that I was tired of seeing my dreams and hopes come crashing down.

I was very frustrated with the situation because I was unemployed, was in pain, and had missed out on racing after a summer of hard training. My prayers sounded more like begging in the days and weeks after the surgery. I yearned for a purpose in life. Eventually, I told the Lord once again to make my life an instrument of his peace. I no longer cared about my personal dreams. I felt that I was chasing my own ideas of success. Too often I was praying for God to make things in my life about my will. However, when Jesus taught us to pray, he instructed us to pray that God's will be done. I thought about this for some time and decided that I needed to pray to God for graces that would help me conform to his will. Even though I had recently made choices to detach myself from the world, it was not until this moment that I completely turned everything over to the Lord. I wanted God to use my life to display his grace and love. Once I made that prayer from my heart, my life began to change—drastically. God answered my prayer—and it turned out his plans for me were greater than any dreams of my own.

CHAPTER FOUR

How you think when you lose determines how long it will be until you win.

G. K. Chesterton

As the weeks after the surgery progressed, the incisions began to heal. I was still in pain, but I felt the urge to get out and walk. My doctor said I would eventually be able to run again, but that promise seemed a long way off as I stepped out the door to go for a walk. I mapped out a two-mile loop from my sister's condo and took those first painful steps. It was difficult not to feel defeated. I prayed for strength because it was clear that even a short distance was going to be a battle. My chest was tight, and it felt as though my body was forcing me to hunch forward. I had to stop a number of times to catch my breath and allow the pain to subside. After nearly forty minutes of walking, I finally returned to my starting point and collapsed on the floor. I was exhausted but was proud of myself for not giving up.

My goal was to get slightly faster each day. I pushed myself very hard and always returned home completely spent. It was extremely difficult, but I improved gradually and started to jog parts of the loop. Within two weeks, I was able to run the entire way. Each run of the loop was an all-out effort. I thought my days of running quickly were surely over but found great satisfaction in giving everything I had every day. I thanked God to be healthy enough to still be active. I realized life was a beautiful blessing, and I owed everything to the Lord.

Running was difficult, but it was the high point of each day as I continued to recover. My pace began to improve, but I kept all my runs under five miles for the next five weeks. The confidence I gained made me feel like I could do anything. I often prayed to God for direction in life during those runs. Almost as if God was sending me a direct answer, I felt called to do two specific things with my life.

I explained the callings to my family as something I believed I was supposed to do. The first yearning in my heart was to go after something big athletically. My mind drifted toward another marathon, but it did not feel quite right. I remembered hearing of some endurance runners who participated in one-hundred-mile ultra marathons. For some reason, my heart leaped with excitement. My legs had difficulty at the time running less than five miles, and I had only run two marathons in my life. The thought of running nearly four marathons in a row scared me very much. However, I believed it was something I was supposed to do. I found a one hundred miler on the weekend of my birthday—less than four months away. I started planning an intense training schedule and signed up for the race in mid-October.

The second calling I felt was to find a job I would enjoy as opposed to searching for one that paid well. Without hesitation, I started looking for a job in the running industry. I was fortunate to find a part-time job with Potomac River Running, a family-owned running store in the Washington DC area. The owners treated me like family from the start, and I made quick friends with the other employees at the store. It was an amazing feeling to actually love my job.

I also worked part-time for the Advancement Office at the Dominican House of Studies in Washington DC. Since it was located across the street from Catholic University, I was able to attend daily Mass at the crypt in the basilica. I felt like God was drawing me closer to him. While I did not know what the Lord had in store for me, I believed I was on his path. For the first time in over a year, I felt peace in my heart.

During the autumn season, I also moved into an apartment with my brother. It was located directly next to a running trail. I pounded out the miles during the limited amount of my free time. I had to break down so many mental and physical barriers during those months of training. Every time I felt as though I could go no further, I prayed. Prayer got me through a marathon distance training run in the beginning of November. It helped me conquer a thirty-mile training run on a cold and windy night in mid-November. I had a leg injury that kept my miles down during the winter, but I came back with a personal best time in a January marathon. One week later, I prayed my way through a thirty-eight-mile run, which was the furthest I had ever run. I then began to lower my mileage to prepare for the February race.

I traveled down to Texas for the race of my life. My stomach was in knots as I stood at the starting line. Some people had told me I would not be able to finish. I was only months removed from my lung incident, and my longest training run was only a little more than a third of the overall race distance. I said a quick prayer before it began. I asked the Lord to help me make it through because I did not think I could do it on my own. The reason I was at the starting line was because of my belief that for some reason, God wanted me there. It was a huge leap of faith, but I trusted in God. Suddenly, we were running on the dark trail. My battle was under way.

The race was brutal. I ran when I could and walked when I could not run. My goal was to finish before the thirty-hour cutoff. I fought pains, exhaustion, and failing muscles along the way. However, I kept my eyes on the finish and finally crossed the finish after twenty-eight grueling hours. Because of the date of the race and running overnight, I actually finished a year older than when I had begun. I turned twenty-six years old during the race but felt as though I had aged in wisdom beyond my years. My thought before the race was that I could do anything, as long as God was at my side. After finishing, I knew it was true.

I returned to Virginia feeling extremely proud of myself. I longed to share my feeling of accomplishment through the sport of running with others. Within six months after finishing the race, I was managing one of the running store location full time. Each day was awesome and a new experience. I loved helping people realize their goals, and each person I helped had a unique story as to why he or she was running. By the time autumn came around, I was coaching over thirty novice runners for a half-marathon through a charity program. I was so happy I could run the race with them in December. It was priceless to see the joy on the faces of my runners when they realized they were going to finish. It brought joy to my heart, knowing they had attained their goals.

The experience of running with the people I trained was so inspiring. I watched many of them overcome personal obstacles to reach the finish line. I was so invigorated by the experience that I decided to go for a twenty-one-mile run after returning home from the race. It felt great.

After my first ultra, I thought I was done with long races. However, I felt a restlessness in my life. The thought of running a one-hundred-mile race a second time was exciting and still scary. The same race I ran previous year was less than three months away. I knew it sounded odd, but it felt like I was supposed to run it again. I trained as hard as I could in those few months. I put in a forty-miler in December and a thirty-seven-miler in

January. By the time February came along, I was beyond excited for the race. It was another difficult race, but I was healthier and very confident. My coworker, Joan, acted as my pacer for miles 60 through 80. She also served as an amazing one-woman crew when I passed through an aid station every twenty miles. I went through a few tough stretches but finished nearly six hours faster than the previous year. I thanked God for all the blessings in my life and for being with me during another brutal run.

CHAPTER FIVE

What great thing would you attempt if you knew you could not fail?

Robert H. Schuller

My job managing one of Potomac River Running stores was awesome. I was confident I had found a place where I would be for a long time. The running scene was phenomenal, and I participated in a couple of spring marathons for fun. Racing was great, but it was the training I enjoyed the most. I continued using my training miles as time to spend in prayer. It was during one of these runs that I felt a call to completely change the direction of my life.

My brother, who was still my roommate, had recently gotten engaged. His wedding was planned for the summer of 2010. I had the choice of finding a new place to rent or doing something else. When I asked God for direction, I was immediately reminded of the thought I had after my first marathon—to run across America. My first instinct was to simply dismiss the idea. However, I decided to keep my heart open to the possibility that I was being called to follow through with it.

I prayed on the matter incessantly. My life was so good just the way it was. I was surrounded by people I loved, and my job was perfect. Leaving it all to run across the country sounded ridiculous. The idea of a literal cross-country run began with the desire to help others. I had thought of different charities to raise money for, but I did not know what to do. I asked God about this very issue while running along the Potomac River one morning. Immediately, the memory of my mother running with her rosary ring came to my mind. She had always prayed for people when she ran. I admired her for finding time to pray. I knew right away that I had my answer. By taking requests from people, I could pray for them as I ran. It would be a way to include as many people as possible in the run. Additionally, I believed lifting up everyone's concerns to God was the best way I could help them.

I returned from my morning run with a purpose. It was then that I realized I was faced with the actual decision. Deciding on a cause for running across the country was the easy part. Making the commitment to undertake a transcontinental run was going to be very difficult. I thought and prayed about the decision for weeks. The more time went by, the more I felt pulled in the direction of taking up the journey. I made the decision while out on a route I ran almost daily. I had just asked God to give me some sign that he wanted me to take up the journey when I came upon a section of red roses on the side of the path. They were gorgeous, and I always enjoyed running past them, but this time there was a yellow rose in the center of all the red roses. The yellow rose was special because it was connected to a devotion my family had to St. Therese, "the little flower." At that moment, I made the decision to follow through on my plan to run across America. I was going to do it—with the intention of bringing myself and others closer to God.

CHAPTER SIX

To do anything worth doing, I must not stand back shivering and thinking of the cold and danger, but jump in with gusto and scramble through as well as I can.

Og Mandino

Once my decision was final, I resigned from my job. My employers were so excited for me. Ray, one of the owners, offered to send me supplies along the way. It was such a great feeling to know I had people who believed in me before I took a single step. After my brother's wedding in August of 2010, I moved in with family in New Jersey. My Aunt Barbara and Uncle Alex let me stay there while I worked on the basic preparations for the run. I loved spending time with them and appreciated their generosity. Financially, I planned to pay for the run with my own savings. Therefore, being able to live with minimal expenses was a huge help.

I constructed a training plan that I believed would have me in good physical condition to begin the run in late January. I originally planned to start on my birthday in February. However, I decided to make a change to those plans. I had a devotion to Saint Sebastian, the patron saint of athletes, so it made perfect sense to start the run on his feast day: January 20.

Upon my arrival in New Jersey, I began to lay down a solid base of seventy to ninety miles per week. Additionally, I designed a route for the run. Each day was broken down into individual turns and mileage markers written down on an index card. My family and friends were scattered all over the country; so I planned my route through Phoenix, Oklahoma City, Notre Dame, Virginia, my hometown in New Jersey, and finally New York. I found a good spot along the Pacific Ocean to begin my journey. One of my college roommates, Brendan, owned a running store in Long Island,

New York. I made plans to finish at the Atlantic Ocean near his store. The mileage added up quickly, totaling three thousand seven hundred miles. The thought of running that far was intimidating, but I believed it was possible with the Lord by my side.

As the weather began to cool down in October, I drove out to Phoenix, Arizona. My family there, Aunt Sharyn and Uncle Kevin, offered to house me while I finished up my training. The weather was gorgeous, and I took full advantage of it. I would run two or three times a day. The weekly totals gradually increased from one hundred to one hundred sixty miles. Eventually, I put in a two-hundred-ten-mile week. It was my plan to average thirty miles per day on the road, so it was a good test to see how my body responded. I was extremely tired but made it through quite well.

My list of items to purchase dwindled as I entered January. I assembled my jogging stroller, in which I planned to push all of my supplies. In it would be my tent, sleeping bag, clothes, medical supplies, food, water, and spare parts. I practiced with the jogger a few times. It felt very awkward. Even though the wheels rolled smoothly, it was still quite heavy. I figured I would get used to it quickly once I started the run.

My nerves were acting up as the days in January passed by one after another. Physically, I was feeling very strong. Runs of two hours did not feel bad at all, which helped me feel confident about putting in days over thirty, forty, fifty, or even sixty miles. I did need to stay injury-free, and thanks to a visit to Arizona Pain Specialists, I was assured of beginning the journey in good health. I went to them for a lower leg problem, and through a few treatments, they were able to get me back to 100 percent. They were also very excited for my run and gave me a tiny camera to record videos while out on the road.

The day before I drove from Phoenix to California, my sister gave birth to a little girl. Kristina and her husband Roberto named her Valerie, after my mother. I was excited to begin running but was crushed that I would not meet my niece until I reached Alexandria. I looked at it as a source of motivation to run strong.

On the morning of January 18, my aunt dropped me off at a car rental facility. I rented a one-way car and drove out to Coronado, California. Through a connection of my brother, I was hosted for the evening by Jeff and Candy. They were such wonderful and generous people. Jeff and Candy showed me around their town and had a send-off party for me. Some of their friends came over to wish me luck and to hand me prayer intentions.

For months, people asked me what I hoped to accomplish by running across the country. I wanted to encourage prayer across the world and help bring people closer to the Lord. My personal relationship with God was helped tremendously through a devotion to Mary, so I could not think of a better avenue to use than praying decades of the rosary as I ran. I believed Mary would bless my journey and lead people to her son as well. I believed God would listen to our prayers and would help us desire his will instead of our own. I did hope for healing, but more than anything, I wanted everyone to receive what they truly needed—Jesus Christ.

PART II

The Run

THE BEGINNING

Have I not commanded you? Be strong and courageous.
Do not be afraid; do not be discouraged, for the Lord your God will
be with you wherever you go.

Joshua 1:9

January 19: Oceanside, California.

I am sitting alone in my motel room the night before this massive undertaking. It is a strange sensation to feel so alone before such a daunting task. My thoughts turn to the countless people who have me in their thoughts and prayers. My emotions are currently in a state of contradiction. I feel a huge pit in my stomach, yet I am unable to contain the overwhelming sensation of excitement.

I am looking forward to the experiences and the adventures on the journey. However, I am also anxious about the people, animals, or cars that may harm me. These worries are only subdued by the belief that I am doing God's will. I truly believe everything will work out in the end. There is no doubt this run will be extremely difficult, but I also know the high level of my determination. Jesus will be with me every step of the way, so I know I will make it to New York. I have to—I have no home, no job, and no significant other to get back to. I did not put a life on hold to do this. This run is my life, and the beautiful thing is that it is not for me, but for others. No matter the physical difficulties or emotional struggles, I will make it because God has led me here. He has called me to run across America to bring people closer to him.

I won't let myself down, I won't let down those who have asked me to pray for them, and I won't let God down. This is my motivation. I am confident this reason to run will be strong enough to result in a successful journey. I pray that I stay healthy, stay humble, and remain steadfast in prayer. I do this to honor God, and I pray to be an instrument of his peace. This is my prayer. Starting tomorrow, I will bring that prayer to life.

January 20—Day 1: Oceanside, CA-Rincon, California, 34.4 Miles. 34.4 Total Miles.

The emotions I experienced taking those first steps away from the Pacific Ocean were simply indescribable. It was essentially an emotional overload as it seemed every fiber of my being was filled with hope, excitement, and anxiety. I wanted to laugh and cry at the same time without knowing why. It was difficult to even think, although that was partly because I only slept two hours the previous night due to the excitement.

There was no formal send-off. I just went to the ocean and took pictures to prove I started at the Pacific Ocean. I also hooked up a satellite program on my phone so people could track me in real time, which was added incentive to move quickly! I grabbed some sand to carry with me to the Atlantic Ocean before dipping my hand in the water as it came toward me. As the waters pulled back again, it looked almost as if the ocean was waving goodbye.

I was so relieved to finally get under way as the ground beneath my feet turned from sand to pavement. I had talked about the run for so long. There was a strong degree of anxiety inside of me to begin making good on my promise of praying across America. Soon after taking those first steps, I felt a growing burden on my shoulders. I knew it was there because I had many people counting on me and looking to me as an example. I never doubted my ability to succeed, but the feeling made me want to follow through despite any obstacles in my way. I could almost sense the hope of the people who I had promised to keep in my prayers. My level of confidence in completing the journey kept that pressure from getting to me. This confidence was derived from the belief that the run was an answer to God's call. I felt that God would bring me safely to the shores of the Atlantic. As my footsteps found a rhythm, I hoped that people would recognize the complete trust I put in God. I also prayed they would realize how much more of a spiritual journey it was as opposed to merely a physical endeavor.

I had beautiful, sunny weather as I started out by picking up a paved trail for the first eight miles. It gave my mind a chance to get into the run before jumping onto the roads. Once I pulled myself together after the first five minutes, I dove right into my personal intentions before making my way to the list of requests. As long of a day as it was and as many requests as I prayed for, I barely made a dent in the intentions I received from all over the globe. Many of the requests tore at my heart. I prayed for a man dying of cancer, a few young men and women fighting addictions, and a single mom who was struggling to pay the bills for her children. As difficult as those and others were to read, it was encouraging to know that people had so generously allowed me to help bring their concerns to God.

The run itself was difficult as I entered hilly terrain almost immediately. This was made more challenging by having to push the eighty-pound stroller up the hills and attempting to control it on the descents. It was clear that I needed more time to get used to handling it. Toward the end of the day, I had a member on a construction crew ask me where I was going. When I answered by saying New York, her was response was, "Good luck!" with a little bit of a laugh that seemed to suggest she thought I was crazy. After finally making it to my destination over thirty-four miles from my starting point, my body and mind felt completely trashed. I could not imagine keeping up that pace for four months. I thought that sounded a bit crazy—just like the construction lady suggested.

I am staying in a motel room at a casino tonight where I ate dinner earlier this evening. I am already feeling sore and know that I will be hurting tomorrow, but that can be expected. I am happy with this first day but also realize that this journey will have to be taken one mile—if not one step—at a time.

January 21—Day 2: Oceanside-Santa Ysabel, California, 17 Miles. 51.4 Total Miles.

I woke up this morning sore but managed to get packed and out on the road shortly after the sun rose. The first eight miles were brutal as they averaged about two hundred and fifty feet of elevation gain per mile. Then after a dip for a couple of miles, I hit nothing but inclines until the end. I did have to walk briefly at a couple of points but was proud of myself for running the vast majority of those mountainous miles with the jogger. Even without the heavy baby jogger, it would still be considered an extremely tough run in the mountains.

Despite the tough physical battle I was fighting on those narrow and winding roads, I got in a groove from a prayer perspective. I found myself feeling very connected with the intentions. I was able to focus as I said a decade of the rosary for each request through the hilly terrain. I prayed for a woman having a heart transplant, a young man struggling with drugs, and a man who was fighting cancer. It seemed to me that the more I removed myself from the distractions of everyday life, the more I was able to concentrate on and devote myself to prayer. While my body felt exhausted, I arrived at my beautiful destination with a smile on my face.

I am currently relaxing in my cabin at Lake Henshaw, where I finished up for the day. The sun is setting, and the pink glow is reflecting on the water in front of the mountain range surrounding the lake—truly remarkable. I just finished updating my list of prayer intentions that have continued to pour in from all over the world. It has become clear to me that all these requests speak volumes as to how much people all over the world are in need. The first and best step to take in addressing those needs, struggles, and concerns is to lift them up to the Lord. If I can help more people do just that, then I will consider this mission a huge success. I hope and pray this happens, as it will be more than worth any discomfort it takes to get to New York.

January 22—Day 3: Santa Ysabel-Borrego Springs, California, 31.6 Miles. 83 Total Miles.

I started running early in the morning, taking in the scenery as I hit the road. The weather started off a little chilly but warmed up quickly as I ran up more narrow roads. I made my first friend on this trip at that point! His name was Lawrence, a volunteer who helped to clean up preserved land in the area. Upon inspecting my jogger, he said, "You seem to only be missing two things—a baby and the kitchen sink!" That comment had me laughing for a few miles. We talked for a bit, and he showed me where the Pacific Crest Trail intersected my route. I heard about the path before because it went all the way from Mexico to Canada. I would have missed it had Lawrence not pointed it out, so I was psyched to cross that trail.

I kept running with an even rhythm and eventually hit the tiny town of Ranchita, at an elevation near four thousand feet. After reaching Ranchita, I stopped at a small convenience store and chatted with some of the locals who were all very nice. They warned me to be careful of the upcoming "Glass Elevator," which they explained was a steep road that dropped approximately three thousand four hundred feet over ten miles. It also offered an amazing view of the upcoming desert. A cyclist was at the store as well and told me "It is going to hurt!" He was right. I was thankful for a distraction when a motorcade of corvettes passed me going up the mountain. I also met a nice woman, JoAnn, who stopped to see if I was okay and gave me some prayer intentions of her own.

The ten-mile downhill stretch was insanely difficult to get through while controlling an eighty-pound stroller. It felt like it would never end. I spent most of that section praying for my own safety! I managed to complete it safely, but it completely trashed my legs. It was one of the most physically challenging things I had ever done. The outside of my left knee was in severe pain toward the end of the drop. My first thought was that my IT band, which is the band of tissue connecting the hip down to below the knee, had become inflamed. It was extremely painful to even bend my knee. I clenched my teeth together and gutted out the final miles into town as the unrelenting sun continued to beat down on me.

My spirits were lifted when I called my family and spoke with them for some time from my motel. After talking on the phone, I went out to a Mexican restaurant for dinner. I took ice from the water and held it against my sore leg while I ate, which raised more than a few eyebrows. I did not care at that point what anyone else thought. I finished eating a large plate of tasty burritos and tacos before stopping at a convenience store to load up on food and water supplies.

I am going deeper into the California wilderness and further away from the charm of the run. It is sinking in that I have signed up for a very painful and challenging journey. I have ice on my leg tonight and plan to stretch before going to sleep. With such a long run ahead of me, I know even small problems can turn into major obstacles. I am going to pray that it goes away soon, and I can get through it because I still have virtually the entire country to run across. I am also praying tonight that I have the courage and strength to make it to the end. If I don't possess it already, then I pray that God gives me the strength I need to complete this journey.

January 23—Day 4: Borrego Springs-Salton City, California, 27.5 Miles. 110.5 Total Miles.

I awoke to my leg feeling worse than when I had fallen asleep the previous night. Running was excruciating from the onset and running on the rolling terrain with the jogger only made things worse. During the uphills, it was like trying to run and do resistance training with an object that weighed half as much as I did! On the descents, I had to pull back while braking to keep it from dragging me down. As if that were not difficult enough, I had to make sure there was enough of a shoulder so cars could get by. If there was not sufficient space for both myself and a vehicle, then I had to pull off to the side before hopping back on the road. This was not easy to do on any road and was even more difficult given the narrow, hilly, and winding roads—to do all this while running a long distance and in prayer made for some very intense miles.

As much as I struggled physically, my attention was captivated by the gorgeous scenery. I descended on a road overlooking the beautiful Salton Sea just after I ran through a section of the Anza-Borrego Desert. It was such a rush to run alongside the desert landscape while looking at a majestic mountain range. It was overwhelming to see such beauty. I attempted to appreciate it without being intimidated by how vast it all appeared. I tried to use the scenery as a distraction from my worsening leg problem. Every time I bent my knee, it screamed in pain.

The commitment I felt to my mission grew stronger with every Hail Mary I prayed. When I struggled, I found myself lifted up by the intentions of others. I was humbled so many people asked me to pray for them. In the span of an hour, I found myself praying for a single mother in Columbia, a woman in Ecuador, a Polish priest, and a woman in Spain. Many of these people requested prayers for their own direction in life, that the Lord leads them exactly where they were needed. I was able to relate to those feelings and hence felt very attached to the people sending in those intentions. I also felt so blessed that nearly everyone who sent me a prayer request promised to pray for me as well—what a beautiful gift!

The last few miles were very rough. The road was rocky, and I was baking in the heat. The sun was burning hot, even though the temperature stayed in the seventies. I was thrilled to get done and bought a few cold drinks at a convenience store. Mike, a friend of a former college roommate, picked me up and took me back to his house. He was so joyful as he told me about the area of the state and some funny stories about our mutual friend. After our brief chat, I took a hot shower and changed into some clean clothes. When we headed out to the grocery store, Mike was so kind and insisted I stay in his car while he went in and purchased supplies for me. We then drove over to his friend's place to eat pizza and watch football. I was so dazed. I simply sat on the couch lost in my own world, feeling very concerned about my injury. I felt bad Mike and his friends were so nice to me and bought me dinner, yet all I could do in return was smile and say thank you. They were clearly excited and asked me many questions about my journey. One of the questions was about what I found to be the most difficult part of the run to that point. I answered with a description about the pain from the volume of miles. However, the true answer was likely more of my mental battle in dealing with that pain. I tried to answer their questions with a smile, but I was in no mood to talk to anyone.

I am happy to be hosted by such kind people tonight, but I am worried about my attitude. I normally love talking to people. However, my desire to keep quiet, especially about what I am doing now, does not sound like me at all. I knew this was going to be challenging, but to have feelings of depression on the fourth day is not something I expected. I am praying tonight for healing and a turnaround in my outlook.

January 24—Day 5: Salton City-Brawley, California, 37 Miles. 147.5 Total Miles.

This morning made me recall the feeling I had in my gut when I changed schools as I entered the sixth grade. I switched from a small Catholic school where I knew everyone to a larger school where I did not know anyone. Although it was something I needed to do, my stomach was in knots because it was not something I wanted to do. I had the same nervous feeling this morning in my gut when Mike drove me back to where I left off the prior afternoon. My leg still hurt, and I had thirty-seven long miles to go on a hot day while running with my jogger on the side of a busy road.

Fortunately, my leg pain was bearable for the first half of the run. I was able to move at nine to ten minutes per mile for the first few hours. I let myself get lost in prayer during the second part of the day. I prayed for a dad having knee surgery and a child battling cancer with an impending surgery of his own. It was easier to face a long mileage day knowing that people were counting on me to pray for them.

I forced myself to grind out the miles in the unrelenting sun, just briefly taking a break under the shade of a stop sign for a snack. I did not meet or talk to anyone on the road, but I continued to be humbled by the prayer requests. I spent a lot of time focusing on a prayer intention for a two-year-old boy who was diagnosed with leukemia. It broke my heart to imagine the pain the child and his family would have to endure as the treatment began. I thought of how blessed I was to be healthy. It was prayer intentions like this one that helped me realize just how good I had it. If I was hurting, I thought about those in chronic pain. If I was hot, I thought about the homeless who dealt with extreme temperatures without a roof over their heads. If I found myself complaining about how much my leg hurt, then I thought of those who could not walk or run at all. If I was lonely, I thought about how fortunate I was to have a family that both loved and supported me. I realized through my uncomfortable situations just how truly blessed of a life I led. It gave me determination to finish for those who were less fortunate. I felt a strength arise from within every time I thought about those who asked me to pray for them. I thought that if they had the courage and strength to get through their daily battles, then I could surely endure mine.

Tomorrow begins a three-day—and ninety-mile—journey to Arizona that passes through the desert. There are no motels, restaurants, or grocery stores between here and there. This is one of the sections I am most nervous about, and it comes at a time where I am feeling tired and dealing with an injury. I just limped over to the closest convenience store and loaded up on supplies. I am also fully loaded on prayers and hope others continue to pray for me as I approach the desert. I have a feeling I am going to need it.

January 25—Day 6: Brawley-Route 78, California, 32.5 Miles. 180 Total Miles.

My first thought upon waking up this morning was that there would be no easy days on this journey. My left leg continued to give me problems as I hit the road. I periodically experienced a sharp pain shooting from my knee, which radiated up toward my hip. I audibly gasped each time, trying unsuccessfully to release some of the pain with a loud breath. I was reduced to walking a few times, which I really did not like doing. However, I had no option other than walking it out until I could get running again.

My heart was beating out of my chest as I ran toward the desert. The town had given way to sparse farm houses. The green farm country eventually led me through a citrus grove. After passing through the grove, I ran over a canal, which was the unofficial start of the desert. I was on a road with the occasional car and semitruck. Off to both sides was desert brush and lots of dirt and sand—as far as I could see. I received many strange looks from people in the vehicles as I continued running into the uninhabited land. Once I was several miles in, I realized there was no turning around—I was in the desert until I emerged on the other side.

I came across a desert oasis near a sand dune where people were riding dirt bikes. I met a man there who ran a small business out of a trailer. Although I was stocked on drinks and snacks, I was able to buy a cold water, and he gave me a hamburger for free. At that time, the cold drink and hamburger was like having a nice steak and my favorite beer. I made sure to say a prayer of thanks for that gift when I began running again.

The temperature was once again tolerable, in midseventies. However, the sun continued to burn bright, so I fashioned a bandana under my hat to protect my ears and neck. A couple of miles after I left the oasis, a truck driving by created a strong enough wind to knock both the hat and bandana off my head and down a steep sand embankment. I immediately put the brake on my stroller and slid down the embankment to retrieve my items—only to realize I had a steep climb back up to the road on a surface made completely out of sand. It felt like the saying of "two steps forward and one step back" for the next few minutes, but I eventually made it back to the road with my leg hurting more than ever. I prayed for strength as each step sent waves of pain through my body. I went as far as I could before the sun started to fall along the horizon. I pulled my jogger a few hundred feet off the road and set up my tent for the night.

The sun has just set, and I finished my dinner of packaged tuna. I may be in for a long night as I already hear coyotes howling. I am exhausted, and my leg is in a lot of pain. If it were not for this injury, I would be in much better spirits and further down the road as well. I am just trying to focus on the prayer intentions and hope that I can have my leg looked at in Phoenix. If I can make it there and let this injury heal, then I will be in good shape. However, I cannot comprehend possibly finishing this run in the condition I am in at the moment. I plan on doing just over thirty miles again tomorrow, which will take me to the Colorado River and one day away from civilization. I am hoping and praying tonight that I will make it.

January 26—Day 7: Route 78-South of Palo Verde, California, 32.7 Miles. 212.7 Total Miles.

I did not need to see the weather forecast when I broke down my tent this morning. I could tell it was going to be sunny and warm. The shoulder disappeared shortly into the run. To make matters worse, there was a strong wind blowing directly in my face. I was in dire spirits just a few miles into the morning. At that point, I pulled off the side of the road, sat down, and hung my head. I felt so lonely and was hurting both physically and mentally. I really wanted to stop and thought for a moment what it would be like to hitchhike my way back to Phoenix. It was simply a fantasy as it was not something I truly considered doing. I was frustrated with myself for even thinking those thoughts.

What was going on that I was only a week into the journey and already having this type of experience? I wondered if I was doing something wrong, but then I remembered why I was on the journey. My days on the run were meant to be spent in prayer—and that is exactly what I needed to do at that moment. I asked God to give me the strength to deal with the pain, the loneliness, and the frustrations. I desperately wanted the pain to go away, but the bottom line was that I felt God called me to run across the country. I had complete faith he would not abandon me in my journey. Those thoughts and feelings had me thinking of when Jesus entered the desert, where he prepared for his upcoming mission. I thought it was very appropriate the desert came at the start of my journey because I also needed to prepare for my journey in a spiritual way. As miserable as I felt, my only joy at that moment came in knowing that I was doing God's will, and it was more than enough to fuel me for the upcoming miles.

Prayer intentions also fueled my progress as I prayed for a family who lost their son in the war. I could not imagine how my pain could in any way compare with their breaking hearts. I offered up my suffering for them. It somehow helped me to continue moving forward. I did my best to not look at my shadow because it clearly showed a bad limp in my running gait. As I continued down the road, travel was made more difficult by the surprising number of large dips in the road. I normally ran facing traffic, but because of the terrain and lack of shoulder, I felt it was safer to run with traffic at that point. Fortunately, I went through a border patrol checkpoint, and the officers there were really nice. They told me they would warn the vehicles coming through after me to look out for a runner on the side of the road. It was intense and scary as I had a few close calls. At one point, there were trucks traveling both directions. They converged on me at the bottom of one of the dips. I was running downhill and had to pull my jogger up over the sidewalk at the last second to get out of the way because there was nowhere for the truck behind me to go. The driver would have been unable to stop in time because of the steepness of the descent. After a few of these intense scenarios, I eventually made it through that dangerous section unscathed. My leg was still giving me major problems, and it took everything I had to keep running. As evening approached, I finally made it to a dirt road that led to the Colorado River. I found a spot to setup camp just across from the Arizona border and pitched my tent for the night.

I am so exhausted. I had another package of tuna for dinner tonight and only a little water. My supplies are running low as I have about two liters of water remaining. I am also having a difficult time fighting off the grips of depression. The past few days have been extraordinarily tough, and I believe God has given me just enough strength to get to the end of the day. My sleeping bag is all set up, but I do not feel like camping out again because of my sore back. I also have a tough time sleeping when I can hear coyotes nearby. I cannot imagine the remainder of the run being as taxing as it has been thus far, but if that is what I must endure to reach the end, then so be it. If all goes as planned, I should reach civilization again tomorrow. This gives me hope that things will start to improve.

January 27—Day 8: South of Palo Verde, California-Ehrenberg, Arizona, 24 Miles. 236.7 Total Miles.

After breaking down my camping supplies in the early morning, I immediately crossed into Arizona. From there, I started heading north on an unpaved, rocky road that paralleled the Colorado River. It was not a smooth run at all, and I had to take some walking breaks to give my body a rest from the bumpy run on the rocky surface. I lost my index card with the directions for the day on it. To add to the frustrations of the day, my phone battery went dead. Therefore, I was running blind and got lost twice, which added on unnecessary mileage.

About six miles into the day, I suddenly saw movement in front of me about thirty feet away. Then a mountain lion emerged from the side of the road. Its massive shoulder muscles bulged each time it took a step. I froze in my tracks as it started to slowly look around and cross the road. I silently grabbed my knife and pepper spray in case it decided to attack. I held my breath and prayed silently as I could feel my eyes go wide and the hair on my neck and arms stand up. I hesitantly let out a sigh of relief as it continued to the river for a drink. I waited for a minute before moving along. The rest of the day was spent looking over my shoulder as I slowly progressed forward.

Five miles after the mountain lion incident, I came across a cliff that had just collapsed across my road. I was somehow able to navigate my jogger up and over it, but the few cars on the road had to wait for a bulldozer to come and clear the road. I continued on, praying for protection and endurance. A few times during the rest of the run, I found myself stopped for no particular reason. I did not think I told my body to stop, but there I was—suddenly not moving. I had gone as far as I could, and the thought of another step seemed impossible.

Once again, I found motivation in the prayers I was saying for people. The sad situations of illnesses, financial troubles, and people struggling in their marriages made me feel like my troubles were not worthy of complaint. As tough as things were, I knew that God was with me and encouraging me to press on. I forced myself to move forward one step at a time. At one point, I was able to see Interstate 10 in the distance. Soon after the sighting of the highway, I spotted a sign for a hotel and fast food restaurant rising above the horizon. It was one of the happiest moments of my life as I realized I had made it out of the desert and back to civilization!

I just finished checking into my motel, where I was put on the second floor. There is no elevator here, so I had to carry all my supplies up the stairs to my room. At this point, I am just so happy to not be camping out in the desert again. I am about to go eat a ton of food and restock my supplies, which are very low. Somehow, I made it out of the desert low on food and with less than a liter of water remaining! I am looking forward to falling asleep in a bed tonight, which is something I promise to never take for granted again!

January 28—Day 9: Ehrenberg-Quartzsite, Arizona, 20 Miles. 256.7 Total Miles.

After a few miles into the day, I thought to myself how fortunate it was that I did not know what was coming between Ehrenberg and Quartzsite. If I had, then I would have spent a great deal of time dreading the section. Interstate 10 runs between the two towns, cutting through a mountain range along the way. Since I was not allowed to run on the interstate, I found an unpaved path to run on. I did not know what I was getting myself into when I mapped it out because it turned out the trail was always either very soft or quite rocky. Neither was conducive to running, especially with a jogger. The situation was made even more difficult because the path undulated the entire distance. Just a couple of miles into the day, a man who was out hiking that area came up to me and showed me scars on his leg. He said he was attacked by a pack of wild dogs in the area and told me to be careful. It gave me one more worry to deal with on an overwhelming day.

There were countless hills I had to navigate on the trail. As I approached the top of one particularly huge incline, I felt confident it was the final hill, but I was quite wrong. When I crested it, I saw that the trail was about to weave its way through a mountain range. I was devastated and demoralized. I also had no choice but to continue on. The drops were so steep that I had to go backward down a number of the hills in order to maintain control.

The uphills were a different story altogether as running was impossible. I lifted up the back two wheels of the stroller and pushed the front wheel as hard as I could before quickly engaging the break and throwing my weight behind the stroller to keep it from sliding backward. I repeated this action all along the brutal path. Just a couple of hours into the day, my entire body felt like I had been hit by a truck. It hurt to walk or even move my arms. While I moved along slowly, I prayed for many different intentions. It seemed many of the prayers I was sending to God were cries of desperation. I prayed for a man battling an addiction to drugs. I prayed for a teenager with cancer. I thought it was appropriate I was praying for them to overcome seemingly insurmountable issues while I fought a dire physical challenge of my own. I just took one step at a time and offered up the burning I felt in my muscles for those who were really suffering. Without God, I would not have been able to get through those miles as well as I did. I hoped that those in my prayers would feel the presence of God just as I had during that vicious section.

I learned toward the end of the day that the path was generally used for all terrain vehicles. An elderly couple in one of the ATVs stopped to see what I was doing. They had seen the tracks of my jogger in the gravel miles back and could not figure out what was making the grooves in the sand until they came up on me. It was humorous because they could not believe I was pushing a stroller on that trail. The couple said they would be impressed if I made it because they had never heard of anyone doing anything like it. I finally made it to the town only to find out that the motel where I was planning to stay was all booked up. The nice woman at the reception desk told me about someone in the town who rented out a trailer, so I ran a few more miles into town and got set up to stay in a trailer for the night.

I could not be happier to be done and have a roof over my head for the night. I also just made it back from a fish and chips dinner. I totally deserved the large serving of fried ice cream for dessert. I am hoping it energizes me for a long day tomorrow. It is closing in on 11:00 p.m., and I do not think I have ever been more ready for bed in my entire life!

January 29—Day 10: Quartzsite-Salome, Arizona, 39.3 Miles. 296 Total Miles.

I woke up early this morning feeling somewhat refreshed, but beyond sore. I packed up my things and forced my body to get into something resembling a run. My initial plan was to hop on I-10 for five miles to get to Route 60. However, when looking to enter the highway, I saw a sign indicating pedestrians were not allowed on I-10, and there was a cop car parked next to it. I decided not to chance it and took the long way around. I did not know exactly how I would get across I-10 as it was a section I had not mapped out very well. My only hope was that I could try to sneak on the highway for a few miles to get to Route 60 if there was no way across.

I quickly found out that my time pushing the jogger up and down rocky hills was not quite over. I made it to the other side of the interstate through an underpass. I found a road much like the one I was on the previous day. There were not as many hills in comparison, but they made up for it by being incredibly steep and long. I took a video of some ATVs that had trouble getting up the climbs, which did not make me feel better about my situation. I also struggled, taking about an hour and fifteen minutes to cover just a two-mile stretch—not exactly what I had in mind for running across the country.

I felt I had reached my limits after getting through that difficult section. The same trail went on for another few miles parallel to Route 60, as the path continued to pass through low brush and cacti. I could not stand being on that trail any longer, so I found a barbed wire fence and unpacked my stroller. I then tossed everything to the other side before getting my body over as well. I managed to do so with only scratching my cell phone. All things considered, I was happy to get onto the smooth surface of the highway and started running again. Despite already getting through fourteen miles rather slowly, I was faced with a marathon to run to my destination. To keep things interesting, I was racing the sun to finish before sunset. I had a great respect for the marathon and tried not to think about how far the distance was, especially after already running fourteen brutal miles.

I started picking up the pace, running many of my miles in the eight—to nine-minute range. My leg was still in some pain, but it was not severe. I took full advantage of feeling decent. I ran through a town named "Hope" before finally reaching my destination motel in Salome. It was tough to fight the mental battle of getting through the long miles on the highway while looking at small mountains dotted with green brush all around me. It felt like I was not going anywhere. I managed to deal with the mental obstacles by concentrating on prayers for families affected by war, people who were terminally ill, and a young woman in a coma. I offered up my discomfort for those requests as I ran. It did not make the miles any easier. It did, however, give me a strong sense of purpose and deepened my determination to finish strong. I did just that as I rolled up to the small motel with plenty of time to spare before the sun went down.

I am so happy to put this day behind me. It is a strange feeling to be all alone and far away from anyone I know. It has me reflecting on how I arrived at this point in my life. I believe it is impossible to predict where God will call each of us. I am having a hard time letting the feeling sink in that I am on this run by myself and staying in a small town tonight. As for the run, I know I am my biggest critic, but right now I am very proud of how far I have come. I don't know how I can keep up this same intensity for over one hundred more days. I have no control over that right now, so I am just going to focus on today and trust in God to take care of tomorrow.

January 30—Day 11: Salome-Aguila, 30 Miles. 326 Total Miles.

I was thrilled to have a good start to the morning. I had a shoulder to run on, and the sky was partly cloudy, so I did not completely bake out on the road. Because of the wide shoulder on Route 60, I did not have to worry about avoiding vehicles. I was happy for the light traffic and that there were no turns to think about. I enjoyed the scenery as I ran next to mountains all day long, thankful that I was able to run around them! It was beautiful to see the jagged brown peaks pierce the horizon. It was easy to get lost in both the prayers and God's wonderful creation.

My IT band started bothering me at about mile 17, making it extremely painful to bend my knee. My run continued on with a bit of a limp. I was doing everything I could to offer up any discomfort or pain I was in for the intention I was praying for at the time. Reading the requests made me want to be a better person to those around me. I realized so many people were struggling with something, and many of those struggles seemed incredibly difficult. I could not imagine dealing with some of the burdens people had to face on a daily basis. I surmised that there were many people who I dealt with on a daily basis who must have also been fighting battles I did not know about.

I took a moment to look back on my own life. I admitted that I had been short with others or passed unnecessary judgment on them at times. I resolved to change those actions immediately. Passing judgment on people was not only the wrong thing to do, but there were likely other factors as to why people acted the way they did. I had no right to judge them, especially without knowing the circumstances behind their actions. This experience taught me that the best thing I could do with any situation was to pray to God for that person.

The overall mileage today was not too bad, which was a good thing considering the hotel at the end of town did not take credit cards for payment. I had to run an extra couple of miles to withdraw cash from an ATM. Of course, the machine was out of order when I arrived there. I was fortunate the owner of the hotel, Rita, was nice enough to drive me to an ATM a little ways down the road. She was so kind, and her concern for my well-being reminded me of how my mom always acted. Rita wanted to know the details of my run to ensure I knew what I was doing and that I would be safe on the roads. When we returned, I stocked up on supplies and got a quick bite to eat.

I am so exhausted from this daily routine. I am praying for a good night of rest. If the past week is any indication, much of it will be spent awake from the soreness. Although my physical limits are already being tested, I can sense that this journey is going to be much more of a mental battle. I would love nothing more than to sleep in tomorrow morning, but in five hours I will convince myself to get up to face another day.

January 31—Day 12: Aguila-Wickenburg, 26.8 Miles. 352.8 Total Miles.

This morning had a nice surprise waiting for me as I hit the road. It was a cool morning, and just after sunrise, I saw an awesome sight in the sky. Past the dull-colored grasses and open fields were magnificent mountain ranges. They were bathed in a pinkish hue from the sunrise, and a single bright ray of light shone down through a gap in the clouds. It was beautiful, and I felt as if it were a light at the end of a tunnel. I knew how little ground I had covered compared to the size of the nation, but the thought of arriving in Phoenix lifted my spirits.

I planned to knock out about a marathon as I continued to reel in Phoenix. For probably the first time since day 3, I was able to run without significant pain from my left leg. It was also nice having a wide shoulder to run on for most of the day, which made it so much easier to pray without interruption. Intentions continued to pour in from all over the globe. In the midst of a short stretch where I was struggling, I prayed for a woman's intention from Mexico for the health of her grandfather. Another intention of a man from Ecuador struck me because he was praying to stay close to the Lord as he felt he was starting to fall away from his faith because of a heavy burden. I felt as if I could almost sense his pain and prayed intently as I ran through my own aches for his relationship with the Lord. It was amazing how taking the focus off myself and placing it on those in need helped me to get through my own struggles.

It may have been because the road was easier, but I felt very confident running with the jogger and believed I was getting quite good at handling it. In a moment of comic relief, I thought to myself how awesome I would be at pushing my future children around!

I took full advantage of an early check-in at my motel by taking a short nap. I then showered before heading out for pizza, a taco, a burrito, a soda, and chocolate milk. The woman who took my order at the counter watched me inquisitively as I downed enough food for a family of four. I was really hungry and enjoyed every bite!

I made it back to the hotel lobby after dinner, and the clerk asked me where I was going the next day. I mentioned I would try to make it the fifty-seven miles to my aunt and uncle's house in Phoenix. A man in the lobby overheard me and said I could never make that kind of mileage in one day. I knew all the motivation I needed was someone telling me I could not do something. I told the man I believed all things were possible with God. I walked away from the lobby with the intention to prove it.

Despite the lower mileage, my body is still hurting. Regardless, I am going to give everything I have to get to Phoenix within the eleven hours of daylight I have tomorrow. Either way, tomorrow is going to be a real challenge, so I am going to get as much sleep as possible before sunrise.

February 1—Day 13: Wickenburg-Phoenix, Arizona, 56.8 Miles. 409.6 Total Miles.

Once I woke up this morning, I told myself that I was going to see my family by the end of the day. There would be no excuses, and I would not give into the temptation to stop short at a hotel before I arrived at my aunt and uncle's house. Normally, I waited until the sun rose to begin, but I put on my blinking light and hit the road about thirty minutes before the sun came up. The first mile or so was a dangerous stretch in the dark as there was no shoulder to run on. It opened up after that, and I was really pushing the pace at that point. My body was running hard, and my mind was praying with equal intensity. I lifted up in prayer a woman who was in pain after suffering a stroke, a child with epilepsy, and another child with a heart defect. I prayed that my discomfort would in some way ease their pain. I wanted them to feel God's presence in their lives.

One of the most welcoming sights I experienced on my trek was the familiar face of Robert, who worked for Arizona Pain Specialists. As one of my sponsors, they took some video footage and photos of me for their publications. I looked like a disaster as I was exhausted and was sporting an unkempt beard. At that point, the only thing I cared about was seeing a friend and eating a fast food meal he had brought me. I was intent on moving fast to finish the high mileage for the day, so I inhaled the meal and only spoke briefly with Robert. He was so filled with energy. Robert told me how great I was doing and that he was amazed at how far I had already run. It was very encouraging to be around his overwhelming positive attitude. He filmed me from mile 27 through mile 30 before taking off. It was a great mental break to see someone I knew, and it helped to break up the day's run.

The terrain was slightly hilly at parts, but not bad enough to slow me down as I continued plugging along and praying. No single mile went by quickly, but praying for people struggling with all different types of things certainly made the distance seem easier. I received a request a few days earlier from a person with cancer in his bones. He said that he was close to the end and was asking me to pray for him and his family. When I read this intention off my list, it made me run and pray even harder. It was requests like that one which really got me going. Praying for the man helped me to run by a hotel deep into the run without even a thought about stopping.

I hit the fifty-mile mark, and my legs really started to cramp up and give me trouble. The cramps reduced my stride to a mere shuffle. I told myself, "Fine, a shuffle it is for the last seven miles!" and continued trudging on in a race against the sun for the final miles. As the sun was setting, I picked up the final stretch of road on a route I had been on hundreds of times in getting prepared for my journey. It was surreal to run the same section with my jogger at the end of a very long day. All I cared about at that time was getting to my destination. I did just that as soon as the sun disappeared behind the mountains. Kevin was surprised to see me as he thought it was Sharyn getting back home. I gave him a big hug and was happy that he did not care how bad I looked or probably smelled! My aunt came back soon after I arrived and was equally surprised to see me a day early. It was so awesome to see them again, and the terrible feeling of loneliness quickly dissipated. I joked with them that they should never question how much I loved them because of how far I had just run to see them!

It is now time to handle some logistics and take a few days off before heading out on the next section of my journey. I am looking forward to some rest, the company of my family, and seeing some of my friends in the area. The difficulties I have faced these first two weeks have only made the joy I feel in my heart more meaningful.

February 2—Day 14: Rest in Phoenix, Arizona, 409.6 Total Miles.

I was thrilled to sleep in this morning, but I did not necessarily relax as much as I had originally planned. I was able to do my taxes and take care of some bills during the down time. I took a break from the paperwork to treat my legs nicely by getting a sports massage—it felt awesome and was paid for by some good friends of mine from New Jersey. It was funny to see the massage therapist's reaction to the tightness in my legs. He asked, "What the heck have you been doing to your legs?" My explanation of running the equivalent of nearly sixteen marathons in the previous thirteen days seemed to be a satisfactory answer!

Arizona Pain Specialists hosted a dinner tonight to celebrate my arrival in Phoenix. It was held at a family-style Italian restaurant, and I ate nonstop for a couple of hours. While the food was great, it was my conversations with people that were most special to me. I heard from the owners and some of the employees what my run meant to them. One of the owners, Joe, described how the run had brought people together in a way he had never seen before. I felt such joy knowing that my journey was making a difference in this world. I felt so honored that they had faith in me from the very beginning. I was beyond humbled by their continued support of my mission.

There was one very funny moment at dinner. Another patron in the restaurant learned of my run, and he sang me an impromptu song opera-style about how what I was doing was crazy. It caught me off guard, and all I could do was laugh. I thought at the moment that it would be difficult to top that kind of reaction!

I am so excited to be in Phoenix. The past couple weeks have been so lonely because I am out on the road by myself. The chance to see in person how my run matters to people is priceless. It only intensifies my drive to complete this mission. I cannot describe the happiness I feel to be around my aunt and uncle again. They are so generous, loving, and concerned. I have enjoyed talking to them about my stories from the run and simply love their company. It was well worth the long day yesterday to see them. I feel that my loneliness has disappeared because of my time with both them and my friends. I am not sure if it is because of a deeper appreciation of life, but I have never felt so blessed.

February 3—Day 15: Rest in Phoenix, Arizona, 409.6 Total Miles.

I headed out to Arizona Pain Specialists to get some work done on my leg this morning. I was surprised to see just how many people had become interested in my run. The group had a big board with my picture and a map that kept track of my progress. The employees were also wearing "Where's Jeff?" shirts! I thought this was especially appropriate because I was never where I was supposed to be when I was growing up and someone in my family was always saying, "Where's Jeff?" Another patient in the waiting room told me she had just picked up one of the shirts for herself. Although I received comments from people online, it was completely different to experience the excitement people felt about the run in person. My chiropractor, Dr. Moore, worked on my leg; and it started to feel better almost immediately.

To cap off the night, I went to a party at a country western bar in the evening. A church group I joined while in Phoenix was holding the celebration in honor of my arrival. I always loved country line dancing but passed on it in favor of saving my energy. My friends were so nice as they also had made treats to celebrate my upcoming birthday. They proceeded to throw money into a jar to cover the expense of an upcoming hotel night. I was still tired, so I called it an early night and headed home to spend a few minutes with my aunt and uncle before going to bed.

I continue to be humbled by everyone I talk to in person. I can sense that this run is bringing them hope in some way. After seeing this hope in their eyes, I know I have to make it to New York. I cannot—and will not—let them down. I am a man of my word, and I intend to keep the promise I made. I will finish this run for them and for the intentions they have entrusted to me. It is a burden, but one I am happy to carry—and I know that I do not have to carry it alone.

February 4—Day 16: Rest in Phoenix, Arizona, 409.6 Total Miles.

I started this morning off in an awesome manner. I was honored to have the opportunity to speak to a group of kids at a grade school. I was blown away at how perceptive and insightful they were. I had nine-year-old kids asking me how I planned to deal with the weather and hardships on the road. They were aware of the loneliness factor and asked how I planned on handling it. The children were so caring and were unbelievably supportive of my run. I heard from the director of the school at the end of the day as to how much they all loved hearing about the run. She also told me that one child said he would be nicer to his parents because of how I talked about loving all those around us. One of the teachers gave me a heartfelt intention to pray for her nephew who was battling cancer. I left the school not only with additional prayer intentions but also with the feeling that I received more from the talk than I gave.

I spent some much needed time today looking over some logistics of my remaining journey. I also repacked everything. Additions to my supplies included some heavier clothes since the high temperatures were supposed to drop from the sixties and seventies to the twenties and thirties within a week's time.

I have enjoyed my time off. It was great seeing friends, and I cherished the time with my family. However, I have a commitment to fulfill and a dream to live. I am looking forward to continuing that journey tomorrow!

UP AND OVER

No matter how steep the mountain—the Lord is going to climb it with you.

Helen Steiner Rice

February 5—Day 17: Phoenix-Gilbert, Arizona, 33.6 Miles. 443.2 Total Miles.

I realized getting back into running after a few days off was not easy. After stepping out of my routine for a few days, I found it difficult both physically and mentally to find a groove again. I left my aunt and uncle's house just after 8:00 a.m. to a familiar path along a canal. I was rolling along just fine but started to feel more tired than usual about fifteen miles into it. I was psyched to break up the run at the twenty-mile marker, where my aunt and uncle were going to meet me on the road with lunch. However, about a mile before our rendezvous point, my IT band flared up badly, and I had to limp into the parking lot outside of Arizona State University. I was happy to take a break and eat a sandwich from Subway and drink a shake from McDonald's. As good as the food tasted, there was no hiding from Sharyn and Kevin my frustration or the amount of pain I was in. I did my best to move on, but it was painful and tough going. At least I had a long list of new intentions compiled from my days off to keep me plenty busy in prayer and give me causes for which to offer up the pain.

I had about thirteen miles to go after lunch with my family, so I pushed on and ran by a man standing on the side of the road. I stopped and talked to him as he looked like he was having a rough day. He said he was looking for work and that he would even work for food. I felt so bad this man was struggling with something as simple as hunger. I had a package of beef jerky in my food bag I offered him. He was reluctant to take the food but finally accepted it. As I ran on, I couldn't help but think that I was just where God needed me to be. All I had to do was put one foot in front of the other to keep it that way.

I finally made it to my destination, which was a woman's house in the town of Gilbert. Carrie had seen me on the news and offered her guest bedroom for the night. I was so thankful for the place to stay and was excited to take a ride on her Harley as well. After talking to her for some time, I discovered she had a sad story of her own. Her husband had been killed, and she was having a difficult time finding work. I thought that it was another example of people needing prayers. I wished I could do more to help but understood the best thing I could do for her and everyone else was to pray.

I am happy with the progress I made today and hope I can remain focused on my mission as I move forward. This run is about bringing people closer to God through prayer, and I intend to see it through to the end. I have a strong feeling it is going to be prayer that will ultimately carry me to the finish.

February 6—Day 18: Gilbert-Gold Canyon, Arizona, 24.4 Miles. 467.6 Total Miles.

I did not exactly move quickly this morning, but I consistently moved forward. I felt extremely tired as the day progressed but was content with a slight improvement on my leg injury. The day was made easier by light traffic on the road. I had my eye on a flat-topped mountain range in the direction I was headed—it never seemed to get closer. I became frustrated with the feeling that I was not making progress as it continued to loom in the distance for mile after mile. Eventually, I got lost in prayer for a couple of hours. I prayed for someone's cousin who was fighting in Afghanistan, a woman's family who was left behind after she passed away from cancer, and a couple going through a divorce. It was difficult to run while thinking and praying about those people. Their situations in many ways made my burden even heavier. I felt saddened about the troubles of the people in my prayers. At the same time, it made me realize that as much as I wanted to help them, the best thing I could do for them was to pray. I continued running and the sadness remained on my heart. However, I felt a strong sense of hope and peace simply knowing that I had placed those concerns in the hands of the Lord.

Before I realized it, I was right up on the mountain range that seemed so far away only an hour earlier. I made my way back to Route 60 and was soon rolling up to my motel. I was relieved to be done with the fairly short distance but wished I had a place to stay further down the road. I found myself a little obsessed with the mileage, and I felt bad about stopping well before thirty miles. My mind was feeling the burden of the overwhelming mileage, and I simply wanted to make a bigger dent. However, I took comfort in being able to shower and put on some clean clothes.

For now, I am enjoying some snacks in my motel room while watching the Super Bowl. I was so happy that Sharyn and Kevin drove to my motel to drop off dinner for me. Seeing family means so much to me. It certainly lifts my spirits to have their support. I'll need all the help I can get as tomorrow marks the first day I start running into higher elevations. My dad is also planning to come in for a couple of days. He is scheduled to meet me at my destination tomorrow. It will be nice to have some company, even if it is for a short time. I believe there is a lot of good being done through the prayers. While my body and mind are feeling the weight of the physical journey, my spirit feels stronger and closer to God with each step. This is what keeps me going mile after long mile.

February 7—Day 19: Gold Canyon-Superior, Arizona, 29.9 Miles. 497.5 Total Miles.

I started this morning on the road that began a climb to my highest elevation of the trip. I felt nervous because much of the winding section of road was supposed to be very dangerous. As such, I tried to focus solely on the ground in front of me with the belief that everything would work out.

The first ten miles were relatively flat, and I found a dirt path that followed my route for a few miles. It was slower going than pavement, so I eventually found a way back to the road and continued on my way. The road started to rise, and I felt my legs begin to burn as they climbed. The fact that gravity was working in conjunction with the stroller to put even more resistance on me did not help the situation.

The prayers continued as I ran along the side of the road in the warm weather. I once again fashioned my bandana around my hat to protect my neck and face against the sun. There was just a brief interruption when I stopped to tend to my nose when it suddenly began to bleed. I took care of my nose and continued running through the beautiful scenery. Beige and green brush covered the ground, which was periodically broken up by brownish-colored mountains rising high into the horizon. It was not long until I was in the heart of some of those mountain ranges. There were a few tense situations where the shoulder became extremely narrow or disappeared altogether. I finally made it to my motel in Superior and waited for my dad to show up, which he did within minutes after my arrival.

My dad fits right in with the scenery as he stands tall and wears his white cowboy hat everywhere. His concern for my safety is obvious, but I can tell he is happy to see me doing fairly well. My spirits are also in good shape because I've had some type of company the past few days. I am looking forward to my dad's company over the next three days as well, which helps me feel less intimidated by the upcoming treacherous roads. I am off to bed because I know I will need all the rest I can get.

February 8—Day 20: Superior-North of Globe, Arizona, 35.3 Miles. 532.8 Total Miles.

I woke up this morning, on my twenty-eighth birthday, to a pit in my stomach. It first took shape the previous day but returned with a vengeance as I hit the road. I was fortunate that the first few miles of the day, while uphill and winding, did have two lanes going my direction. Since my dad was around, he drove behind me for those miles with flashers on to warn the cars and trucks coming up from behind me. It was still quite tense during the first hour or so, but I was moving at a good pace because I wanted to finish the section as quickly as possible. The scenery was absolutely gorgeous. The mountains were rocky and dotted in green brush. I took in my surroundings while focusing on the gray road that rolled ahead of me in the distance. Under almost any other circumstance, I would have paused to enjoy the scenery more.

The road eventually went back to one lane in each direction, so I told my dad to check out the road ahead for a few miles. It was definitely scary at times as on more than one occasion I had to jump off the road into a small ditch because of traffic. One time it happened on a sharp curve that had no visibility. I was forced to use my sense of hearing to guess which direction the vehicles were coming from. It was windy with a fair amount of traffic on the road, so trying to make that determination was rather difficult. I said a prayer for safety because if I jumped out on the road at the wrong time, then there would be no chance to get out of the way of the vehicle. The run and quite possibly my life would be over. I realized in those moments how short life was and that it could always end at any moment. I was happy to be at peace with God and desired to feel that way each and every day for as long as I lived. I prayed for safety and made it through each of those dangerous situations unharmed. I was relieved that I survived and felt blessed to continue both my journey and my life.

My legs felt like lead weights. I somehow had to find a way to move forward one arduous step at a time. I was just thankful I did not have to navigate my stroller through that stretch since my dad had it in his car. I decided to take a short break, so I met my dad at a McDonald's at mile 23. He bought me a soda and fries, which seemed to give me enough energy to continue on as I turned north just after the town of Globe. I was pleased with my progress, but Show Low was still about eighty-five miles away at that point.

Once I hit mile 29, I really felt like stopping and calling it a day. My IT band had behaved most of the day, but it started to act up, and the rest of my body told me to stop. However, with the next town so far away, I needed to push through it. I told my dad to wait for me at the spot that would make it a thirty-five-mile day. Once I made it to mile 33, my mental tenacity and steadfast focus on prayer had me feeling better. I picked up the pace and was so happy to climb in my dad's car at the end of the day. While not a monster day from a mileage standpoint, it was a very strenuous mental day. I was sure that having my dad nearby, along with the constant prayers, helped me push through to the end. I was starving by the time we drove back to Phoenix for the night. I downed twelve slices of pizza and a couple of pieces of chocolate cheesecake. It was awesome and well-deserved.

I will always remember where I was and what I was doing on my twenty-eighth birthday. Running over thirty-five miles through hilly terrain on dangerous roads may not be most people's idea of a great birthday, but getting through it with both my dad and God by my side made it a unforgettable day. I feel like I truly celebrated the gift of life on this birthday.

February 9—Day 21: North of Globe-South of Show Low, Arizona, 36 Miles. 568.8 Total Miles.

After a short night of sleep, I arose early to drive back out to where I left off the previous evening. I was all bundled up to start the run since the temperature was in the high twenties. I was able to relax and move fairly quickly during the first four downhill miles. However, it quickly turned into a literal uphill battle after those early miles. The road began to rise with no end in sight, and a strong headwind appeared, which ended up hanging around for the remainder of the day.

In order to stay positive, I tried to remember how blessed I was that my dad was around because it meant I did not have to push my stroller through the rough terrain. The combination of running up the hills and against the cold wind made things difficult and had me frustrated. It felt like I was running in place for most of the day. I took walking breaks at times in order to ensure I would have enough energy to make it through the mileage. Despite snow on the side of the roads, much of the route was quite runnable, and I carried a short list of prayer intentions in my pocket. I continued to pray as I put the miles behind me one by one.

My mind was focused on the road and prayers for the first twenty miles, but I was still nervous about an upcoming stretch of narrow and winding roads through Salt River Canyon. I was warned by a local reporter to be careful through the section as it was supposedly an extremely dangerous stretch of road through the canyon. When I finally got there, I understood the warning. The scenery was beautiful. As I descended, I looked up to see different colored layers of rock rising high above me. It was as if I was running in a smaller version of the Grand Canyon. I did not look too much at the surrounding view because traffic was heavy and the vehicles were moving fast. I was jumping across the street and back again since it varied as to which side of the road I felt it was safer to run on.

After descending approximately two thousand feet, I had run twenty-six miles on the day, and I was at the bottom of the canyon. The descent trashed my legs and aggravated my leg injury. I had a five-mile climb back up the canyon to go before another five miles to reach my finishing point. Looking up at the impending ascent, I felt overwhelmed and demoralized. Before turning up the incline, I took a brief pause to remind myself of how far I had come despite the physical pain. I said a short prayer for myself and those on my list of intentions who were fighting uphill battles of their own. I then started moving as steadily as possible. It was excruciatingly painful, and I had to limp up parts of it. I did take a short break to speak to my dad and to take a photo together in the scenic canyon. I felt bad he had to watch me struggle so much. He was very understanding of my attitude when I was short with him in some of our conversations. He continually forgave me as I routinely apologized for each time I let the pain get the best of me. I admired him for forgiving me so easily. I thought it was a glimpse of how God forgives us over and over as well. I had made my share of mistakes in life, but he never abandoned me and continued to give me chances to do things right. These thoughts kept me motivated to finish the miles as strong as possible.

I am proud of myself for pushing through the difficulties of the day once again. I'm absolutely thrilled my dad is here, and we just returned to the motel after an awesome dinner together. I ate a burger and had a Fat Tire, one of my favorite beers. I know I earned it and look forward to finishing this tough stretch to Show Low tomorrow.

February 10—Day 22: South of Show Low-Show Low, Arizona, 37 Miles. 605.8 Total Miles.

The first thing I did this morning was turn on the television to check the weather. The temperature was a freezing eleven degrees—and I learned I would be facing a cold headwind on the road! I was as bundled up as possible given the clothing I brought with me. We had a continental breakfast, and the television in the lobby of the motel showed Times Square in New York City. It was overwhelming to even think about what I would have to endure before finally passing through Times Square. Seeing a landmark near the finish made me realize that I had to focus on the current day and not get weighed down by the vastness of the country. I centered my attention on the fact that it would be millions of small steps to my final destination—not one big one.

My dad drove me to my finishing spot from the prior afternoon, thirty-seven miles away from the motel in Show Low. By the time I started running, the temperature was at best in the low teens, and the wind made the biting cold feel even worse. I really began to take notice of just how difficult it was to breathe as I ran to approximately six thousand three hundred feet above sea level. I said a prayer of thanksgiving that I did not have to run through any canyons or winding roads. The scenery turned very green as grass and evergreens populated the side of the road, with the tops of hills breaking up the horizon. I saw some more wildlife as a fox ran out on the road right in front of me. He did not seem bothered by my presence at all, and I was too exhausted to care. We took a quick look at each other before continuing on our separate ways.

The running was slow but was at least steady. It was thankfully much less worrisome than the previous days as the roads were not too dangerous. There were a few spots with no shoulders or where a guardrail made the road narrow, but travel was mostly pleasant outside of the cold and wind. Just like the previous day, my leg acted up at about mile 25. As much as I struggled physically, a bigger battle was taking place mentally. While I did not consider stopping, I began to feel sorry for myself for the first time since I started the run. My dad had driven to the motel to shower and wait for me toward the end of the day, so I took some time over the final miles to have a talk with myself. Things were not going well as I had a noticeable limp in my stride. Given the situation, it was easy to get down. While I certainly felt sad and exhausted before, this was the first time I had feelings of pity for myself.

I jogged slowly and even walked parts of those final miles, taking time to talk to myself and to God. I was reminded of why I undertook the endeavor and also of those who were truly suffering. My run would come to an end at some point, but many of those who I was praying were battling terminal illnesses, life struggles, life-long afflictions, or addictions that would not end so easily. I reminded myself that I did not take on the challenge to avoid difficulties in life, but rather to face them—with prayer. By the time I finally reached the motel in Show Low, I was still in pain but had found new mental strength. I also replenished my physical strength with a well-deserved pizza and a big dessert.

Unfortunately, my dad just left for Phoenix as he has an early flight in the morning, so I am back on my own again. It was fantastic to have his company for a short while, and I am sure it is a time we will remember for the rest of our lives. I have decided to take a day off tomorrow to recover from these past few days of climbing, cold temperatures, and wind. It was difficult to say goodbye to my dad, but I am looking forward to seeing him again somewhere down the road on this run.

February 11—Day 23: Rest in Show Low, Arizona, 605.8 Total Miles.

Today was quite relaxing as I took a much needed rest day. I could have continued on, but my next destination was forty-seven miles away. I thought I could benefit from a day of rest after the tough elevation I ran through in the mountains. It was very difficult on my legs, and running on the dangerous roads definitely took a toll on my mental state. Not having him around today made the isolation very real, and the road forward seem more daunting. I knew my family was concerned for my safety, but seeing it on my dad's face made it very real. I noticed the worried look on his face a number of times. It was most apparent when he came back to check on me and described the dangers of the upcoming miles. I did the best I could to pretend like is wasn't a big deal and that I was not scared at all. The truth was that I was quite nervous through many of those sections. My thought was that there was only so much I could do, and the best plan was to leave the rest to God.

I am so grateful for the chance I had today to catch up on sleep. I also went out a couple of times during the day to eat in an effort to keep my weight up. It is now just after 6:00 p.m., and I am getting ready for bed. I'd be lying if I said I wasn't anxious about the upcoming long mileage days. My plan is to not worry about the miles tonight, but to simply sleep and get after the long road tomorrow.

February 12—Day 24: Show Low-Springerville, Arizona, 47.4 Miles. 653.2 Total Miles.

Today started out as another cold morning. The temperature was only eighteen degrees when I hit the pavement. I was moving well for the first twelve miles and met Karen, a local reporter, on the side of the road to give a quick interview. It was so nice to not only take a break but also to talk to someone so supportive and encouraging of my mission. She was so down-to-earth and was quite excited for my run as well as the people I was praying for. I spent more time talking to Karen than I had initially planned, but it was well worth the chance to have some great company for a short while.

I continued on after the interview through some of the most gorgeous scenery I had ever seen. As far as I could see were beige-colored grasses with dark green bushes spotting the landscape. Snow was laced through the grasses and colored the hills dotting the horizon in white. If nothing else, it provided a welcome distraction from the long miles of the day.

The shoulder was narrow to nonexistent, so I was forced to jump on and off the road as the traffic passed me. It was frustrating, but I was really able to concentrate on the prayer intentions people asked me to pray for. Many of the people sending me requests asked me to pray for our military, if not specific people in the armed forces. I placed an American flag on the front of my stroller at the beginning of the run to display my love for the nation. I was really feeling the heaviness in my legs when a few military vehicles drove by me going the opposite directions. I could not believe they appeared when I was in prayer for the military at that moment! I waved to them, and their simple act of waving back inspired me to continue running strong.

The elevation made it tough to push too hard because I was running in thinner air as I climbed to over seven thousand five hundred feet above sea level. My body was already exhausted, and forty-seven miles was a long way to go. However, I just did my best to put one foot in front of the other while praying one Hail Mary after another. I pushed it as hard as I could to make it to a 5:00 p.m. Mass in Springerville. I kept doing the math and figured out how fast I had to go in order to make it to my motel. I also budgeted time to shower and hobble over to the church, which made the timing very close.

I ran extremely hard and had a tough time surviving the final ten miles. My mind had to get past the amount of miles the GPS watch displayed on my wrist. I continually put it behind me and focused on what I had to do to make it through the current mile. My throat made audible grunts as I pressed hard through the pain. I wanted to stop but instead continued to run each mile faster than the one before. I finally reached my motel and showered before heading over to the church. I was so tired and exhausted that I had to close my eyes and take a deep breath a few times because I thought I was going to pass out. Outside of my physical issues, I had a great sense of peace come over me as I entered the church. I felt as if I was being welcomed home from the moment I walked into the building.

After going to church, I walked over to a small restaurant and was the only customer there. If it was not for the lone waitress, I would have started to cry. I did not know why I felt that way, but I was in great physical discomfort and missed being around my family and friends more than ever.

I realize this run has already worn down my emotional barriers. Everything feels so raw and extremely real. If I get a note from someone saying that I reminded them to pray or a post on my website thanking me for what I am doing, it makes me feel unbelievably great. At least on the inside, I feel a gigantic smile. However, when I feel lonely or sad, it does take a toll. I feel like I would like to talk to someone about it, but I don't think anyone truly understands what I am going through. At the end of the day, I bring my concerns to God because I know he understands. He is also the one who will ultimately carry me through this journey.

February 13—Day 25: Springerville, Arizona-Quemado, New Mexico, 48.6 Miles. 701.8 Total Miles.

I began this morning as I always do—in prayer. I said the prayer to St. Michael the Archangel, asking for protection and strength on yet another day. The terrain was still quite hilly, and most of the day was spent between seven thousand and seven thousand six hundred feet above sea level, which made breathing difficult. I focused on the positive fact that for the first time since I left Phoenix, I had a wide shoulder to run on the entire time.

Arizona was certainly a struggle, but fourteen miles into the day, I came across the sign indicating that Arizona was behind me, and I had entered New Mexico. It often seemed like I was going slow and not making much progress, but seeing the sign lifted my spirits because it showed me that my small steps were adding up to something much bigger. I had over thirty-four miles to go until I reached Quemado, so I only stopped for a brief moment to snap some photos before continuing on the open road.

I appreciated the opportunity to relax and focus on prayer since the road was wide and traffic was sparse. It was very peaceful as I could see far across the expanse of arid grasses dotted with green shrubbery. I realized just how much I loved spending time with God each day. The physical pain and mental battles I faced was more than worth the opportunity to bring my own concerns and those of others to the Lord. I felt encouraged by his presence and also took to heart the small gestures of kindness shown by the vehicles that passed me. I doubted any of them had any idea what I was doing, but so often they smiled or extended a friendly wave in my direction. Some were even kind enough to stop and ask if I needed anything. Similar small gestures may have gone unnoticed in the past. Since I had quite literally slowed down my pace of life, I took notice and was so appreciative of their small acts of kindness. I heard my whole life that we should look for Jesus in other people. For the first time, I felt like I saw him without even trying to look. Perhaps it was the simple fact that I eliminated all the distractions in life that typically clouded my vision. For the moment, I did not care about why I felt that way. I simply enjoyed the tremendous opportunity to run, pray, and see Jesus in those around me.

The scenery surrounding me was gorgeous, but despite enjoying the beauty of the country and my happiness to be in New Mexico, it still seemed like I was making little progress. At one spot, I could see a huge drop and spotted the road far off in the distance as it climbed its way to the top of a large hill. The telephone poles were so far away that they appeared to be tiny sticks emerging from the ground. I guessed it was only five or six miles to that point, but it turned out to be closer to eighteen miles! I actually checked my watch on a few different occasions. I needed to make sure I was running at an honest pace and had not succumbed to a false sense of movement. My legs were so sore, and my right foot was in burning pain for the final fifteen miles. I tried to run without stopping, but with about six miles to go, I had to take a breather. I just sat on the side of my road with my head hung down, staring at my feet. The previous forty-two miles of the day had worn me down, and the thought of continuing to pound out the miles for another hour felt like an eternity. A few miles later, I could not recall actually standing back up to get going again. Somehow, I found myself pushing the jogger at a good clip as I finally rolled into the tiny town of Quemado.

I checked into the small motel, which was attached to a cafe. The woman saw my stroller outside and asked if I was biking across the country. When I told her I was running, the look on her face was priceless, but I was too tired to talk about it any longer. After showering and reloading on supplies at a gas station, I went to the cafe for dinner. Despite being starving from all the energy I expended, I was not able to finish my dinner because I was about to fall asleep in my food. I quickly paid my bill and walked back to my room.

I don't think I have ever felt this tired in my life, but I need to get ready for another day over forty miles tomorrow. I have been praying continuously for others, but it is at moments like this I take comfort in knowing others are praying for me as well.

February 14—Day 26: Quemado-Datil, New Mexico, 43.3 Miles. 745.1 Total Miles.

I was definitely hungry when I woke up early this morning. I ate a nice breakfast of French toast with a cup of hot chocolate before getting under way at sunrise. The hot chocolate looked awesome and was appropriate given that the temperature was in the low twenties. Trying to get my legs going felt like trying to start a car without a battery, which was not a good sign, considering I would be running through mountains at over eight thousand feet in elevation. I continued to plug along and tried my best to focus on the prayer requests. Once again, I ignored the signals of my body that were begging for mercy.

After eighteen miles, I unexpectedly found an oasis of sorts. It was a convenience store far removed from the nearest town. I stopped in for a cold drink and a snack. There was also a Laundromat connected to it that I wished I had time to use! A number of locals were hanging out there, and they already knew all about my run. They had apparently spoken to the reporter who interviewed me back near Show Low. One of the kids said that he could not believe I was still running because he had seen me a couple of days earlier out on the road. They were all so nice, and a woman there gave me some snacks as I sat down on the front porch to catch my breath for five minutes. I heard all about the area and others who had passed through that part of the country. It was a great break and encouraged me to continue running strong for the remaining miles.

I was reluctant to get going but had almost a marathon yet to go, so I said goodbye and hit the pavement once again. The next town up the road was called Pie Town, which supposedly had pies, just a few miles away at eight thousand feet in elevation. I was so looking forward to downing a pie. My spirit was broken when I finally got there because a sign was up saying that the place was closed on Mondays. At the time, it felt like a crushing blow. I said I would make it up to myself by getting a nice dessert at my destination.

I ran past Pie Town, which thankfully was the highest elevation I would reach on the run. I then started a descent and ran past the Continental Divide. To know the largest mountains were behind me gave me a great boost of energy that seemed to fuel me for the next stretch of open road.

I continued running in prayer. In addition to my normal intentions, I also prayed for the people I met at the convenience store as well as the construction crew I passed shortly after Pie Town. I was truly thankful I had the chance to pray for those I met on my journey. I remembered how before the run began, I meant to do so many things but always found myself busy and distracted. I suddenly found myself with as much time as I could ever want. With all that time, all I wanted to do was pray. I felt so blessed at that moment. I realized how much the journey had given me the chance to not only pray for others but to also deepen my personal relationship with the Lord.

The final few miles of the run were exceptionally difficult. The thought ran through my mind to unpack my sleeping bag and take a nap on the side of the road. I shook off that thought and gave everything I had to keep moving through those miles. Finally, I reached the small town of Datil. Once again, my motel was attached to a restaurant and convenience store. This made me happy because it meant I did not have to walk far for anything! When I checked in, the desk clerk let me know my sister called to see if I had checked in yet. I quickly sent her an e-mail letting her know I arrived safely and asked her to let the rest of my family know I was making progress.

I showered and came back to get dinner, only to realize it was Valentine's Day. The restaurant was all decked out with a special menu, red tablecloths, and flowers. I sat down and ordered a piece of steak to reward myself for making it through a tough day. When I looked up, I couldn't help but smile to myself as I noticed a few couples looking at me with what I assumed were looks of pity. I realized that to anyone who did not know what I was there for probably thought I had been stood up on a Valentine's Day date. I laughed a little on the inside before downing a nice dessert and loading up on supplies at the convenience store.

The daily battle with fatigue is wearing on me. My only explanation for being able to run so many miles is that the Lord is giving me additional strength. I am beyond tired and happy to have a chance to sleep for six or seven hours before getting after a thirty-five-mile day tomorrow.

February 15—Day 27: Datil-Magdalena, New Mexico, 35.8 Miles. 780.9 Total Miles.

Today was another beautiful day in both the scenery and the weather. I was especially thankful for a wide shoulder to run on as I began the day. Although it started out chilly, the sunny weather helped it to warm up to about sixty degrees.

Soon after I began, the road opened up to a long, twenty-mile straightaway through the desolate New Mexico highway. The scenery was beautiful and serene as I passed herds of wild deer with gorgeous mountains in the distance. Parts of the scenery that were not completely natural were large, white satellite dishes. The dishes were huge and appeared to be close, but it took a very long time to get to them. I guessed it was a great place to study the sky because I saw signs for an observatory about four miles out of the way. I would have stopped at it if I were in a car, but I was in no mood to run any additional mileage!

The long straightaway gave me a great chance to relax and pray. I was happy to pray for intentions sent to me from friends, so many of the prayers were said for people I knew very well. One in particular was for my former roommate Matt, who was scheduled to be ordained a priest the following year. I thought that if he could give his entire life to the Lord, then the least I could do was give everything I had to God during my journey. It helped me to push my body very hard, which allowed me to gain ground on the mountains in the horizon.

By the time I reached the town, I was sure I looked like I had nothing left to give. I was exhausted and in a lot of physical pain, as I had also battled stomach issues on top of my normal leg problems. On my way into the town, I waved to a police officer sitting in his car, and I could tell by his response that he thought I was out of my mind, pushing a stroller in a place where towns were very far apart. I was too tired to talk, so I continued moving on until I reached my motel at the end of the town.

The woman at the motel counter was very nice and directed me to where I could get food. After a quick shower and an e-mail to my family, I hobbled over to a nearby bar and ordered a soda and pizza. It was a quiet little bar with only a person coming in on occasion to purchase a six-pack of beer or a lottery ticket. It seemed to be a poor area, and I made a mental note to keep all the poor in my prayers. Since the next town was going to be much larger and was only twenty-seven miles away, I decided to pick up some snacks and soda at the bar. My waitress paid for my purchase of supplies despite me telling her that it was not a problem. I thanked her and said I would keep her in my prayers while on the road.

As I limped back to my motel, I felt as though I had once again seen Jesus in someone. I could only assume from our conversation that this woman did not have very much, but she was willing to help me out anyway. The waitress said she had a son and would want others to take care of him, so she took care of me by making sure I had enough supplies to reach my next location.

I can only imagine what this world would be like if more people had the attitude of my waitress this evening. The experience of being helped by this woman truly makes me want to be a better person and act as generous as I can with the blessings the Lord has given to me. Physically, I am very tired. Spiritually, I feel rejuvenated. If I had to choose between the physical and spiritual, I wouldn't have things any other way than how I feel right now.

February 16—Day 28: Magdalena-Socorro, New Mexico, 27.1 Miles. 808 Total Miles.

I was thankful to be in short sleeves by 10:00 a.m. despite a cool start to the day. Twenty-seven miles seemed like a long distance but was relatively short given some of my recent mileage days. It was such a relief to relax a little from a mental standpoint because I did not have to psyche myself up for a very long day. Once again, I was blessed with beautiful mountain scenery everywhere I looked. I tried not to get distracted because the road was narrow in some spots, and I had to periodically jump off the road to allow vehicles to pass.

The key for me today was the encouragement I received from the drivers on the road. Traffic was far heavier than I thought it would be for the area of the country I was running in. I guessed the truckers had seen me on their route over the previous few days because on so many occasions I received honks, waves, and smiles from them. The good nature and smiling faces of the drivers helped my mood for the first fifteen miles of the run. The next section wove down a fairly steep road that dropped about two thousand feet to the town of Socorro. It was a tough stretch of road that only made my pesky leg problem feel worse. I used the promise of a decent-sized town up ahead to keep my mind off the pain.

A few miles outside the town, I was treated to a small laugh when an officer in a police vehicle waved at me and gave me a strange look. Obviously, he didn't think I was threatening in any way, but watching him trying to figure out what I was doing had me laughing to myself for the final few miles. I finally rolled into town, and I wound down my prayers for the day. They had helped me stay focused, and I ended on a prayer a teenager sent me asking me to pray for my own determination. I thought it was so thoughtful of him to remind me to pray for myself. I gladly obliged as I asked the Lord to help me to stay focused.

As I hit the streets of Socorro, I saw a signal appear on my phone for the first time in about a week! I made my way to the motel, and before I even finished checking in, I confused a woman who peeked into my jogger. She walked away disappointed there was no baby inside and did not seem at all interested as to why it was filled with supplies. I chuckled to myself at the misunderstanding.

After taking a hot shower, I gave an interview over the phone as quickly as I could because of an intense craving for good food. Once the interview was wrapped up, I walked down to a brewery, calling my family on the way. I was happy to talk to my aunt back in Phoenix and was also psyched to eat a fantastic burger paired with a very tasty dark beer. After being away from any sizable town for a long time, eating at an awesome restaurant was such a treat.

I made it back to my motel in time to take my laundry to a Laundromat next door. It was difficult to wait for the laundry as I sat there with my head nodding, doing my best to stay awake. Once my laundry was mostly dry, I grabbed my clothes and began walking back to the motel with my clothes in hand. On my way out, I held the door for a man named Vernon who was going in. He was so thankful that I stopped to help him. He insisted on giving me a soda. I could tell he did not have very much but also saw that it gave him great joy to return to the favor, so I graciously accepted the soda.

It is clear to me that many people are willing to share what little they possess. I hope to treat others the same way many kind people have treated me since I began my run. It is one more unexpected lesson I have learned on this journey. I will be thanking God for this learning opportunity as I go to bed tonight. I am also going to shave for the first time on the trip because my reddish, unkempt beard is starting to look terrible!

February 17—Day 29: Socorro-San Antonio, New Mexico, 11.4 Miles. 819.4 Total Miles.

I was finally able to catch up on some much needed sleep. I began at 11:00 a.m. since I had a short distance to run. It was my shortest planned run of the entire journey, and it started out absolutely gorgeous—sunny with the temperature rising to the high sixties. There was a small headwind, but I was not bothered by it all that much.

The first five miles were uneventful, but then my leg injury flared up again. The pain made me wince each time I bent my left knee. Despite the discomfort, I actually had bigger problems. At least ten different dogs chased me down the country road I was running on. I got the distinct impression that they wanted to hurt me. Fortunately, I had the foresight to purchase a device that delivered a sound annoying to dogs but one that people could not hear. It seemed to confuse them more than anything, and it gave me about ten feet of space. It was extremely frustrating to be in pain while I tried to fend off dogs for about six miles. I was badgered for such a big part of the day that I was not able to get through many intentions.

I was simply happy to finally arrive in one piece at the bed and breakfast in San Antonio. The owners were so nice, and it felt like they could be my grandparents. Simply talking with them made me miss growing up with my family and having a place of my own. They were in awe of my task and wanted to make sure I was eating enough! They suggested a good place to eat and set me up with a very comfortable room. I made my way to a small restaurant called Buckhorn Tavern where I ate two green chili cheeseburgers. They were unreal and quickly became the highlight of my day, although not becoming dinner for the dogs was a close second.

I definitely miss my family and friends as the loneliness of the run has sunk in deep by this point. It is about sixty-five miles to the next place with a motel, but I am hoping to camp out about thirty miles down the road at a tiny town that consists of two houses. If nothing else, it should certainly be an interesting day. I am not going to spend energy I do not have worrying about it now. As I have done the entire run thus far, I will leave it in God's hands, and I have no doubt things will work out just fine.

February 18—Day 30: San Antonio-Bingham, New Mexico, 29 Miles. 848.4 Total Miles.

I was so thankful to my hosts at the Casa Blanca Bed and Breakfast for making me a fantastic breakfast before I took off down the road. They were kind enough to send me off with a bag of cookies as well, which were very addicting and also completely consumed before 10:00 a.m.

I crossed the Rio Grande in the morning and continued at a slow pace on a seemingly endless stretch of uphill road. The scenery was beautiful and wide open. I could see for miles around as beige grass and small bushes surrounded me. I could see small hills all around me in addition to impressive mountains climbing out of the horizon. As tired as I felt, I was happy there was not much traffic. The people who did drive by were all waving. I imagined that people were just very friendly in the area because my hands were as tired as my legs from waving so much!

While running down the highway, I saw a man riding a horse with another one in tow. I said a quick hello to him and figured he was a local rancher, but I found out later in the day he was riding from Arkansas to California. I did pray for him as I had made a habit of praying for each person who I passed on the roads. I promised myself to continue this after the run was over because the world would be better place if we all prayed for everyone we met. Since the miles were long and somewhat slow, it gave me a great opportunity to pray for others. Many of the requests today were simple requests of parents asking prayers for their children. I sensed the pain in some of their requests as I could tell they loved their kids but were torn apart by seeing them struggle with anything from drug addictions to their faith. I felt bad for them because of their helplessness. Like everything else on this run, I knew there was no better route to go than to pray for them. I asked that they would accept the Lord and see his presence in their lives. I hoped they would find the peace in their lives that only Christ could provide.

After what felt to my legs like an eternity, I finally saw two houses down the road and surmised that it was the town of Bingham. Upon arriving at the second house, I met the owners, Don and Allison. Allison was a sweet motherly figure, and Don was a tough guy with a great sense of humor. They were so nice to me and not only allowed me to stay on their property for the night but also allowed me to come inside for a home-cooked meal of spaghetti. I was planning on having a package of tuna for dinner, so it felt like I was eating at a fancy restaurant. Allison would not take any money for allowing me to stay on their property. I loved the chance to simply talk to both her and Don. They encouraged me on my journey and also called ahead to a ranch where they said I could stay the following night if needed. It was so nice to relax for an evening and to have some normal conversation with people. I was sure they thought nothing of it, but just spending time with them was a tremendous gift.

Since I left the everyday life behind, I have begun to see just how many things I took for granted. I only hope I continue to treasure the small things in life after the run is over. I am tired from the distance but feel beyond thankful for all the blessings that continue to come my way each day. I truly feel the presence of the Lord, and this serves as confirmation that I am exactly where God needs me.

February 19—Day 31: Bingham-Carrizozo, New Mexico, 35.8 Miles. 884.2 Total Miles.

After a short night of sleep, I had some snacks and hit the road just after sunrise. The road began to rise over the first ten miles to six thousand nine hundred feet above sea level. The hills finally leveled off and then started to drop over the following twelve miles. I was extremely exhausted and decided to sit down for a few minutes. No sooner had I sat down than Troy, a man riding a motorcycle, turned back around to see if I was okay. We talked for a little while, and he gave me some sugared coffee from his canteen, which helped me wake up. He was visiting family down the road and was looking for work. Despite his situation, he offered me a twenty dollar bill out of his wallet. I just couldn't accept it but was completely overwhelmed by his generosity.

I started to pray for Troy as I continued running east, and he continued to ride west. The wind began to pick up to twenty-five miles per hour and was coming at me on an angle. It made forward movement very difficult, but I proceeded to push on at a slow pace. The scenery changed from a mountainous setting to a science fiction environment of black rock on either side of the highway. I was running through the lava flow remaining from volcanic activity a few thousand years earlier. It looked awesome, and the change of scenery helped to pass those windy miles rather quickly.

A few miles outside of town was the ranch I was set up to stay at for the night. I was feeling tired and knew I would feel better mentally if I put in a couple of extra miles on the day. When I finally reached town, an elderly man asked me what I was doing. When I told him, he walked off shaking his head and muttering to himself. I was not sure if he did not believe me or thought I was simply crazy. If nothing else, it provided me with a much needed laugh. After getting showered and changed, I made my way over to a diner. For dinner, I downed chicken fingers, a hamburger, and ice cream. It was the perfect meal.

Tomorrow is supposed to be about forty-six miles, so I know I am going to need as much rest as I can get. I feel blessed to not only feel connected to the prayer requests that continue to come in online but to also pray for people like Troy I meet along the way. As much as my body is taking a beating on this journey, the spiritual growth makes it more than worthwhile.

February 20–Day 32: Carrizozo-Corona, New Mexico, 46.8 Miles. 931 Total Miles.

Last night was not a good time to have trouble sleeping. I kept waking up during the night, and my legs were so sore that it made getting back to sleep nearly impossible. When I started out, the wind was quite strong. Thankfully, it was not in my face but was sustained at over thirty miles an hour and coming at my back on an angle. As I started heading north, there was an unbelievable sunrise to the east. There were a couple of mountain ranges in the distance with sections of clouds over them. The sunlight hit them with a gorgeous pinkish-orange hue. Even though I had just started, I stopped to enjoy the view and take a few pictures.

It was not easy to move forward on the highway with the strong wind and a shoulder that became narrow to nonexistent. The wind never died down, and the constant howling wore on me as I developed a pounding headache. It was persistent and stayed with me throughout the day. Not only did my leg decide to act up again, but the constant jumping on and off the road also had my left wrist burning in pain.

The aches and pains were one thing, but the road conditions and traffic were another story. The road itself was rolling, so it was often the case that I did not know what, if anything, was coming over the crest of the hills. In the past, I had been able to use my sense of hearing to listen for vehicles, but I was essentially running blind because of the wind. As if to give me a warning, there were many more roadkill on the stretch of highway than anywhere else I had run. My solution was to stray off the highway as I approached the top of each hill in case a car or truck came over the top.

Even at that, I still had a few cases where I came within a couple of feet of speeding vehicles. There were a couple of times where I just went off the road completely for a minute to take a breather and gather my thoughts. I spent so much of the day praying for strength and especially for safety.

The final five miles felt like they were never going to end as I continued to avoid cars and eighteen wheelers alike. I was distracted from my own desperate situation as I prayed for an intention of a family who was struggling in their relationships with each other. The son was estranged from his parents, and none of them seemed to know where to begin in trying to repair the broken bond. I sensed the pain they all felt as I prayed for them. There was no doubt in my mind it was these prayers that carried me through those final miles. I was never so happy to arrive at such a small town. It was a long and dangerous day with just as many prayers said for myself as for others. I checked into the small hotel in town and was thrilled they had a room available. Since there was no place open to eat dinner, I walked a distance back to a gas station to pick up dinner and additional supplies.

I just made it back to my room and microwaved five large burritos for dinner. It may be the food in my stomach, but I can barely move and feel beyond fatigued. The mileage is a definite struggle and has not become any easier. I cannot believe I have continued to run so far day after day. It is purely a mental and spiritual battle at this point. If it were not for my faith and my promise to pray for others, I believe I would have quit long ago.

February 21–Day 33: Corona-Vaughn, 34.8 Miles. 965.8 Total Miles.

This morning started out very rough. The temperature was in the twenties, but the wind chill factor made it feel like twelve degrees. Forward progress was still difficult as the road was narrow, and there was a fair amount of traffic, mostly semitrucks, on the road. In addition to those conditions, my hands immediately became numb, and I had waves of pain radiating up through my leg. By the time I was a few miles in, I was beginning to feel incredibly dejected and had a difficult time imagining how I would reach my destination, still well over thirty miles away.

I truly felt the loneliness of the run from a mental standpoint. The physical discomfort was also sinking in quite deep. As always, I turned to prayer. I prayed for a person who passed away from cancer. I also had an intention for an infant in a life-threatening situation. The requests reminded me of how life was so precious. I remembered how my mother never gave up in her fight against cancer. I thought of how difficult it was for those who had to watch their small children suffer in pain. I knew Jesus had suffered while he was on earth and prayed that he would be with these people in their sufferings as well. These thoughts made me run even harder. I also made sure to pray for myself. I asked God to give me the grace and strength to get through the day.

The prayer intentions either gave me enough inspiration or I had a direct answer to my prayer for strength because things quickly turned in my favor. The wind died down, and the temperature climbed to where I was quite comfortable. A shoulder appeared on the road, and my leg began to feel much better. My mile splits started to drop as I continued to run much faster. I was even blessed with some conversation on the road as there were a couple of construction crews working on the road at miles twenty-two and thirty-three. The men all had a great sense of humor and joked with me about how crazy yet awesome my endeavor seemed. It was just what I needed and helped put me in a great mood as I continued on mile after long mile to town.

My spirit was unexpectedly lifted when I was about a mile away from my motel. A car drove by me before pulling a sudden U-turn and then drove up beside me. It startled me at first. I said hello, and the man asked me where I came from and where I was running. When I told him, his eyes lit up, and he said, "God bless you!" about five times. He then asked me if I liked running in New Mexico, and I told him I loved the scenery. Evidently, that was the answer he was looking for because a big smile covered his face, and he drove off, pumping his fist in the air out his open window. The encounter caught me off guard but made me feel great and helped my attitude.

The day was productive, and I was very content with my progress by the time I rolled up to my motel. When I stopped in a convenience store to load up on supplies, I heard the song "In My Life" by the Beatles. It was the song I danced to with my mom during the mother-son dance at my wedding. It brought back so many memories, and in an instant, I found myself overwhelmed and actually started to tear up. I paid quickly and left before anyone noticed. It was clear that my emotional barriers were no longer existent. Because of the extreme exhaustion, I found myself once again having a hard time concealing anything I felt. I was sad because of how much I missed her, and it was only compounded by being so far away from anyone I knew. It was tough moments like this where I found myself relying on my faith to pull me through.

I have complete trust that God will carry me through the difficult times because the distances between the next two towns are fifty-eight and sixty miles. I am weary, sore, and feel I cannot make those types of distances in a single day. However, I know that all things are possible with Christ, even if those things feel out of reach. I will do my part by getting to bed early tonight and allow the Lord to lead me as far as I am meant to go tomorrow.

February 22—Day 34: Vaughn-Fort Sumner, 58 Miles. 1,023.8 Total Miles.

I knew today was going to be brutal. I made sure to start out right by eating breakfast at 3:30 a.m. at a twenty-four-hour diner. I quickly packed up my stroller and hit the road just before sunrise. In one of the most awesome sights I had ever seen, my vantage point on the highway allowed me to witness the orange glow of the sun sweeping across the land as it turned the darkness of the land into the brightness of day. On a day where I was feeling anxious, that beautiful sight brought to my heart such a wonderful feeling of serenity.

The first few miles were tough as the road was rolling with little to no shoulder. I quickly realized there were very few vehicles traveling on Route 60. Therefore, I was able to run much more relaxed. I continued making calculations about how fast I was running. I felt a constant pressure to move quickly in order to make it to Fort Sumner before dark.

The view was nothing to keep me occupied as I could see for miles on end over the flat terrain. I would focus on a telephone pole or a cell tower in the distance and was constantly surprised at just how long it took me to get there. Once I arrived, it felt as though I was rewarded with the identical view as the previous stretch of miles. The repetitiveness of the scenery and the quietness of my surroundings all day long would be enough to normally drive me crazy. Instead, I used the time as an opportunity to continue to pray for the intentions for the sick, the unemployed, the unborn, those with relationship issues, and those with nobody to pray for them. As long as fifty-eight miles took to run, I learned that it would take much longer than that to run out of people to keep in my prayers.

Only two things distracted me from my immersion in prayer during the long stretch of miles. The first was about twenty-two miles into the run, when a fighter jet flew extremely low directly over my head! I could not believe the noise it made and how low it flew. I gathered I was running through an area used for military aircraft training. The experience was so cool as I essentially had a flyover all to myself. If the sound of a military jet flying a couple of hundred feet over my head was not enough to get my blood flowing, just thirteen miles later, I hit the one-thousand-mile marker of the run. It was a huge milestone. More than anything else, it made me feel like I was actually making progress on the journey. I calculated the distance as the equivalent of more than thirty-eight marathons. As good as it felt to pass one thousand miles, the thought of so many marathons in a short period of time made my legs feel the heaviness of the run even more than usual.

I was totally spent when I hit the fifty-mile mark, but two good things happened simultaneously. The road widened and gave me a shoulder to run on for the first time all day. Additionally, I saw the town of Fort Sumner in the distance. At the time, the town was about eight miles away but simply being able to finally see where I was going made a huge difference in my mood. I pushed hard those final miles to reach my motel with plenty of daylight to spare.

After such a long day, I was psyched to find a place to eat that had a massive burrito, which was unbelievably tasty. I polished it off with a cold beverage and dessert. I stunned the waitress by completely clearing my huge plate of food in a matter of minutes and following it with more food!

I somehow made the stumble back to my motel after that awesome dinner. I feel as though I can barely move, so I plan on sleeping in tomorrow. I look forward to enjoying a well-deserved day off before tackling another daunting day. Fifty-eight miles seemed endless, so I cannot even begin to think what sixty miles will be like, which is how far it is to the next town. I am thanking God I can take a day of rest to prepare myself for that kind of monster mileage.

February 23—Day 35: Rest in Fort Sumner, New Mexico, 1,023.8 Total Miles.

I was glad to have a day off because every muscle in my body was deeply sore. Simply walking down the hall to do laundry took a long time. As much as I had run, my love for the sport was not diminished. On my walk into town to load up on supplies, I walked by a track. I briefly thought about jumping on it for a quick workout. However, I reminded myself how crazy that idea was given the circumstances. After replenishing my supplies, I did laundry and napped like a champion. At over one thousand miles into the journey, I still considered it a very productive day!

I enjoyed going back to the same place I ate the previous night to get another awesome burrito and dessert. There were a couple of times

I noticed the waitress looking at me with a surprised look on her face. I guessed they had never seen anyone eat so much in such a short period of time. I laughed to myself on my hobble back to the motel, trying to take advantage of every opportunity I had to help my mood.

As long as yesterday's run was, the thought of running even further tomorrow has made it tough to completely relax today. Resting my legs, writing down new prayer requests, doing laundry, and restocking my supplies for the upcoming miles have been a good use of my time. Staying busy and resting did little to calm the anxiety I feel for tomorrow. I am confident that with the Lord's help, I will make it. I know I cannot avoid the discomfort that awaits me tomorrow, but I take comfort in knowing I will not have to face it alone.

February 24–Day 36: Fort Sumner-Clovis, New Mexico, 60.5 Miles. 1,084.3 Total Miles.

The longest single day of my run began this morning as I hit the road well before sunrise. Since it was still dark out, I ran with my headlight, three blinking lights, and as much reflective gear as I had packed. To anyone passing me by, I must have looked like a Christmas tree in motion. I could not even think about the overall distance of the day for quite some time. I was purely focused on staying on the road and avoiding traffic at the early hour. By the time the sun finally broke across the horizon, I had run over ten miles. It was a nice start to the day but did little to minimize the fact that I still had over fifty miles to run before I could rest.

I took a picture of myself at sunrise and immediately became concerned when I looked at it. For the first time on the run, I noticed how much of a toll the journey was taking on my body. My face was sunken in. I had clearly lost weight, and it appeared as if I was barely keeping my eyes open. I looked tired and completely beaten down. I tried not to let it bother me as I continued down the road. I had to fight off a multitude of negative ideas. These thoughts made me question if I could make it to not only the end of the day, but to the end of the entire journey. My body was certainly taking a beating, and the truth was that I did not know my limits. I prayed that my limits were sufficient for what I had planned. If the picture was any indication, my limits were quickly approaching. I knew I would have to rely on God even more than I had already done to carry me through to the end.

My saving grace today was that the terrain flattened out so I did not have to deal with dramatic elevation changes. There was a rail line that paralleled Route 60 for most of the day so I was able to wave to the trains periodically. I was not certain if the train whistle was supposed to sound or if the conductor was making the noise for me. I did not really care which it was, but I took it as an encouraging sign.

The miles passed by slower and slower, even though my pace was maintained at a steady clip. Physically, I was starting to run out of steam at about the thirty-mile mark. However, it quickly became much more of a mental battle. I had to focus on the fact that I already put in thirty miles. It was difficult to not concentrate on the thirty plus miles I still had to run. My head bowed down momentarily as I prayed for guidance and strength.

Once again, the prayer intentions helped to keep me focused on why I was putting my body through such a challenge. I had a variety of prayer requests, but one involved praying for a woman who passed away from liver cancer, which I could relate to because of my own mother's death. There was also another woman I spent time in prayer for who was battling cancer. Another request was for a couple about to lose their home because they could not keep up with their bills because of medical issues. It was very difficult to think of what those people were going through, but it drove me to pray intently for them. They helped me to run strong even when my body wanted to give up.

I did take an occasional break from praying to simply relax my mind. I even said hello to the cows and horses that frequently came up to the perimeter fences as I ran by. Since there were no people I encountered on the road today, I did my best to envision the animals as my personal cheering section.

When I finally reached the fifty-mile mark, I could feel my body start to shut down. The aches I experienced throughout my muscles quickly turned into intense pain. My run shifted into more of a shuffle as my legs locked up. My eyes felt heavy and were begging to close if I would simply pull off onto the side of the road and take a break. As much as these forces tried to pull me away from my task, I focused on the prayer intention for a young girl who had been both emotionally and physically abused. She was in the midst of a custody battle at the time of the request. I offered up my suffering and pain for her over those final miles. I prayed she could live a happy and peaceful life without unnecessary pain. I knew my run would eventually come to an end, but her battle did not have a clear time of when or if she would be placed in the custody of a caring family. When I received the intention for the little girl, it broke my heart and encouraged me to keep going and to keep praying. I understood that as long as I had people like that little girl to pray for, I would continue to run and pray until my legs were physically unable to move forward any longer. I trusted God would hear and answer those prayers.

I finally entered the town of my destination just in time to have two pit bulls come out from a yard and start chasing me. I turned around to face them. I was so weary that I did not think I could fend off the dogs on my own. I braced myself for an unpleasant encounter when I was startled by an eighteen-wheeler that drove by while honking its horn. It was enough to scare the dogs back to their yard. I was beyond thankful to that driver for his kind act.

The final miles into town felt just as shaky as on the outskirts where I was chased. I did my best to continue running hard. The effort was finally rewarded when I made it to the motel unscathed, but in a lot of discomfort and extremely tired. I was so relieved to be in a decent-sized town and ordered pizza to be delivered to my room so I would not have to walk anywhere.

The absence of movement has never felt so good. I say this as I lay in my motel room, sprawled out on the mattress after eating two pizzas I had delivered to me. I'm not certain I could move much of my body right now even if I wanted to. I am ridiculously sore in my legs from all the running. My arms and upper body are equally sore from pushing the eighty-pound jogger the entire day. As sore as I am, I have a huge smile of relief on my face for finishing such a long day.

Today was a perfect example of how God was with me out on the roads. I know I would not have made it on my own. Without help, I would have been in much more trouble with the attacking dogs. My best explanation is that God is taking this run with me and will continue to be at my side through every step of the way. In my mind, there is no other way I can make it to New York. I am completely reliant on the Lord and, as such, have never felt more confident in the success of my mission.

February 25—Day 37: Rest in Clovis, New Mexico, 1,084.3 Total Miles.
After the run to Clovis, my body demanded I take a day of rest, so I obliged. Despite being off from running for the day, it was actually quite productive. I gave a radio interview over the phone before speaking with a local reporter, Liliana, in person. She was kind enough to drive me into the main part of town where I received a much needed sports massage for my

legs. Thankfully, there was a mall nearby, and I picked up another pair of running shoes since I went through my shoes rather quickly. I did not think the two pairs I had with me would last until the next time I was scheduled to be restocked on running gear outside of Oklahoma City. The mall was a couple of miles from town, but the walk back was a nice way to keep my body loose. After getting prepared for the next day, I went to a small diner and absolutely crushed a few entrees in addition to a large dessert. The poor waitress kept bringing me a check. In turn, I would then order more food. I was slightly embarrassed but figured I needed the calories!

I hope that my body stays healthy and strong because I still have some long miles ahead of me. As I get set to run another day well above fifty miles, I can't help but think back to just a few years ago when I had trouble getting through ten miles a week. I never could have imagined doing this type of mileage, but I think it is a perfect example of how God helps us achieve things beyond our imagination if we only trust in him.

RUNNING THROUGH TROUBLE

The angel of the Lord encamps around those who fear him, and he delivers them.

Psalm 34:7

February 26—Day 38: Clovis, New Mexico-Dimmitt, Texas, 54.5 Miles. 1,138.8 Total Miles.

Once again, I started my run at sunrise to give myself the best chance of finishing before I ran out of daylight. The first milestone of the day came only eight miles into the run. I reached the Texas border and had a Texas-sized smile on my face to enter the state! I took some photos before moving on and also allowed a few moments to enjoy my progress. I felt like I was moving well because the panhandle of Texas was close to the middle of the country. This thought had me riding high emotionally as I continued running in the warm weather into Texas.

I enjoyed the scenery around me of farm houses and wide open land. Large rolls of hay were scattered throughout the massive fields. It was quite peaceful and serene. I was not even bothered by the dogs that came out to chase me. The only thing that slightly irritated me was the smell of cattle farms. After more than a few trucks transporting farm animals drove by, I did start to feel nauseated. Since the weather was warm, each time one of the trucks passed me, I got hit with a gust of warm air that smelled quite terrible. I quickly learned to turn my head and hold my breath for a few seconds each time one of them passed.

The lift I got from entering Texas began to dissipate about twenty miles into the day. My body began to sink into a deep soreness. I kept running and was extremely grateful the terrain was flat. I also continued praying as I had a fresh list of prayer intentions I copied onto a sheet of paper during my day off. I was thankful for that because of the long road that still lie ahead. I was encouraged by the continued support and prayers of people following my journey. Encouragement also came in the form of answered prayers, as one person wrote on my site that a family member whom she asked me to pray for was in good health again, which she called a miracle. This type of message made the journey more than worth the effort.

After running on Route 60 for a number of days, I finally turned east on Route 86 and ran through a small town before hitting the open road again. I was about a marathon into the run when I experienced a truly amazing occurrence. I had the feeling someone was near me. I turned around completely. The terrain was very flat, and I could see for miles in every direction. The scenery was completely still, except for one thing: there was a man running the same direction as I was, but on the other side of the road. He was dressed in white from head to toe. I turned back around and asked myself what someone else would be doing out there because we were far away from any towns or even houses at that point. I decided to take the opportunity to speak with him and see what he was doing. I turned back around to say hello, but he was gone despite there being nowhere to go. I believed that I saw my guardian angel for a moment. It made complete sense my angel would be following closely behind me. I was sure I was keeping my angel quite busy as I had come so close to disaster on many occasions. It was the highlight of not only my day, but of the entire run.

I still had close to thirty miles to run, so I didn't pause too long to think about it. The final ten miles were challenging because I became very nauseous and dry-heaved many times. I felt terrible and tired but was thrilled when I finally saw the sign welcoming me to the town of my destination. I checked into the motel, where the owners were so nice and gave me a low rate for the night.

After a much needed shower, I walked into town. I found a Pizza Hut and sat down with a large, two-topping pizza and a big glass of sweet tea. Before I started eating, I was joined by a gentleman named David, who had been eating with his family nearby. He saw I was eating alone and asked if he could join me. He thought I may have been a new sports coach in town because I was dressed in athletic gear. I then proceeded to tell him my story. Dave told me that he was a former pastor and current city manager. It was so great to talk to someone about faith and life in general. I was accustomed to eating alone because of the nature of the trip, but it reminded me of how much I missed interaction with people. Before I left, Dave gave me a few prayer requests of his own, including one to pray for rain because of the extreme drought that part of the country was experiencing.

Today was packed with lots of miles and a few great situations. It has me feeling rejuvenated and inspired to continue pushing on as hard as I can when I continue making progress through Texas tomorrow.

February 27—Day 39: Dimmitt-Tulia, Texas, 31.5 Miles. 1,170.3 Total Miles.

Because of the previous long mileage day, thirty miles did not seem terrible in comparison. I started later than normal because of both the mileage and a time I was supposed to meet up with a reporter outside of Tulia.

The first fifteen miles were not bad, although it was slightly windy. I had dealt with wind before, so I was not worried when I heard the wind would be around fifteen to twenty-five miles per hour. However, all that changed after I passed the town of Nazareth. I had been running along pretty well, but suddenly the wind picked up incredibly fast. It was as if someone had turned a switch on from low to super high. When the high winds were combined with an area in a severe drought, conditions were perfect for a dust storm. The wind came from the southwest. When I turned toward that direction, I saw a huge wall of dirt barreling at me as high and as wide as I could see. There was no doubt in my mind things were about to become quite rough and that there would be no outrunning the storm. I could only hope and pray to endure.

I furiously changed my running cap into a thin winter hat. I did this so that it would not blow away and would simultaneously protect my ears. I then pulled out a bandana from one of my bags and wrapped it around my mouth and nose. I also ensured my sunglasses were tight on my face. I then braced myself for the impending storm just as the wall of dust swallowed me up.

Visibility became limited, and since the road I was on was not very wide, I had to be extremely careful to avoid the oncoming cars. I felt as if I were in the middle of a Hollywood movie as large tumbleweeds quickly rolled across my path. Some of the tumbleweeds hit my legs. I quickly discovered I should do my best to avoid them if possible because they were thorny, and it really hurt when they struck my body. I was only partially successful in that endeavor. I would often hear them coming up on the road, but they were moving so fast that I had no time to react and would get a quick sting in the leg.

The tumbleweeds, debris, and avoidance of cars were not my only problems. The wind and dirt were relentless. I would continually get knocked off my feet, and I would have to catch myself from falling all the way down. The wind was strong enough to push my stroller off one of its wheels. I constantly had to push it back on the ground to keep it from falling over. On top of it all, I had to do my best to move forward for over sixteen nasty miles.

After fighting the elements for what felt like hours, I looked down at my watch and realized I had not even gone a mile since the storm first hit. Despite my best effort to cover my face, there was dirt in my eyes and mouth. I was also coughing violently from the filthy air. The situation was extremely demoralizing, and the conditions completely sucked all the energy out of me.

I had to pull off the road on a couple of occasions and sit with my back up against the stroller for some protection from the wind. I checked the weather on my phone and saw the winds were steady at over forty miles per hour and gusting between sixty and seventy miles per hour. I regretted checking the severity of the wind because of the toll it took on me mentally. I believed I would be protected but knew I was in for a battle nonetheless. The remaining miles took everything I had. I remained in constant prayer but had little memory of what else occurred in those miles. I needed protection and strength more than ever. Somehow, I eventually stumbled into my motel. When I looked in the mirror, I had two dark circles around my eyes where the edges of my sunglasses were, and my face and neck were also caked in dirt. Before getting dinner, I showered and brushed my teeth for a long time. I had the feeling it would be days until I would feel clean again.

I don't think I've ever felt as I relieved as I do now. I am so grateful to be out of the elements. There is dirt everywhere, and I just spent a long time shaking the sand out of my belongings. If nothing else, I have a new appreciation for good weather. I also have a new appreciation for answered prayers. It was absolutely brutal out there, and I know it was the hand of God that brought me to safety.

February 28—Day 40: Tulia-Turkey, Texas, 54.4 Miles. 1,224.7 Total Miles.

I had another long trek scheduled for today, but the absence of high winds and blowing dirt made it much more bearable. However, I put myself in a predicament by starting later than I had originally planned. The run through the elements the previous afternoon took everything out of me. I still felt the effects of it in the morning as it took much longer than usual to get dressed and get my stroller packed. I had well over fifty miles to get through before reaching my destination and felt nervous because of the limited amount of daylight.

The time constraint worried me. I pushed it very hard for the first fifteen miles to give myself a cushion. However, once I hit the fifteen-mile mark, I also hit a terrible wall. My legs wanted to quit, and my mind felt like it had no more fight left in it. I decided to walk for about four minutes. I tried my best to give a pep talk to myself. Neither effort worked. A young man in a pickup truck stopped to see if I was okay. He had a strong southern accent and told me, "I didn't know what you were!" He was very kind and offered me some water. We both continued on our respective ways, and I said a decade of the rosary for him as I continued my attempt at a run.

The prayer requests definitely helped me to keep moving forward. I prayed for a family who seemed at the end of their own rope because the father could not find work. I read messages of encouragement, and people told me I was in their prayers as well. Knowing that people were still praying for me also gave me strength. However, I still felt extremely weak and had great trouble putting one foot in front of the other. I slowed down even more and finally found myself at a complete standstill. Then it hit me: I had nothing left. I asked God to help me once again because I knew I could not continue under my own power. I was stopped on the side of the road with almost forty more miles to go on the day and thousands of miles to go before reaching the Atlantic. I spoke to God not by looking up to heaven but prayed as if he was standing right next to me because I felt in that moment he was that close.

It wasn't easy, but somehow I got moving again and was able to keep moving all the way to the small town of Turkey. It hurt, and I even strained a muscle in my lower right leg, but I finally arrived at the doorstep of my motel as the sun went down. It was a close call, but I made it just in time. The hotel clerk, Albert, was very nice and gave me a couple of dollars for dinner at a small cafe in town. I was exhausted but could still see very easily that people were so generous and kind.

After a long day, it feels fantastic to put my legs up and relax. I have another long day tomorrow, but I am not worrying about it now. If God can pull me through over fifty-four miles with the way I felt today, I have no doubt he will find a way to carry me through whatever tomorrow may bring.

March 1—Day 41: Turkey-Childress, Texas, 45.9 Miles. 1,270.6 Total Miles.

I had another high-mileage trek planned for today, but it started out perfectly when Albert made a big breakfast for me at the motel. A few locals joined me, including a farmer who I waved to the previous evening when he brought in his tractor from the fields. The people in town worked long hours. After talking with them, I had a new respect for how hard they labored. I was happy to see I was building friendships with people in small towns along the way. I started out the journey thinking the most memorable parts of the run would be the beautiful scenery along the way, but I learned the best parts of the run were much more about the people I met.

The breakfast with the locals of Turkey made me really miss being around others, especially my family. I tried to keep my attitude positive and enjoy everything around me. I was able to do this today by seeing humor in the cattle I ran by in the early miles. The road curved through some hills where cattle were grazing, and they would often gather together and just stare at me as I ran by them. I guessed it was a sight they did not usually see. I started laughing when I heard them mooing but could not see them because of the terrain. I had my personal soundtrack of echoing cows as I ran through the hills. At the time it seemed quite funny, and if nothing else, it kept my spirits up. I felt like I really needed it as my body continued to feel the heaviness of the miles sinking in to every fiber of muscle in my legs.

I always tried to run the entire distance through the day without stopping. However, the tiredness I felt in my body called for a break. There was not much around as I continued east on Route 86, so I stopped at the first place possible, which was a very small diner in the town of Estelline. I sat down at one of about seven bar stools and ordered a grilled cheese sandwich with a sweet tea. It may have been a simple meal, but it tasted absolutely phenomenal. I spoke to the woman who ran the diner and answered a handful of questions that her young son asked about my trip and the stroller. Also at the diner was a middle-aged gentleman who was local to the area. He offered to pay for my meal, and I should have taken him up on the offer. I got the impression he did not have too much to spare, so I graciously declined. It was a situation I experienced frequently. I once again struggled with how to react to the offers of help. I thought it may be better to accept the offers of assistance in the future and resolved to make a conscious effort to accept help that came my way. I knew I often looked to help people around me, but I realized that we all needed help at times in our lives, and this was clearly one of those times where I could use assistance. As I jumped back on the road and turned onto Route 287 toward Childress, I told myself that I should not be proud and to simply accept any help that came across my path.

Sometimes I am taught a lesson about life or about myself, and today I learned to be a gracious recipient of kindness. As I was thinking about this, I was almost immediately presented with an opportunity to act on what I learned. It was about fifteen miles from Estelline to my destination in Childress, and the road I was running on was having some work done on it by road crews. I waved and smiled at the crews as I ran past them. When I came upon the last crew, one of the workers came up to me without any prompting or discussion and pulled a five dollar bill out of his wallet and gave it to me. He said, "Something tells me you could use this." I had to smile inside because it looked like it was everything he had in his wallet, so my immediate thought was to politely decline. However, given what I had just been thinking about, I graciously accepted. His nickname was Lefty because he did not have a left hand. I told him about my mission of prayer and that I would say a prayer for him. I prayed a decade for Lefty before I reached Childress and also thanked God for the opportunity to have a second chance to be a gracious recipient.

I was so exhausted when I finally made it to my motel that I wanted to go straight to bed. However, I was also starving. I quickly showered and went out to eat at a nearby restaurant. After downing a big sandwich, I loaded up on supplies and packed up things for the following day's journey. I was about to get ready for bed when I realized I was still very hungry, so I went out and ate a few burgers at a fast food place nearby.

I am making a conscious effort to eat more because I feel like I am losing weight and I cannot afford to go into a calorie deficit if I hope to be successful. I am really looking forward to a shorter day tomorrow, but I am even more motivated by putting Texas behind me and entering Oklahoma. I am so blessed to meet great people on this journey and to learn valuable lessons in the process. My experiences do not take away the pain but continue to help me run through it. God is so good.

March 2—Day 42: Childress, Texas-Hollis, Oklahoma, 33.5 Miles. 1,304.1 Total Miles.

Most days seem to throw some type of curve at me, but thankfully there was not much to worry about on the road this morning. I started out a little later than normal because of the manageable distance to my destination. I was promptly greeted with a section of road that was mostly downhill as I made my way north. Despite some nagging pains from my left leg and some lingering soreness on my lower right leg, I was able to make decent time. It was easy to get lost in the miles because the scenery stayed fairly constant throughout the long miles. I ran by open fields of grass with low trees on a road that disappeared straight into the horizon. I did not feel like I was making progress, but my GPS watch continued to click off every mile.

I made it through many prayer requests as the road was mostly flat with at least a slight shoulder most of the way. Among the intentions I prayed for was a middle school boy fighting cancer, a family who lost a young boy in a tragic accident, and another family faced with the possibility of losing their young mother to a fatal disease. Simply reading the requests made me feel very sad. I wanted to take away their pain more than anything else in those moments. I prayed that the Lord would give them peace. I prayed for healing if it was in his will. Although I desired healing for everyone I prayed for, I also realized that the Lord's ways were so far above our ways. I believed God had a plan. I had to trust in that plan despite my inability to figure it out. As such, I did the only thing I could do. I continued to run and kept on praying.

My road finally turned east as I followed Route 62 toward the Oklahoma border. I wanted to enjoy the crossing because my schedule indicated it would be another two weeks until I ran into another state. The toughest part of the day hit a few miles before I reached the state sign. The wind picked up and was coming from the direction I was headed. This made forward progress even more difficult to my tired body, and my pace slowed drastically as a result.

I finally saw the state line landmark and took a few quick photos to commemorate the event. It felt great to put Texas behind me, but I made the mistake of zooming out on the map of my location. Instead of focusing on how far I had come, I saw how far I had in front of me. My thoughts turned to how difficult it would be for my beaten body to make it to the end. I did not see how I could make it to the finish with the way my body was feeling. It was at that time I reminded myself of Philippians 4:13, which says, "I can do all things in Christ who strengthens me." After a rough final stretch of miles, I finally pulled up to my destination, where a friend of a friend put me up for the night and fed me well.

Tomorrow starts a long trek through Oklahoma, and I am looking forward to the adventures that await me in this state. It was a tough mental battle today, but I think of the Philippians passage each time I feel as though this task is too much for me. I am reminded that it is too big for me to take on alone, and that is where my faith in the Lord strengthens me. I know that when I make it to the finish, it will be because of the strength Christ so lovingly bestowed upon me.

March 3—Day 43: Hollis-Mangum, Oklahoma. 35 Miles. 1,339.1 Total Miles

I got off to a slow start this morning because I did not sleep well at all the night before. It was extremely difficult to make the first few steps out the door in the morning. Everything hurt, and my body was crying out for rest. As difficult as it was to get started just before sunrise, I was rewarded for my efforts with the most beautiful sunrise I had ever seen. The sun was huge and shot out various shades of orange across the sky, lighting up the clouds as if I were watching them being painted by an invisible brush. I stopped to enjoy it for a minute before continuing on my way.

My body felt so weak, and I was moving slowly for the first two hours. I ran on back roads as I wanted to get off the main highway for some miles. The quiet was nice, but the often unpaved and sandy trails did not exactly help me make quick progress. The rut that my body was in slowed my physical progress, but it only increased my prayer life. I realized I had once again completely run out of energy but continued to place the day entirely in God's hands. I offered up the pain I endured for the prayer intentions I went through each mile.

I did not pray for as many intentions as a normal day, but it was because of the amount of time I spent in conversation with God. I felt as though he was right next to me on my journey, and I could talk to him as a friend. I found myself not looking up to heaven as much, but rather looking right next to me because I felt as though the Lord was right there by my side. I couldn't help but think that was how things usually were, but I had been too busy with my life to notice. I believed I felt so close to the Lord because I slowed down my life and spent so much time in prayer. I wanted the feeling to last, so I made a personal resolution to make more time for God in my daily life whenever the run ended. I promised myself that prayer would become a bigger part of my life. Additionally, I told God I would try my best to make my daily life look like I was living a prayer by my actions and my words.

I faced my toughest challenge today just outside of Mangum, when I came upon a bridge with no shoulder. There was a decent amount of traffic, and I had to time my crossing of the bridge to avoid when cars came across. I did not want to risk there being two cars going the opposite direction at the same time I was crossing because of limited room. I waited for a few minutes before taking my chance and sprinting across the bridge while pushing the stroller. As soon as I began running over the bridge, another car appeared coming my way, and there was a short line of cars behind me coming the opposite direction. It was too late to stop and go back. I somehow found another gear, which was not easy to do after already running thirty miles. There must have been a powerful source helping me because it felt as though I had a hand pushing me across. I absolutely flew over the bridge and made it to the other side just in time to pull off onto the side of the road, allowing the cars to pass without incident. I was exhausted but unscathed. There was barely enough energy in my tank to land on my feet for the final few miles into town.

I worried my motel was no longer in existence because of how far it was past the main part of town. Once I finally spotted it, I checked in and was able to get clean. I then gave an interview to a nice reporter from the local newspaper. He was more impressed with my reasons for the run as opposed to the run itself, which I was thrilled about. We had a nice discussion of how faith helped us through difficult times. After the interview ended, I ate a quick dinner and restocked my supplies for the next stretch of road.

My schedule from a mileage perspective is not too bad through Oklahoma, for which I am extremely thankful. I am so glad I planned some lower-mileage days at this section of my adventure. I am realizing it is not only good for my legs but is also a wonderful chance to get some extra sleep. I just hope I will be able to sleep well so that I can continue running strong.

March 4—Day 44: Mangum-Hobart, Oklahoma, 28 Miles. 1,367.1 Total Miles.

The frustrations started early this morning. A strong wind hit me head-on for the first four miles. The simple amount of distance was difficult. Pushing my heavy jogger on a road with no shoulder and against a powerful headwind made it exponentially more challenging. It felt like I had to work twice as hard to move forward, but even at that I was moving slowly and became drained very quickly. Perhaps the most frustrating thing about the start was that I could not get to the prayer requests because I was so focused on avoiding traffic and making forward progress. I used my time to ask God for strength. I also prayed to St. Michael the Archangel for protection. I laughed to myself thinking that they must have an abundance of patience because I had not stopped asking for protection since the moment I began my journey! There were a few close calls with vehicles on the road during the first thirty minutes. However, I truly believed God was leading my steps and keeping me out of harm's way. I simply gave everything I had and offered it all up for his glory. I trusted I would arrive in New York safely as long as I continued to do just that.

I was provided with a brief respite as I ran through the small town of Lone Wolf. I waved to two men who were out walking on the sidewalk, and they flagged me down to talk. The guys were so nice and invited me into the community center for a meal. I sat with a volunteer and also one of the men, whose nickname was Rainbow. He was a middle-aged man filled with kindness and had the demeanor of a man who worked extremely hard. We talked about my run, my mission of prayer, and farming. Each person I met in the small town was so kind and asked me to keep them in my prayers. It was such a blessing to take time out from running to connect with some great people. Rainbow took a picture of me in front of their town sign before I said goodbye and continued on my way. I felt great because I was fueled by the spaghetti lunch and felt encouraged by the good nature and kindness of my new friends.

The final nine miles of the day were extremely frustrating as the shoulder disappeared completely and traffic was heavy. In that final stretch of road, I was not on the pavement for any more than forty-five seconds at a time. I had to keep pulling the stroller off the side of the road in time to avoid the vehicles coming my way. My arms were burning in pain from the constant shifting of the heavy jogger on and off the road. It finally got to the point where I started to jog slowly through the thick grass because I was tired of waiting on the side of the road for traffic to clear. I finally stumbled into my motel and fell down on the bed in pain. It took a great deal of energy to get up and eat dinner before reloading on supplies.

There is a part of me that wants to stop this run so badly. It has tried to give me every reason as to why I should stop. One of those reasons is that I have gone so far already and should not risk hurting myself. However, I still have a deep sense of responsibility to those whom I promised to pray for. I also feel a responsibility for the requests I have not yet received, but which will undoubtedly come my way. The feeling that God has called me to do this is so strong. Unless I am physically unable to move on, I know I will reach the finish. The end is still very far away, so I am trying my hardest to stay focused on one day at a time. I need to get to sleep because with the way I am feeling now, tomorrow is going to be very difficult to endure.

March 5—Day 45: Hobart-Carnegie, Oklahoma, 34.9 Miles. 1,402 Total Miles.

From the moment I woke up this morning, I knew it was going to be a very difficult day. My right shin area was noticeably swollen. While it hurt to walk, running was nearly impossible. The shin area had started bothering me toward the end of my time in Texas but had never got to the point where it was debilitating. About twenty miles into the day, it got so bad that I could no longer run and had to walk. I tried to run on it every couple of minutes at that point but continued to feel a sharp pain that was beyond excruciating. I had no choice but to walk for the final fifteen miles of the day. My immediate concern was that it could be a stress fracture. I was slowed even more when I was stopped by a police officer who was sent to check on the situation. He said a number of people called into the police department with reports of a man pushing a baby on the highway. I got the impression he thought I was crazy, but he was still nice and allowed me to continue on my way.

As frustrating and painful as things were, I continued to be encouraged and humbled by people I encountered. I stopped in a convenience store on the east side of the small town of Mountain View. I bought a few items and sat down to snack on them while giving my leg a chance to rest. One of the women at the counter asked what I was doing and when I told her how I was running across the country for prayer, she reached in her pocket and gave me some money to help with my expenses. That small act of kindness gave me the strength and motivation to continue on despite my physical struggles. There was no way I could quit after looking her in the eyes, thanking her, and promising to pray for her out on the road.

While I was at the counter, a man about my age came in the store and made a beeline for me, asking if I was running across the country. It caught me off guard, but evidently he was a runner as well. He said his name was Scott and that he and his wife had just passed me on the road in their car. Scott also said that he thought I was running across the country because I was wearing athletic clothing while pushing a full stroller. When they were discussing it, they decided to turn around and come find me to discover what I was doing. I let him know the quick overview of my journey and my mission. He wished me luck before heading out of the store with a big smile on his face. Small encounters like that lifted my spirits enough to make it to the end of the day.

After what felt like forever, I arrived in the town of Carnegie and had to backtrack a few times before I finally found a motel to stay at for the night. While watching the news, I learned something that I already guessed given the previous few days: March was the windiest month in Oklahoma. When I mapped out the logistics of the run, I thought of temperature, daylight hours, and tornado season amongst other things. However, I never thought to factor in the wind.

I am so thankful that my motel has a Laundromat connected to it. My clothes are clean for the first time in what seems like a couple of weeks. I just returned from restocking supplies at a gas station and getting dinner at a small restaurant across the street. I am definitely walking with a limp right now because of the injury, so I am slightly worried about the damage that may be done to my leg. I have already started praying intently that I do not have a stress fracture. I have also enlisted others to pray on my behalf for healing. I am in a small town right now but will have it looked at in a hospital tomorrow evening. There is nothing I can do for it at the moment, so I am going to do the only thing I can think of—pray.

March 6—Day 46: Carnegie-Anadarko, Oklahoma, 26 Miles. 1,428 Total Miles.

I got out of bed this morning with bags under my eyes. I had a sleepless night because of the intense pain in my leg. Upon starting my run, I quickly discovered that it was going to be a very long day despite a seemingly manageable distance to my next destination. I could run on my leg for only a minute or two at most before the pain would take over, causing my eyes to tear up because of how much it hurt. However, I felt pressured to get to my motel as quickly as possible so I could drop off my belongings and make my way to the hospital. I wasn't sure if I wanted to get there to find out what was wrong with my leg, but stopping for the day seemed like a pretty good incentive at the time.

It only seemed fitting that on the day where I was in the most discomfort was also the day I got chased by a multitude of dogs. It started early and only became worse as I made progress throughout the day. I was not entirely sure where they came from, but all of the sudden there would be dogs roaming around that became interested in following me. For some reason, the dogs often became quite aggressive toward me. At one point, I had ten dogs at once surround me while barking loudly and baring their teeth. I tried to face as many of them as possible and slowly (which was the only speed I had) back away in the direction I was headed. A few of them got close to me, but thankfully none ever attacked or bit me. It was sad to see all the dogs roaming free because I saw a few on the side of the road who were struck and killed by vehicles. I tried to look at it as one more thing to add to my prayers.

The silver lining to the day was that I had a lot of time to spend in prayer. I continued to receive requests from school classes, family, friends, and strangers. They kept me busy, although I was sure I could keep God plenty busy with my own intentions at that time. People continued to motivate me with their concern for their friends and family around them. Quite a few of my intentions were from parents praying for their children to find their way back to God. It gave me a deeper faith in people and their concern for the ones they loved. I was humbled by the opportunity I had to join with these people in prayer. There was no doubt in my mind God was listening to these requests and answering them, even if it was not in the way we hoped he would answer. I was happy this element of the run brought me great peace in the midst of so much discomfort.

Once I arrived at the motel, the first thing I did was take a shower. I then took the ten-minute walk over to the hospital to get my leg checked out and was very worried because I had a distinct limp. I sent a text to my sister saying that I may be in serious trouble because of how much my walk was affected by the injury. The doctor took a look at my leg and was clearly concerned that I could not move my right foot much without extreme pain. My foot was also unable to lift its toes up in the air at all. It felt terrible, but I knew there was little I could do. As I waited for the x-rays to come back, I simply prayed that everything would be okay.

When the doctor returned with the x-rays, he told me that sometimes small fractures could be difficult to detect on x-rays, but he could not see one. He advised that it was a severe case of anterior tibial tendonitis, which would make sense as it was an overuse injury. The doctor also told me to rest for a few days and take some anti-inflammatory medication along with some painkillers. I imagined I was the happiest patient to ever be diagnosed with that injury. I was still in pain but was so thankful I did not fracture anything. I smiled the entire hobble back to the motel as I gave an interview to a reporter over the phone. The pain was still there, but the outlook on the remainder of the run became much brighter.

I just received word that my brother is coming in for a couple of days to run with me when I reach my sister-in-law's family outside of Oklahoma City. I will rest there if I need to, but I am looking forward to having some company for a change. As tough of a day as this was, I don't think it could have ended any better. I know I am still in for a long battle, but my attitude is much more positive now. I am going to bed tonight, thanking God for the blessings I have received that continue to make this run possible.

March 7—Day 47: Anadarko-Chickasha, Oklahoma, 17.4 Miles. 1,445.4 Total Miles.

I woke up this morning thankful for a short-mileage day. I did try to run but was only successful in running a portion of the day's mileage because of the swelling and persistent pain. My legs were still giving me problems, and it was difficult to find any distractions as I ran past fields with scattered tree lines for miles. However, the combination of a positive mental attitude and completing my run by noon made for a fairly easy day despite it being windy once again.

One issue I continued to battle was my ability to take in enough calories to support the long distances for which I needed to fuel my body each day. I knew I did a great job in that aspect for the first leg of my run to Phoenix. Since then, I had run longer distances, and my focus was solely on finishing in daylight. Consequently, I lost fifteen pounds over the prior month and needed to refocus on calorie consumption. Today was a great start on that new goal as I ended my run at a Sonic and downed some hot dogs and a shake while I waited for my hosts for the night to pick me up. Sheila and Tiny were my hosts, and I was connected with them through my previous boss, Ray, at Potomac River Running. I considered myself blessed to have friends looking out for me. Ray had been nothing but supportive and helpful from the moment I told him about my plans to run across America. This particular time in the run was where I felt like I needed some company and support, so things could not have worked out any better.

Tiny and Sheila picked me up and took me to Jake's Ribs for lunch. It was one of the best meals I had ever eaten and satisfied my craving for tasty barbeque. My hosts made me feel like I was relaxing with my grandparents.

They were so generous and fed me well the entire stay. They also set up an interview with a local paper and talked about God with me. It was a great day, and I could tell that I would not want to leave in the morning.

I am continually humbled by the support and prayers I receive along the journey. As difficult as things are, the intentions and positive messages help me to keep going. It makes me feel like my message of encouraging prayer is being heard and that people are making time in their day for God. I received a message today from Scott's wife (I met Scott in the town of Mountain View a couple of days ago). She sent me a prayer intention for a friend of theirs who is currently battling cancer and also gave me an encouraging note that brought tears to my eyes. It read,

"While you are hurting, struggling, and sore, know that you are certainly leaving people along the way inspired, our family included. Inspired to not only take on great challenges, but as the Lenten Season approaches, to focus on prayer and that which really matters."

This message of gratitude and encouragement is just what I needed tonight. I simply run and pray every day, often unaware of the effect it may have on the people I am praying for, those who send me intentions, or anyone following along. I am running not for myself, but for everyone else. When I read this e-mail, it feels like I am where God wants me to be. I know I need to keep running and keep praying until I run out of real estate. This is my plan, and I will continue to do whatever is necessary to reach the finish line. I have publicly promised to complete this mission, and with God's help, there is no doubt I will follow through on that promise.

March 8—Day 48: Chickasha-Purcell, Oklahoma, 34 Miles. 1,479.4 Total Miles.

I was sad to leave this morning as Tiny drove me to where I left off the previous day. My hosts were so great and even sent me off with a great breakfast in the morning. I said goodbye and took off toward my destination just after sunrise. It was still a bit dark out since clouds had rolled in. For the first time since I started the journey, I got rained on. The skies opened up, and rain started to fall steadily. Within a couple of miles, it began to pour, and I was getting soaked. Just thirty minutes earlier, I was still sleepy. Navigating through pouring rain on a narrow road and coming within a foot of a semitruck traveling fifty miles per hour woke me up quickly.

I was not happy to be drenched but counted my blessings to still be in one piece when the rain stopped after about an hour. I made fairly good time until the shoulder ended about eleven miles into the day. The terrain was rolling and had no shoulder for the final twenty-three miles of the run. This certainly made progress tedious, but I considered myself blessed to still be on the move and that both the drugs I was taking and the prayers I was saying were helping my leg. While my left leg was still sore, the swelling on my right leg began to go down, and the pain began to subside along with it. I ran at least two-thirds of the miles today, which was a huge improvement given the recent struggles I experienced.

The prayers I said today mainly centered around giving thanks for the many blessings in my life and for my health. I also made progress on the many intentions people continued to send me. I prayed that they would not only sense the presence of Christ in their lives but also receive hope from their involvement in bringing me across the country.

I have been thinking over the past couple days of just how blessed I am to be able to use my talents for God. I want to continue to do the same once this run is finished because the feeling of knowing that I am on the path the Lord has laid out for me is extraordinary.

IN GOOD COMPANY

The truest help we can render an afflicted man is not to take his burden from him, but to call out his best energy, that he may be able to bear the burden.

Philips Brooks

March 9—Day 49: Purcell-Lake Thunderbird, Oklahoma, 24.1 Miles. 1,503.5 Total Miles.

The morning started out quite well as I was actually running at a solid pace for the first time in days. However, things turned sour quickly when the shoulder I was on suddenly ended, and I had to jump on and off the busy road to avoid vehicles. I had enough of avoiding traffic, so I turned north on a side road, directly into a cold wind. The day was dreary and cold, so the wind did not help the issue.

My biggest mistake was eating vegetable sticks I had with me for breakfast. I did not realize until about eight miles into the run that they had cheese in them. This was bad news because I had carried them around for a few days. There was no question they were not safe to eat because I quickly became nauseous and began to throw up. The sick feeling did not go away for the next ten miles. I tried to run, but I did not get far as I constantly stopped to throw up. I counted thirteen times I got sick on the side of the road in a stretch of ten miles. I felt confident after each round of getting sick that there was no way I had any more food in my stomach. Unfortunately, I continued to surprise myself.

In the midst of being sick on the side of the road, I had about ten dogs chase me. Needless to say, those were some long and frustrating miles. However, I finally hit mile 18 and started feeling decent again. The absence of sickness made me feel so much better. I was able to put in some

104

solid miles until I met up with Coleen, my sister-in-law's mother, at a gas station. It was such a great feeling to not only surpass the one-thousand-five-hundred-mile mark, but to also see a familiar and friendly face. I was thrilled to be with someone I knew. I originally planned to run all the way to Coleen's house in one shot, but I decided to split it up into two days, given my leg issue.

Upon reaching their house, I unpacked my stroller from her vehicle and took a much-needed shower. There were packages waiting for me at their house! I must have looked like a kid on Christmas morning opening them up. My friends at Potomac River Running sent me running shoes, new socks, and nutritional supplements. To top it all off, we went to Ash Wednesday Mass, and I could not have been happier to be with people I knew for the beginning of Lent.

This season of Lent is a special time to focus on the events that led up to the death and resurrection of Jesus. Traditionally, prayer is one way of preparation to mark the celebration of the resurrection. I think it is appropriate that much of my run will take place during this holy time in the liturgical calendar. I know I still have a long ways to go to get where I want to be in my spiritual life. I hope and pray I continue to grow in my own faith through prayer during this time and that I can play a role in bringing others to deepen their own prayer lives as well. I am anxious to complete tomorrow's mileage because my brother Dave will be flying in for a few days. I cannot wait to have some company on the run. I have not had anyone run with me over the first one thousand five hundred miles, so to have my brother with me on the road is going to be a huge lift!

March 10—Day 50: Lake Thunderbird-Seminole, Oklahoma, 30.4 Miles. 1,533.9 Total Miles.

Coleen dropped me off near Lake Thunderbird about thirty minutes after the sun came up. We were joking on the way to the start that anyone watching was likely wondering if I was in trouble because they would see me get out of the car so far from anything! I used that humor to keep my spirits up for the first few miles. I barely even noticed all the odd looks I received as I plugged along the wide shoulder of the rolling highway.

It felt so much easier running without the stroller! Upon reaching my first mile, I looked at my watch and could not believe I was running under eight minutes per mile. Without the stroller, I did not have to work nearly as hard as I was accustomed to and could thus move much faster. I told myself that I better enjoy the opportunity to run without having to push anything up or down hills because it would not come along very often on my journey. There was also little to no wind, which helped me to make progress without becoming exhausted. I continued to crush the miles one by one, and my legs did not even bother me beyond being sore. I did have to keep about a dozen dogs away from me today, but I was in such a good mood that it didn't bother me at all. I was happy with being able to relax on the rolling terrain. It allowed me to go down the list of intentions I carried with me and to concentrate on praying for each of those requests. I felt so touched by a request of someone praying for a friend. She said that her friend was a wonderful person who was lost and needed God. I remembered when I had felt lost and imagined that nearly everyone could relate to that situation. I prayed for the woman as I ran. I asked God to help her to trust in him. If she did this, then I believed the Lord would take her back with open arms and lead her to a beautiful life in accordance with his will.

Since the weather and my legs did not fight me today, I was able to breeze through the thirty miles as if it were a short jog. This seemed unbelievable to me because it was only a few years earlier when thirty miles an entire week felt too much. I thought it was proof that our bodies and minds could bear much more of a load if we trained them correctly and allowed the Lord to work through us. I could not believe how much better my leg felt already. I credited the great feeling to all the prayers people said for me. There were numerous texts, e-mails, and posts of people who offered up prayers for my return to good health. While I was sure the drugs and pain medications were helping, I believed with my whole heart I was back to normal because of the prayers being lifted up for my health. I set out to pray for others, but it turned out I had a multitude of people praying for me. I was both grateful and humbled by the outpouring of support. Rest had been recommended, but somehow running on it during time spent in prayer was just what I needed.

I was also thankful to be picked up at my ending point by my hosts and enjoyed sweet tea and pizza to replenish my calories. It tasted phenomenal, and I was even happier to have company around me once I finished running.

I have been very lonely on the road. Having family with me at the end of the day makes me realize just how much I want to be around people. I have already proven I can get by on my own. However, I find life is much easier and filled with greater happiness when we can share both our joys and our struggles with those close to us. I can already tell it is going to be very difficult to leave this part of the country, but until then I am going to enjoy it!

March 11—Day 51: Rest in Shawnee, Oklahoma, 1,533.9 Total Miles.

Today's rest day came at a perfect time. Since my brother Dave flew in late last night, we had the entire day to relax and catch up. Dave is similar to me in so many ways. We are both tall, athletic, have a passion for our faith, and enjoy relaxing with a good beer. We also have the ability to talk very quickly. I did not think anyone around us had any idea we were talking English because of how fast we spoke to each other, trying to catch up on things as quickly as possible!

We eventually made our way to see the kind folks at the Shawnee Medical Center Clinic. They were so benevolent, and my legs were thrilled to be treated nicely for a change. I had some of the knots pushed out of my muscles and had an ultrasound machine do some other type of work. I did not fully understand it at the time but was too tired to ask questions at that point. The two women who took care of me could not have been more helpful and accommodating. I enjoyed answering their questions about the dangers on the road as well as all the different types of requests I prayed for on the run.

I thanked them and promised I would keep them and their entire practice in my prayers. It was part of a resolution I made early in my run to pray for everyone I met on my journey. Since that resolution, I prayed for people who helped me, people I met along the way, and even those who passed me in their cars on the road. My thought was that our world would be a much better place if we all prayed for those we came in contact with each day. I understood I would never know the effect my prayers or even the run would have on the world. However, I also believed it would change me. I figured that was a great place to start.

After the visit to the medical center, we went to a fish fry at the local church. Not only was the food fantastic, but the people were also so sweet and supportive. I felt like I was surrounded by a multitude of new friends and supporters. We also went to the Stations of the Cross after the meal. It was a solemn reminder of what Jesus sacrificed for each of us.

As I sit in my bed, I am only thinking of what I saw at the stations tonight. It is a reminder to think of Jesus every time I want to complain. My most desperate moments do not even compare to his life and the sacrifice he gave to save our souls. This run has already made my love for Jesus even stronger than it was before I started. I have learned to truly appreciate the love God has for us. People have been interested in me because of the distances I run. However, I would love to see people recognizing the love of Jesus for them through my run. This journey is not about me. It is about pointing everyone to the Lord, whom we should be focusing on each and every day of our lives. He can work in amazing ways in our lives if we allow him to do so. It is my goal to encourage everyone, including myself, to do just that each and every day of our lives.

March 12—Day 52: Seminole-Cromwell, Oklahoma, 20.1 Miles. 1,554 Total Miles.

Not only did I wake up to a fairly short day, but I also had my brother's company the entire way. Dave and I often trained together in high school and even more recently when we were roommates for well over a year. Today felt just like one of those long runs we would typically go on together. We kept a steady pace and talked the entire way as if it were any other run. We discussed my adventures, our family, and life in general. Even though we did not set any speed records, I never felt twenty miles pass by so quickly. I considered it a huge blessing to simply take the time to talk with my brother. After running over one thousand five hundred miles on my own, I felt that his company was the greatest gift anyone had ever given me!

When the miles were completed, Dave's mother-in-law was kind enough to pick us up and take us to Sonic to get some cold ice cream shakes. If that were not enough, we hit up a phenomenal barbeque place for dinner. We had been talking about eating good Oklahoma barbeque for so long that we ordered much more than was necessary. The man taking our order said that if we finished everything, it was the type of order that he would give us for free. After an epic food battle and multiple glasses of sweet tea, we finished everything except a slice of bread. The owner said that he was thoroughly impressed. I did not mention what I was doing, but I knew I had run enough recently to warrant the extra calories. At the end of the day, I figured it was a good start to regaining some much needed weight.

I am so blessed to count my brother Dave and my sister Kristina as my best friends. Like any other kids, we certainly had our times together when we fought with each other. However, we really pulled together as a family after our mom died and have been close to each other ever since. I see characteristics of my mom in both of them, and it often makes me feel like she is still here in many ways. I know she would be so proud of all of us, and I am certain she was with Dave and I as we rolled through the miles today.

March 13—Day 53: Cromwell-Okemah, 13.7 Miles. 1,567.7 Total Miles.

I was thrilled when I woke up this morning. I had less than fourteen miles to run, and Dave was going to run them all with me. I was able to focus on our conversation instead of my injuries. The miles went by very quickly. They were often filled with dogs chasing us, including a friendly one that decided to run with us for about two miles. We laughed and talked for the duration of the run. The humor was very much appreciated. While running with Dave, I thought back to all the times I forced myself to laugh at anything I could think of in order to keep my spirits up. It was so awesome listening to Dave joke around about running, the dogs that chased us, and the craziness of my run. It was as if I discovered jokes for the first time in my life. I was so happy and continued to run well despite a couple of short breaks I had to take for some lingering pains in my leg. We made it to Okemah early enough to sit down and eat pizza at a local restaurant for lunch.

As we ate, I thought of how much easier the prior two days felt. It was not only because of Dave's company but also because of his in-laws, the community at the church, and even the medical personnel in town. Everyone had come together to help me in some way or another. It made me realize how important it was to rely on and seek help from our brothers and sisters in the Body of Christ. This run turned into much more than a solo effort because of the physical, financial, and spiritual gifts people had offered for me along my journey. I believed the same was true in life, in that even the smallest gestures toward those around us have the ability to make an immense impact on their lives.

After dinner, we checked into my motel. We then waited for Dave's in-laws to come pick him up and drop off my stroller. William and Coleen were so generous in not only hosting me for a few nights, but they also treated me like one of their own sons. They arrived in the afternoon, and we talked for a few minutes before they had to leave. William and Coleen gave me my stroller back, handed me an envelope with two gift cards to fast food restaurants, and then took Dave to the airport. It was really tough to say goodbye to all of them, especially to my brother. When I started the cross-country trek, I thought there was a chance I might not survive the run. As their van drove away, I was comforted by the belief that God was protecting me on my journey. I had no doubt in my mind I would be just fine and see him again soon.

My recent experiences have taught me that life is so much easier to handle when we allow others to assist us. It is also very rewarding when we offer up our own talents to help those around us. Personally, I have not always acted in this kind and thoughtful way. The people I have encountered on my journey have taught me to act this way as often as possible, and I intend to change. I plan to help not only those I know but especially those I do not know. Part of my original mission was to change the world and to bring it closer to God. I realize now that this run is only a small part of my mission. The best way to make an impact is not a monumental endeavor but to make the extra effort to support all those around us on a daily basis. If I can act in this manner toward all those I meet on the road of life, then that is something I will consider truly remarkable. It is the manner in which my mother lived her life and in which so many of the saints lived theirs. My personal goal moving forward is to walk in their footsteps for all the days of my life.

March 14—Day 54: Okemah-Henryetta, 20 Miles. 1,587.7 Total Miles.

I hit the road this morning with my trusty jogger once again. I was spoiled the prior couple days in that I was able to run without the jogger and had the luxury of running in the company of my brother. It was difficult to be on my own again, and the loneliness set in immediately. It was even deeper than I had experienced before. I felt beat up and extremely tired when my feet hit the wet pavement. I knew it was going to take some extreme mental toughness in order to keep running strong as I continued to make my way east.

I kept my mileage short in order to allow my leg to recover. Both legs still hurt but were beginning to feel slightly better. Unfortunately, my stomach gave me some problems through most of the day. I finally threw up well into the day, which seemed to help me feel marginally better. One of the things that made the day bearable was the limited amount of traffic on the road. I was running on a country road that paralleled Interstate 40, so I only encountered a small amount of local traffic. The road was rolling much more than expected as I continued to run past "amber waves of grain." It felt cool to be in the middle of America while running by a staple of American imagery. I wished I wasn't feeling sick so I could have enjoyed it more!

Since there was not much to look at on my country road and I was feeling terrible physically, it was a perfect opportunity to pray through my list of intentions. A friend of mine who worked as a substance abuse counselor had sent me a list of prayer requests from her clients. She told the group about the run and used it to show how anything was possible if taken one step at a time. I was honored to learn that my run helped people who were going through a difficult recovery process. Each person had written intentions for me to pray for on the road, and I found them very powerful. Most of the requests focused on a desire to remain clean and sober, to be forgiven for their actions, and finally asking for a chance to reconnect with loved ones and move on with their lives.

As I prayed for each one of the intentions, I felt the sincerity of their words. In many ways, I felt like I could relate to the feeling of wanting to let go of the past and be able to move on with the future. The intentions were very much about the desire to have a second chance. I knew I had held on to the past far too long. Because of my failed marriage, I did not allow anyone to get close to me. It was only shortly before I started the run that I felt like I had completely moved on from the past and allowed myself to let other people get close to me. We all make mistakes, and I thought it was amazing how I felt very united with the people I was praying for. This was just one of the moments on my journey that opened my eyes to the true goodness of people. I hoped that the feeling of being able to look to the future with a positive and confident attitude was something that those I prayed for would experience as well.

I made it to Henryetta without too much trouble and gave a quick interview to Tristan, a local reporter. I was happy for the conversation after a quiet day, and it was refreshing to talk to someone about my mission. He was very generous and gave me some money for dinner, which I graciously accepted and immediately put to use as I grabbed a large pizza for dinner.

My eyes are nearly as heavy as my legs. I do not feel like I have the energy to continue on, but I have learned that God will give me the strength I need. I have never felt so strong in my faith and consider myself incredibly blessed to be where I am at this moment. I am looking forward to the remaining miles and cannot wait to meet more wonderful people along my journey.

March 15—Day 55: Henryetta-Checotah, Oklahoma, 29 Miles. 1,616.7 Total Miles.

This morning started out well with a great breakfast of pancakes at the diner attached to my motel. After I got packed up, I sat on my bed with my head hanging for about five minutes. Although the day was not scheduled to be extremely long and the weather looked nice, I simply did not want to go back out on the road. I said the St. Michael prayer and gave myself the best pep talk I could come up with at that time of the morning. However, I seemed to be running out of material to get my legs moving after almost two months and over one thousand six hundred miles on the roads. The burden of the miles yet to run and the feeling of not wanting to let anyone down finally caught up to me. The burden felt so heavy. While I considered myself a strong person, I knew there was no way I could carry it on my own. Therefore, I ended up doing what always worked when all else failed. I prayed for strength and called to mind all those who were counting on me to pray for them. I opened a prayer request from a teen, asking me to pray that she would be lifted out of a deep depression. I found it amazing how she would ask me to pray with her in a time of trouble. I felt a level of responsibility to help keep hope alive for this girl. I could not bear the thought of quitting. Not today. Not ever. I forced myself out the door and continued my run in prayer.

After dealing with so much wind, I enjoyed the still air and tried to take advantage of it the best I could by moving quickly. Oklahoma consistently had little to no room on the sides of its roads, and today was only slightly better than average. Having to jump on and off the street was tiring, but for some reason, I felt more relaxed as the day progressed.

I could feel myself getting stronger despite the weariness that came with running hours on end. The thought of how much easier this run would be without all the injuries crossed my mind, so I prayed for healing quite often today. It seemed appropriate because I could feel my right shin area feeling much better. I considered myself so blessed because day after day, I reached my destination only on the strength given to me by God.

By the time I arrived at my motel this afternoon, I was completely exhausted. My eyes were heavy, so I took a quick nap before going to a Mexican restaurant. I definitely surprised the waiter by ordering a couple of entrees before pounding a huge bowl of fried ice cream.

Even though I took a nap earlier, I am feeling especially tired. I am concerned about the amount of sleep I am getting, which has only been about five hours per night on average. As a result, my head was bobbing at dinner tonight because of the fatigue. My body may be weak, but the fire of my spirit is fueled by prayer. I may be tired, but I know the Lord will continue to give me the necessary strength to accomplish my mission. For now, I am looking forward to a restful night of sleep before tackling another high mileage day tomorrow.

March 16—Day 56: Checotah-Cookson, Oklahoma, 43.7 Miles. 1,660.4 Total Miles.

I woke up this morning to a pleasant surprise—my lower right leg was feeling much better. It was the first time I felt no pain in that leg since the end of my time in Texas. I knew the distance I had planned would be a true test of its strength. I hit the road shortly after sunrise to see how it would hold up. I was feeling a little tired, but overall I had a strong sense of inner strength. After about two miles, I was out of the town and back on country roads. I decided to make a last-minute change to my route and took some back roads, which ended up being a poor decision. The route turned into rocky dirt streets. They slowed me down and made it difficult to push the jogger. However, I was provided some comic relief as I passed a number of cattle farms. The cattle would come over in herds to the fence and moo loudly while looking at me inquisitively. After many miles on my own, it seemed hilarious and had me in a strangely good mood.

After getting through the back roads filled with cattle, I made it through some small towns. I then crossed a narrow bridge that kept me way too close to traffic for my level of comfort. In an effort to get it over with quickly, I picked up the pace quite a bit and realized that my body responded very well. I did not have an explanation for why I was moving so quickly, but it felt like I had a reservoir of inner strength. I continued to draw from this well and ran strong until mile 30. I prayed as I ran, and one of the intentions hit me hard as it was for a couple who told me that they were both struggling with depression. I knew from personal experience the feeling of the world collapsing down on me and the feeling of sadness that accompanied me everywhere I went. Early on in my journey, I felt feelings associated with depression because of the loneliness, physical pain, and the sense of hopelessness. However, in each of those situations, I was lifted up by remaining steadfast in prayer. It gave me a feeling of great hope to know that this couple was reaching out for help in prayer, because I believed that meant they were on the path to peace. I could not express how humbled I felt to have complete strangers ask me to pray for them. This only made me more driven to fulfill my calling by reaching the end of my run across America.

As the road conditions changed, I realized the final thirteen miles were going to be very treacherous. I laughed to myself, thinking that it was a good thing I was feeling so strong. The road had no shoulder, became very hilly, and was full of twists and turns. If that were not challenging enough, the sides of the road had a steep bank off to the side and traffic was heavy.

As I pulled my oppressive stroller off to the side of the road, I had to hold the left side of the stroller up in the air to avoid sliding down the steep embankment. I was fatigued from the thirty miles I had already run, but now the road was testing my mind as well as my body.

I had a small break when the road opened up, and I was treated to a beautiful view of a large lake. The sun was shining bright, and it reflected off the blue water, which was surrounded by hills of bare trees speckled with evergreens. Looking at the serene setting as I ran put me in a wonderful mood. The respite was short-lived as the terrain became much more dangerous after the break. There were so many times where my arms were burning from holding the stroller up. My legs would almost spasm from using them to anchor the stroller while waiting for traffic to pass. I even stopped a few times because I was unsure how to approach an upcoming turn given the narrow, winding road full of vehicles. However, I was too deep into the road to turn back or find another route, so I used my sense of hearing and said a prayer before each turn. There were many tense moments and times where I pushed my body far beyond what I thought it was capable of handling. It was definitely one of the more dangerous sections of road I had run on to that point.

The road finally opened up again, and I was so excited to see a lodge with a small grocery store. The woman who operated the place was so sweet and cooked me up a couple of hamburgers. She could not believe I had run through the dangerous section of road with a jogger but told me that the worst of the road conditions were behind me.

From a mental perspective, it feels great to complete a run over forty miles again. It gives me great confidence moving forward. I just returned to my room here at the lodge after loading up on supplies for my next section. I am so ready for bed right now. It is usually my legs that need the rest. However, right now, I am most looking forward to my arms feeling normal again. One of the posts on my site from a couple of days ago was from a woman who said she was praying for company for me. I hope that prayer is answered soon because I am feeling very lonely out here.

March 17—Day 57: Cookson-Stillwell, Oklahoma, 27.8 Miles. 1,688.2 Total Miles.

Today was St. Patrick's Day, and I had been looking forward to it since the run began. My friend who created my "Jeff Runs America" shirts made me a green shirt to wear on St. Patrick's Day. I knew I would be closing in on the halfway point around the holiday, which felt like such a long time away and too far down the road to even dream about. I almost forgot when I woke up this morning that it was March 17. When packing my things up in the stroller, I started to roll up my clothes, and suddenly remembered I could finally wear the green shirt! It was a seemingly small moment to put the shirt on this morning. However, it gave me a great feeling of accomplishment because it made me realize how far I had run. I took a quick moment to pray that my mission of prayer was also making progress and that those following my journey were drawing closer to the Lord.

The weather was beautiful as the sun came out and the temperature rose to about eighty degrees. The road was not as bad as the previous day, but the first few miles were still treacherous. My aching body continued to take its daily beating from mile after mile on the pavement. Once I finally escaped from the twists and turns of the winding roads, I felt safer and was able to pray for some additional intentions I received.

I actually paused when I read an intention from a woman who was married for twenty-three years and was dealing with an impending divorce. She wrote that she still loved her husband, but that his feelings for her had changed. He wanted out of the marriage. I did not need the description of her pain because I knew how she felt. I understood the feelings of sadness resonated so deep that it was difficult to imagine ever feeling happy again. I remembered feeling sick to my stomach every moment of each day for months on end after my wife walked out on our marriage. I wanted to be married and would have done anything to make it work, but the distance I felt from her only made me feel worse. It made me feel like I was incapable of being loved by anyone ever again. It took a long time for me to realize that this notion was ridiculous. However, I was only married for less than a year. This woman was married for a long time, and my heart and prayers went out to her. It was almost as if that pain came back with me for a few miles as I prayed for her situation and reflected on my own past. As difficult as it was to relive in my mind, it made me feel very connected to that particular prayer request. I prayed for this woman as I ran, not only for her marriage, but that she would also find peace.

The miles went by fairly slow as I fought both the physical pain as well as the emotional hurt I had just gone through in my heart once again. I was comforted by another message I received from a person who told me I would be in her prayers. There was a great peace that came over me knowing I was in the hearts, minds, and prayers of people following my journey. There was a certain amount of pressure to succeed when others were monitoring my progress, but I just did my best to look at it as an opportunity to show the power of prayer to them in a tangible way.

My stroller tipped over for the first time on the journey when I entered the parking lot of the motel. I turned into the lot and simply did not have any strength remaining to hold it up as the weight shifted to one side. I didn't think any damage was done, but I figured better the stroller falling over than myself! I grabbed some pizza and a celebratory beer for the holiday.

I am back in my motel and continue to limp around as I get ready for tomorrow. It feels like every night I hobble around after I finish for the day—and I am still limping around in the morning. I have no reasonable explanation for my ability to continue running for hours on end day after day while pushing this hefty stroller. I give credit to God because I know I could not run daily with the pain, aching, and injuries that I constantly battle. There is simply no way my body should be able to run at all, let alone for hours on end each day. I cannot pinpoint the exact spot, but I feel as though God has been carrying me for the past number of weeks. Part of my daily prayer is that the Lord continue to give me strength because I know I will need his help to complete the journey. The only thing I can do is say yes each day and put forward everything I have to give. I am confident I can do that. As long as I do, I believe God will carry me all the way to the finish.

March 18—Day 58: Stillwell, Oklahoma-Siloam Springs, Arkansas, 28.6 Miles. 1,716.8 Total Miles.

The weather was beautiful as I stepped out the door this morning. I took a few moments to praise the Lord for the clear and warm conditions. For the first time since the beginning of the run, my left IT band was not in constant pain. I felt very strong from a physical standpoint. This is something I used to take for granted, but after being in pain for so long, I realized how blessed I was to be healthy. That notion was emphasized by prayers for a young man who was disabled and unable to even walk. I knew my run would come to an end, but my thoughts were with people like him, who would continue fighting battles long after my run finished. I made resolutions to count every blessing, to give thanks for all that I had, and to always pray for all of those who suffered in any way.

I was feeling guilty for how I had essentially been blind to so many blessings in my life. I took full advantage of the situation by enjoying the great weather and pushing myself much harder than usual. The day was difficult from a physical perspective, but I found it much easier to move forward when I thought of all the blessings in my life. I had to weave my way through a few construction zones and even decided to go to a hotel down the road an extra mile. Since I was so close to the state line, this actually put me into Arkansas. It was more of a relief than anything to put Oklahoma behind me. It felt like I was in the state forever, and it was not surprising since my mileage had been lower because of injuries. My state crossings always gave me a mental boost, so I ended the day on a very positive note.

This run has made me realize how much I take for granted in my normal life. The simple things like my own bed, good weather, food on the table, and being healthy are all things I admittedly did not pay much attention to in the past. The issues and obstacles I have witnessed and faced since I started this journey have truly opened my eyes not only to the people around me but also to my own outlook on life. I am excited for tomorrow because I am crossing Arkansas on an angle at the very corner of the state. This means I will be in Missouri tomorrow, barring any unforeseen circumstances. I will pray for good weather again tomorrow and will be sure to give thanks for all my blessings tonight.

March 19—Day 59: Siloam Springs, Arkansas-Noel, Missouri, 36.4 Miles. 1,753.2 Total Miles.

I checked the weather this morning and learned I would likely be dealing with rain and thunderstorms later in the day. I anxiously hit the road as I was not going to let the threat of bad weather keep me from running today. In a great start to my time in Arkansas, I had a reporter named Melissa meet me at my hotel. After the interview, Melissa took a couple of photos and then asked if she could pray with me. It was a great comfort to have someone pray with me in person. It was just what I needed to get motivated for the upcoming miles.

Once I started running, my body actually felt very good. I took special notice to the absence of pain in my left leg. It had bothered me almost continually since the third day of the run. Today was the first time I noticed that it did not hurt at all. Normally, it ached constantly with an occasional shock of excruciating pain—but not today. I was hesitant to think the pain was gone for good, but I certainly enjoyed the ability to run without severe pain while I could.

The road was fairly flat as I began, but I had to face traffic without a shoulder after only two miles. It made the distance difficult to get through as there was a fair amount of traffic early on. I found myself often pushing the stroller through the grass on the side of the road to avoid the oncoming vehicles. This wore me down quickly, but the traffic eventually thinned out as I ran deeper into those country roads.

I witnessed many people giving me strange looks as drivers passed me by on the country roads. I hoped someone would stop to talk because I was feeling lonely and longed for conversation. I looked forward to those times when people would stop to ask me what I was doing because I saw it as an opportunity to spread my mission about prayer. I got the chance to do just that when a truck stopped me at a corner, where I was looking particularly lost. There were two gentlemen in the truck, and they asked me what I was doing and if I needed any help. I was so glad they stopped because I was lost at the moment, and they were able to point me in the right direction. I told them I would pray for them. One of the gentlemen, Dave, gave me his address and told me to send him a post card of New York when I reached the finish. I promised him I would and continued on my way, saying the next decade of the rosary for my two new friends.

I was lucky the weather was holding out as I approached the Missouri state line. The day became drearier as the hours passed, but to that point I had managed to stay dry. The sky looked a little menacing as numerous dark gray clouds appeared above my head. I figured there was nothing I could do about the weather, so I simply continued to put one foot in front of the other as I ran past more open fields.

The road became narrow, hilly, and had no shoulder on occasion. There were a few times where there was a drop off the side of the street, so posts with wires connecting them served as a barrier at the edge of the road. Because of blind curves and traffic, there were a few moments when I ended up leaning on the wires since I could go no further off the road. I came very close to getting struck by vehicles on a number of occasions because of the road situation. It was an extremely tense couple of miles, and I was saying lots of prayers for myself during that stretch.

I finally emerged from those tough sections to the motel I was planning to stay at for the night. My heart sank when I pulled up to it with my jogger. The motel was closed, and there was no one around. The only other places to stay nearby were a couple of miles back, and there was no way I was going to risk my life once again on those treacherous roads. The next town was twenty-three miles away, so I did the math in my head and realized I could reach it by dark if I ran very hard. I took a deep breath and forced my tired body back onto the road.

After a mile, I calculated that I could make it if I maintained my current pace. My legs were really aching as both my hamstrings and calves had tightened up. It was extremely challenging from a mental perspective to continue running after putting in thirty-three miles on the day and thinking I was done. I tried to focus on my stride and on the prayers to help get me through it but was suddenly interrupted by a huge roar of thunder. Given the clouds, wind, thunder, and smell in the air, I knew rain was coming very soon. I did not mind if I had to run in the rain, but the road I was traveling on would be far too hazardous in a downpour. It was a dangerous enough section to be running through, but a heavy rain would make disaster almost inevitable.

I began to run very hard as I looked for places to set up camp on the side of the road. It appeared that I was out of luck as I continued pushing the jogger through the increasing wind over the next couple of miles. It was then that it started to rain—hard. I thought I was completely out of options and did not know what to do. As I was on the verge of hopelessness and fear, I came upon a public fishing access area on the right side of the road. I ran down the hill into a clearing next to a river. I began to frantically set up my tent in the increasing downpour and nearby lightning strikes. I finally got the tent to stand up and put on the rain fly. I took my bags from the stroller and tossed them in the tent before diving in headfirst and closing the flap behind me.

Once inside, I took a deep breath and told myself I could take comfort in being done for the day. I was soaking wet, but at least I was inside and out of the elements. Just when I thought I could relax, I felt water on my head. I was sure I put the tent together correctly, so I concluded that the rain fly was defective. Water started coming in from all over. I took a number of plastic items I had with me to catch the water flowing into the tent.

I'm sure this will be a long night, but I am thankful to be off the road, even if it means being damp inside my tent for the night. Dinner tonight involves a package of tuna, which does not exactly replenish the calories I burned today. At this point in the day, I'm glad I have something to eat, and I am certain I will enjoy it. I will go to sleep thankful for yet another day of safety and especially for being directed to this camping location just when it seemed like I had run out of options. I had a difficult day, but the obstacles I overcame make me feel like I am being watched over very closely by the Lord.

March 20—Day 60: Noel-Neosho, Missouri, 20.4 Miles. 1,773.6 Total Miles.

I really needed a short day after the frustrations of the previous afternoon. I had another restless night as water continued to drip in my tent. Also, a few vehicles parked at the public fishing access area while blasting music. It kept me awake for longer than I would have liked, but I was just happy nobody bothered me while I was camped out. Luckily, it was a manageable twenty miles to my next destination.

Packing up this morning was miserable because everything was so wet. I did my best to put on a happy face and look forward to a shorter day. I added an intention of my own for a place to do laundry at my destination—it was desperately needed. From the moment I started running after the sun came up, I received everything I needed to get through the day as comfortable as possible.

The first half of the day was run on a narrow road without a shoulder. I was fortunate there was not too much traffic during the morning hours. I was still very hungry after not eating much for dinner the night before, so I stopped at a Sonic about eight miles into the day to grab some food and a cold beverage. I received the customary strange looks from people as I devoured my meal next to my jogger at a bench outside the restaurant. The food tasted so good and gave me energy to continue running strong.

Upon leaving Sonic, the road widened out and offered a shoulder to run on, which made travel much easier. The sun was out, and I noticed my legs were feeling very good. For so long, I had been compensating for my leg injury and realized I was still running with a bit of a limp despite there no longer being pain. I took the time to alter my stride so that my running gait stayed normal. After doing this for a few miles, I decided to drop the pace by a couple of minutes and ran an eight-minute mile. I couldn't believe how great I felt and continued pushing the pace even faster. By the time I finished mile 19, I had dropped my fastest mile of the day to seven minutes and thirty seconds. It felt so good to run without pain. I was smiling from ear to ear because of it. During the planning stages for the journey, I took for granted that I would feel good enough to run at a solid pace. It was something I overlooked, but after being unable to run without pain for nearly two months, it was something I was sure to never take for granted again. I took in the scenery of green fields as I also made my way through more prayer intentions. I felt so blessed to be in such good spirits while spending the day immersed in prayer. It was one of the most pleasant stretches of miles of the entire journey.

I rolled up to my motel very early in the day. The front desk personnel were so nice and allowed me into a room despite it being well before the normal check-in time. The early finish enabled me to catch up on both sleep and laundry. I also took advantage of the local restaurant and caught up on the calories I missed out on the previous day. My confidence was building, and I prayed for my good health to continue. The chance to do laundry and get a couple of hours of sleep had me rejuvenated and excited to get after the next number of days. I even received news that there were a number of people interested in meeting up with me for a few miles as I rolled through Missouri.

This run is a complete roller-coaster of emotions. Just yesterday I was feeling on the verge of hopelessness, but now I could not feel more excited for the remainder of my journey. People have sent me countless messages of support letting me know that they are praying and offering up Masses for me. I believe with all my heart it is these prayers that are the cause of my healing and continued safety. At the beginning of my run, I thought this journey would be purely about praying for others, but I consider myself so blessed to realize that a big portion of it has developed into others praying for me. It gives me another reason to praise the Lord and offer up additional intentions of my own in thanksgiving for answered prayers.

March 21—Day 61: Neosho-Aurora, Missouri, 42.3 Miles. 1,815.9 Total Miles.

This morning had me feeling anxious to get started for a couple of good reasons: I woke up far less sore than normal, and I felt no pain in my legs at all! Normally, it takes me at least an hour to get packed up each morning, but I had everything tied down and was ready to roll in about half that time. As I walked out the door, I struck up a conversation with a trucker who was staying at the motel. He was so excited for my journey. He told me how he had gone on his own journey when he was about my age, when he had driven around the country to visit various places across the nation. I got the impression we could have both talked for a long time about all of our experiences, but he quickly wished me luck and told me to stay safe on the roads.

For the first time since the beginning of my journey, I felt an excitement to get started. The road cooperated fully by having a nice shoulder to run on for virtually the entire day. It was about sixty degrees at the start, but the sun came out, and it warmed up to about eighty degrees. Despite the warmer weather, I was moving well on the rolling terrain. I actually had to slow down because I did not think I would be able to hold a pace under nine minutes per mile for the entire day. I did slow down, but comfortably made it through the forty-two miles in well under ten minutes per mile. This was the pace I envisioned running when I planned the run, so it was a huge boost being able to finally run that pace.

The day itself was blessed as I had the chance to meet someone I would never have met otherwise. After running about thirty-three miles, I saw a man on the other side of the road hitchhiking with a large backpack. I put the brake down on my stroller and crossed the highway to speak to him. It turned out this man named Ricardo did not have much at all. He was traveling all over the country to see family and friends. To earn money, he stopped in parking lots along the way and sang poetry he wrote himself to music he played on his guitar. Additionally, Ricardo was a man of faith, and he shared with me how Jesus took care of him on the road. I knew exactly what he was talking about and gave him a few dollars for his travels before continuing on my own journey.

I felt encouraged by the meeting and ran strong the final nine miles of the day as I added him to my list of prayer intentions. Just a few miles down the road, someone traveling in a car threw an ice-filled cup at me. The cup hit me and the ice flew out, hitting me in the face and all over my chest. I had things thrown at me in the past, but this was the first time someone connected on their throw. While it caught me off guard, it actually did not hurt, but rather gave me relief as the cold ice felt refreshing in the warm afternoon. It would have been easy to get mad at the person who threw the cup at me. However, I decided I'd do what I had done since I started my run—pray. Just as I had done for the people who passed me in their cars or who I encountered out on the road, I said the next set of prayers for that person. Instead of feeling angry or upset, it gave me a great sense of peace as I finished up for the day.

I just ate a quick dinner before loading up on supplies and catching up on listing the new prayer intentions that continue to stream in online. I feel strong and am looking forward to some company as I am scheduled to have a few people join me on the road as I enter Springfield tomorrow. I also have friends there who will be hosting me for the night. Even though I am tired and sore, I continue to be blessed. It comes in the forms of the people I meet, in the prayer intentions I receive, and in the strength I receive from the Lord to keep running.

March 22—Day 62: Aurora-Springfield, Missouri, 30.7 Miles. 1,846.6 Total Miles.

The feeling of strength and an overall positive attitude continued from the onset this morning. A big part of my outlook was because of the three college students scheduled to meet me later in the run. There was also the promise of friends to spend time with at the end of the day and a couple who said they would run the first fifteen miles with me the following morning. Running in solitude was something I was used to between all the solo miles of training and on the run itself. However, I looked forward to company as it always made the miles go by faster. It also gave me a chance to talk to someone about everything going through my mind.

All the impending excitement had me moving very well. I was fortunate to have a shoulder to run on for almost the entire day. In addition to the prayer intentions I normally prayed for, I took time to say a prayer of thanksgiving for my health and all the blessings in my life. This run and the intentions I received helped me to realize how many great things I had in my life. For many of them, I never stopped to simply say "Thank You." I spent time thanking God for my health, my family, a shoulder to run on, the beautiful weather, my friends, all those I had encountered on this trip, all those who prayed for me, and those who had been kind enough to allow me to pray for them. I made a promise to myself to pause often to appreciate and give thanks for my blessings because I believed they were all gifts from God. I felt bad about how much I had taken for granted in life but was grateful for the situations which led me to recognize them. I made a promise to myself to live my life with a much deeper sense of appreciation.

The miles were going by quickly as I hit the marathon mark at just about four hours. I could not comprehend how my legs were able to move so well. I was sure it had a lot to do with the absence of pain in my legs that I dealt with for the first two months of the trip. As I closed in on the final miles of the run, I had a few college students join me. The three of them were bright-eyed and filled with excitement. It was phenomenal to run in the company of Cody, Sam, and Jessie. We shared a few stories of our running adventures and talked about faith as well. Running with the three of them was so awesome that I did not want our time together to end. After dropping off my supplies at my destination, we ran back into town and got ice cream together while talking some more. I was so encouraged to speak with young people who understood the power of prayer. We bid goodbye as they drove back to campus at Missouri State. We joked about how they would have a good excuse for being late to class. Our conversation and good humor had me smiling as I ran back to my friend's house in Springfield.

I failed to realize just how tired I was because of the excitement of having company, but I quickly noticed once I stopped. I was blessed with being able to have some friends back in New Jersey put me in touch with their daughter in Springfield. Tricia and Dustin took me out to dinner, and I was so hungry that I put away two entrees without a problem. The waiter was very impressed, and Tricia told him why I was eating so much. He replied, "I am not surprised because you are certainly not storing the food anywhere!" Before going to bed, I was able to talk with Tricia's parents, Pat and Tom, back in New Jersey over the computer via Skype. Pat and Tom were like extended family, as they had been friends of my parents for as long as I could remember. It was so great to see them and our conversation only enhanced my positive mood.

Seeing all my friends, both old and new, has me in an extremely enthusiastic mood. I cannot express just how great I feel right now. It is awesome to meet and speak to people who appreciate what I am doing and who support my mission. So much of this run is done on my own. To see in person the joy and hope my run brings people makes me feel incredibly blessed. Days like today really make me feel like I am where God wants me to be. I can only hope and pray I continue to stay on his path long after this run comes to an end.

March 23—Day 63: Springfield-Seymour, Missouri, 38.5 Miles. 1,885.1 Total Miles.

This morning picked up right where the previous evening left off as I had a couple come out to take me through the first part of the day. Marin and Tonya met me at the start. I said my goodbyes to Tricia and Dustin and was off on the road once again. My mind was also eased quite a bit when Marin and Tonya brought me a reflective vest since I had lost mine somewhere back in Oklahoma.

Marin was a tough triathlete who was originally from Europe. I loved running with him because he had a great sense of humor. His wife Tonya was sweet, athletic, and incredibly caring. I got the sense they were both in great shape, and I did my best to hold a solid pace so they would not feel like we were running too slow! We hit it off right away as we exchanged stories and learned about each other. They also helped me navigate toward Route 60, as the original route I had planned was not the safest passage back to the highway. We were so lost in conversation that I forgot we were running and almost missed the fact that I crossed the approximate halfway mark just a few miles into the day. I thought that in a way, it would be mentally easier knowing I had completed over half of the run. At least in that moment, I was correct. I tried not to think about how far I had yet to go, but approaching the halfway mark had certainly been on my mind for the previous few days. After passing that monumental barrier, my confidence began to increase with each and every step.

Tonya had to leave at around the six-mile mark, but I was so glad for the opportunity to meet her. Marin continued on with me until we reached Route 60, which was fifteen miles into today's run. It was tough to see him leave, but words could not express just how grateful I was for his help to start the day. He had talked to me nonstop and helped me to maintain a solid pace. The miles with Marin and Tonya flew by. I was suddenly sad to be on my own once again.

My legs continued to roll at a great pace as I continued east on Route 60. I felt so encouraged by all the new friends I had made over the previous couple of days. I believed in my heart that everyone who crossed my path on the run was meant to for one reason or another. I felt incredibly blessed to meet so many great people all across America. Perhaps even more so, I was humbled at the opportunity to pray for them.

I continued running quickly on Route 60, which treated me well by having a shoulder to run on. The land was still fairly flat with large fields, although I did notice that the amount of trees seemed to increase in comparison with the previous week on the road. I moved along fairly quickly and was enjoying the sunny weather that hovered around seventy degrees. The miles were flying by with only a couple of brief stops to change my drinks and to explain to an officer why I was pushing a baby jogger on the highway. I was getting used to being pulled over and tried to offer some humor when the police officers showed up. I told them immediately that there was no baby in the jogger. I proceeded to explain that if there was a baby in there, then that meant I had taken the wrong one by accident and then we did have a problem! It had not caused any of them to even crack a smile to that point, but I could not blame them for being skeptical in responding to calls about some crazy guy pushing a baby on the highway. Once again, the police officer was very nice and just told me to be careful as I continued running.

The beeps kept sounding on my watch as I clicked off mile after mile. Once I reached my motel over thirty-eight miles into the day, I realized I had run the distance at just a little over nine minutes per mile, which was very good for me. I celebrated by downing a lot of food and dessert at a local pizza place. The people running the pizza store asked me where everyone else was when they brought out all the food. I think I really surprised the owners by finishing everything and then ordering a dessert on top of it!

I am ready to get a good night of sleep before another day of pounding the pavement for hours on end. My spirits are riding high, and I hope it continues as the weather outlook seems bleak. The recent days have been fairly warm and pleasant, but it appears that it is about to get colder with some stormy weather over the next couple of days. I feel so blessed and protected. I know things will not be easy, but I am more confident than ever that I will reach the finish safely.

March 24—Day 64: Seymour-Cabool, Missouri, 38.6 Miles. 1,923.7 Total Miles.

I was glad I made the most of the nice weather when I ran to Seymour because the high temperature dropped about twenty-five degrees from the previous day. The midforties was not a bad temperature to run in, but I preferred it about fifteen degrees warmer since I was on the road all day long. In looking at things on the bright side, I was happy it appeared I would stay dry for the duration of the day.

The morning started out a little rough but was thankfully not an indication on how the day would develop. I did not sleep well at all while staying in Seymour. I was extremely sore and had difficulty falling back asleep when I woke up during the night. Trying to get my legs moving was not easy, and I thought I may be in for a long and slow day. As tired as I was, I began to feel an inner peace inside me. The miles were not bothering me at all, and my pace was steady. I had a hard time believing it, but I was actually feeling good today, if not great.

When I started out this morning, I planned to stop in Mountain Grove at mile 29. After only a few hours of sleep, I was sure I could have benefited greatly from an early finish today. However, my body was feeling so good when I approached it that I decided to continue running. I also felt the burden of the miles, and I knew I would have a better mental attitude if I could run at least thirty miles on the day. The only hindrance to my new plan was a brief pause when I was once again pulled over on the highway. I was tempted to take a photo of the jogger in front of the police car with its flashing lights but decided I should not push my luck.

My spiritual day was fantastic as well. People had let me know through my website that Masses were being said for me. I was humbled by this and so thankful for the support being sent my way. I was especially thankful for the special protection I experienced because of the prayers said for me. The crashes on the highway served as constant reminders of the dangers on the roads. I continued to run by crosses marking the locations of loved ones who died on the highway. From the very beginning of the run, I had said a decade of the rosary in the memory of each person who had a cross on the side of the road. I prayed for not only them but also for the loved ones they left behind. While it was sad, running by multiple crosses each day encouraged me to treasure each and every moment of my life. I realized it could be over without warning and did not want to take anything for granted.

I was so relieved to reach my destination, even though it was set apart from the town I had to walk to for dinner. After a quick shower, I made the mile walk into town and found a very good Mexican restaurant. I was slightly embarrassed by how much food I ordered. I received a few strange looks from people seated near me. I imagined they could tell I was not from there. I also wondered if any of the police officers eating their dinner across the room heard about me from their colleagues who had pulled me over earlier in the day.

I ate everything on my plates and trekked back to the motel to get ready for what promises to be a cold and wet day tomorrow. My body is feeling the effects of the mileage, but my spirit is feeling closer to God than it has ever been before. As I get set to go to bed tonight, I am happy to be where I am and would not trade this feeling of closeness to the Lord for anything.

March 25—Day 65: Cabool-Licking, Missouri, 31.9 Miles. 1,955.6 Total Miles.

I really hoped the weather station was incorrect in its prediction of the cold and wet weather. Unfortunately, they were right on target as it was in the midthirties and raining as I stepped out the door in the morning. I paused before the run to say a quick prayer for safety on the road because of the wet conditions. I would have preferred either snow or a warm rain because a cold rain felt like it seeped into my skin and prevented my body from warming up again. After I began, I made it across a set of train tracks just as the barriers were being lowered. It began to downpour immediately after I crossed the tracks. I was happy to at least be moving in the rain rather than standing still while waiting for the train to pass.

As I turned north on Route 63, I was thrilled to have a shoulder to run on, but I was drenched from head to toe. I wore a poncho, but it only helped so much as my feet were soaked from stepping in cold puddles. I also had to fight through numbness in my fingers for many miles. Since I was running on a highway with heavy traffic, I continually got sprayed by the passing vehicles as their tires kicked up water in my face. It was slow going and very uncomfortable. I did my best to pray, but trying to avoid vehicles all day and hearing a sloshing sound each time I took a step made it difficult to stay focused. Just as I was starting to feel down and sorry for myself, I read a prayer intention for the homeless. I felt awful. Moments before, I was sorry for myself because I was wet, tired, and cold. The reality was that I had money for food and shelter at the end of the day when many people did not. It completed changed my outlook and helped me to stay on track. Once again, God used a tough situation to teach me a lesson about humility.

The temperature never warmed up, but the rain eventually cleared out by the afternoon. The shoulder disappeared shortly after the clouds, but by that time, the end of the day was within sight. I was successfully able to power through the final miles while simultaneously dodging the multiple trucks on the roads. I finally rolled into the parking lot of my motel and was covered in clothes still wet from the rain. I checked in as quickly as I could and continued running directly into a hot shower before changing into dry clothes.

After downing a pizza and reloading on supplies, I am now looking at the weather for tomorrow. It appears as though it may be dangerous enough to keep me off the roads for the day. I am trying to get to St. Louis on a certain day for a talk I am scheduled to give, so things will be much easier if I can at least get some miles in tomorrow. Right now, there is nothing I can do about it, so I will simply do my best to enjoy a quiet night of sleep out of the elements.

March 26—Day 66: Rest in Licking, Missouri, 1,955.6 Total Miles.

Today started out just like each day before it. I pulled myself out of bed and hobbled to the bathroom to take a shower. I then got dressed warmly and put on my poncho since I could hear the rain outside. After packing my stroller, I took a final look at the weather channel and quickly decided that it would be in my best interest to take the day off. The radar had nasty, dark red cells moving around an entire screen of various shades of green. In addition, it showed lightning strikes and reports of hail not too far from where I was located. Getting rained on was bad enough, but I preferred to not get stuck in a hail storm.

A part of me was relieved to take a day off as I was both physically and mentally drained. However, a bigger part of me was uneasy to take a day of rest since I committed to getting to Saint Louis by a certain date. Therefore, I spent a decent portion of the day figuring out how to squeeze the next four days of running into three. Anyway I routed it, I learned that I could not take any type of shortcut. It meant at least one very long day would be necessary to make up for the lost time. This made me apprehensive since the weather was supposed to be cold with the possibility of snow over the next number of days. I started to feel anxious about the next section because of the circumstances but was able to put my mind at rest after saying a prayer for peace and safety.

I have the sense that I am exactly where God wants me to be. So many obstacles have already been overcome and consequently have me where I am today. If I need to take the day off and change my route, then I must believe it is part of his plan. This sense of calmness certainly makes me feel much better. I am not looking forward to the many hours and long miles I have ahead of me in this cold weather, but I believe with all my heart that God will lead me through it safely. I am not afraid of the discomfort or pain that comes with it, but at the same time it is not exactly something I am happily awaiting. I will certainly use the opportunity to get some extra sleep in preparation for a long day tomorrow.

March 27—Day 77: Licking-Cuba, Missouri, 58.5 Miles. 2,014.1 Total Miles.

After looking at the weather forecast this morning, all I wanted to do was stay in bed all day long. I may have done just that if I had not just taken a day off because of severe weather. I had the luxury of being well-rested for a change, and I was certainly going to need it for the upcoming miles. The temperature looked to stay in the thirties all day long with a cold wind, but I was thankful the rain had moved on and at least I would stay dry.

My face and fingers went numb within minutes of heading out the door. It was immediately clear it was going to be a long day. In an effort to warm up, I started moving as quickly as I could, which was not necessarily all that fast. The terrain cooperated by remaining flat for the first twenty miles. This allowed me to concentrate on praying instead of focusing on how many miles remained in front of me.

At one point, I started calculating in my head when I would finish. I became very pleased in my mind with my estimation, except I still had almost forty miles to run. Just when I became confident the day would not be too difficult, the roads became much more rolling. I continued to fight the growing fatigue which was consuming my body. Fortunately, I was able to take a break for a few minutes when I met up with a very nice reporter at mile 34 in the town of Rolla.

My original plan was to stay in Rolla, but because of the unplanned day off, I had to make up about twenty-four more miles. I continually dodged traffic since the roads were narrow and had no shoulder. This was becoming difficult to do since my fingers were still numb, and my level of exhaustion was reaching a peak. As much as I wanted to pull over and take a nap, I yearned to simply be inside and out of the elements. The situation turned from being frustrating to becoming emotional. I remembered the numerous nights I spent in my car during the Chicago winter when I did not have a home to go to. I recalled how the chill set deep into my bones and how difficult it was to sleep or to even feel some level of comfort. Suddenly, my situation did not seem so terrible as I spent some time over the next few miles praying for the homeless, who did not have any shelter night after night in all kinds of weather. It was amazing how every time I started to feel sorry for myself, I realized the many ways God had blessed me.

I did pass the two-thousand-mile marker near mile 45. This gave me a huge mental boost, but one that was short-lived. By the time I hit mile 50, it was starting to get late, and I realized I would have to run hard the remaining miles if I was going to make my motel before dark. If the situation was not challenging already, the temperature dropped rapidly as snow began to fall. The road I was running on became mostly soft. My tires became caked in dirt and forward progress slowed even more—if that was possible.

At one point, I came upon a stream that typically went under the road, but the recent rain had caused it to overflow. It had risen enough to overtake a section of road I needed to cross. I stopped for a couple of minutes and thought about finding a way around it. I was on a back road, and the chances of someone coming along to help me were not great. I was also too exhausted to go back and find a different road that would take me around it. I took a deep breath of the icy air and saw my breath as I slowly exhaled. I then ran forward at full speed. The tires of the stroller made a huge splash, and then my feet hit the freezing water directly behind it. The immediate sense of ice rushing through my veins made me gasp. I pushed through the stream as quickly as possible and was out in a matter of seconds. My socks were soaked in icy cold water, and I could barely feel my feet. As I continued running, the sloshing sound of water in my shoes quickly dissipated. I thought to myself that the water may have frozen in my shoes. I briefly thought about changing into dry socks but then came to the conclusion that my fingers were too numb to untie my shoes. With a few miles left to run and the sun about to set on a snowy night, I knew I needed to run as fast as possible to keep hypothermia or frostbite from setting in. I had been out in the cold all day long, and my body told me that I was approaching serious trouble.

My thoughts turned to the handful of races in my running career I had won. I never liked racing with everyone in the event running behind me. During those times, I was essentially running scared because I could not see the competition. I did not want anyone passing me to steal the victory. The sensation was a powerful one that encouraged me to run fast to ensure nobody caught me. The feeling I had over the last few miles of today's run was similar to that sensation. However, I already had well over fifty miles on my legs, and instead of losing a race, I was faced with the possibility of losing my life or coming close to it. It was a scary feeling, but I prayed for strength and gave absolutely everything I had to get through those final miles.

The sight of the hotel on the horizon was such a welcome sign. I continued running hard all the way up to the lobby. I checked in and stumbled to my room as fast as possible. I took off my shoes and did my best to relax as feeling slowly came back to my feet. I clenched my teeth in pain and tried not to cry out as blood made its way through my feet and hands. The last few miles were so intense that I failed to see just how sore I was from the beating of a nearly sixty-mile run. I tried not to think about it as I showered and made my way to a restaurant next door to grab some pizza.

After being truly scared this evening, the thought of running over forty miles tomorrow does not sound too bad. However, it will not keep me from praying for a restful night of sleep. I was very worried for the final miles of today and have God to thank for giving me the strength to make it through that section quickly. It is evident to me that the Lord is with me every step of the way and that he continues to keep me safe every day.

March 28—Day 68: Cuba-Villa Ridge, Missouri, 46 Miles. 2,060.1 Total Miles.

The snow that started the prior evening continued to fall overnight, so the start of my day involved cold temperatures and running through snow.

I was so exhausted when I finished up my long run the previous night that I went right to bed after eating and did not stretch or ice nearly enough. My body paid for it this morning as all my muscles were stiff, and the soreness in my legs made running quite painful.

I started out the day on scenic, unpaved back roads. The white snow covered the bare trees, while the green of an occasional evergreen added some color to the landscape. The trees reached above the street, creating a white canopy over the dirt road. For a moment, I almost forgot where I was as I enjoyed the pure beauty of my surroundings.

The scenery did not last too long as I soon found myself on Route 66. I was dodging cars by jumping off the road into the snow since there was no shoulder to run on. It was constantly on and off the road, which made for a tedious number of miles. I eventually made my way onto a service road that ran along Interstate 44. It did not have a shoulder but was slightly rolling with a fair amount of traffic. My pace was therefore slow, but I kept moving along and was encouraged by people on the highway who occasionally honked and waved at me as they drove by.

While I somehow managed to keep my momentum going forward, I quickly lost my mental energy and was unsure how I would make it to my destination. Today, my ending point was at a church called St. Mary's of Perpetual Help. I smiled to myself at one point, thinking that my finishing location was quite fitting because I was truly in need of perpetual help.

Shortly after crossing mile 30, I began to struggle both physically and mentally. I did not know if I possessed the mental fortitude to push my body through yet another barrier. I prayed for strength, and the answer came in the form of a man named Dave who showed up to keep me company at mile 36. A few people had contacted me about joining in the run as I approached St. Louis, but I forgot who I spoke to and where we planned to meet up. I felt so much of my mental energy was spent on pushing forward that I often forgot simple things like what day it was or some basic logistics of the run.

I could not have been more blessed to have Dave show up when he did. Dave was a fit ultrarunner himself, and he offered to push my jogger for a few miles. I was not about to turn that generosity down, so I let him take over pushing my heavy burden. I immediately started to feel better as I found it exponentially easier to run without the stroller. I almost forgot what it felt like to not have to run with the jogger—at the moment, it felt incredibly awesome. My pace quickened as Dave and I shared running stories and discussed a number of random topics. Before departing, Dave even told me he was impressed by how well and how quickly I was moving so deep into the run. His words and the company had me moving well through the entire time he ran by my side. Those six miles with Dave helped greatly in lightening my burden. I took the momentum from his company and continued to ride it all the way through some hills and back roads to my destination.

There was no doubt that I looked like a mess when I met Father Mark, the pastor at St. Mary's. As such, he was kind enough to allow me to have the rectory at the parish all to myself for the night. I showered quickly before we went to a restaurant to meet some parishioners for dinner. They were all so nice, but I was too exhausted to talk and was lost in my own little world for much of the conversation. Father Mark could tell that I was tired but not nearly full, so he took me to a fast food restaurant on the way to dropping me off at the church for the night.

I was so happy to talk to him about the spiritual aspect of my run and hear some amazing stories he had to tell. I only spoke to him for the first time earlier in the day because someone had alerted him I would be running through the area. I received his phone number on my voice mail and gave him a ring to get directions. It was interesting how I never knew what was going to develop out of my day when I took my first steps out the door each morning. Having company was always a good thing, and I enjoyed our conversations.

After we ordered at the counter, we took a seat and waited for our orders to be carried out. I had mentioned to Father Mark earlier in the day about my mom passing away a few years earlier. While I was eating my burgers, he mentioned to me in the middle of a separate conversation that he suddenly felt the strong presence of my mother with us. One thing about my mom was her awesome cooking ability. She was the kind of mother who was always telling me to eat more. If she was still alive, I knew one of her main concerns would be about me eating enough food. I found this relevant because within a minute of Father Mark telling me this, the waitress came back with a duplicate order. They had somehow mistakenly carried out double of what I had ordered. I was in no position to refuse free food, so I gladly downed a few more burgers without a problem. After the second dinner, Father Mark dropped me off and wished me well. It was tough saying goodbye to this man who I only met a few hours earlier.

I am making sure to say a prayer of thanksgiving tonight for all the wonderful people I am meeting on this run. I have a beautiful chapel next to the room I

am staying in tonight to say my prayers before I go to bed. I am in a great deal
of physical discomfort but have a huge smile on my face because of how close I
feel to the Lord. As challenging as I find it to put in the miles day after day, it is
an awesome feeling to be able to say I am truly happy in this moment.

March 29—Day 69: Villa Ridge-St. Louis, Missouri, 36.7 Miles. 2,096.8 Total Miles.

I experienced the most peaceful feeling when I awoke at the rectory
this morning. I got out of bed early, so I had a few moments to spend in
prayer at the chapel before hitting the road. It was one of the very few times
in my life where I felt at complete peace. There was an overwhelming sense
of safety all around me, and I felt as if God was saying that he was going
to continue to bless my road and grant me graces along the way. Dave had
told me about a dangerous stretch of road I would be running through later
in the morning. Another runner I was meeting up with in the afternoon
confirmed that I may have some trouble getting through that part of my
route. Those words initially made me somewhat anxious to face that part
of my run, but I suddenly had a sensation of total serenity because I knew
it was going to be okay.

After a few chilly miles, I entered the section of narrow and winding
roads without much of a shoulder. I did hit a few tough spots in that
section and did come close to disaster on a couple of occasions with passing
trucks, but not once did I feel worried or fearful. I was tired, and my legs
were in pain. However, I was able to press on and make it out of that tough
segment without a scratch. As I emerged from the narrow road and onto a
wider highway, I found myself running on a shoulder once again.

My body was still worn down, so I took a quick walking break before
getting my stride going again. The pace started to really pick up and was
only slowed momentarily by an interview and some video for one of the
TV stations in Saint Louis. I went steadily through my list of intentions,
praying for people who were lost, lonely, sick, and abused. I was encouraged
by their own strong wills. It gave me inspiration to stay steadfast in my own
mission.

As I passed through the twenty-mile marker, I started to slow down
once again but tried to stay focused on the upcoming city I was nearing and
the promised day off I planned to take. Just when I was starting to feel the
soreness have an effect on my gait, I was greeted by a fellow runner. Chad
heard about me online and was both a fellow Notre Dame graduate and
ultrarunner. He was thin, fit, and ran with a huge smile. More importantly,

he could really talk. I would say a few words here and there, but he did a phenomenal job of keeping my mind off the pain and the miles. We navigated through the increasing levels of traffic, which seemed odd given how long I had run through empty country roads.

Chad had his wife take some photos of us, and he updated some social media sites with information about my run as we ran. His positive energy carried me through the end of the day. The time I spent with him seemed like five miles but was actually a solid thirteen. Even though it was chilly out, he was kind enough to stay after we finished for the day to take part in an interview for another Saint Louis TV station. The crew was very nice and I was thrilled that they wanted me to talk about the many prayer intentions I was praying for on the road. I was exhausted. The last thing I felt like doing was staying out in the cold for another forty-five minutes in front of cameras. However, I felt it was important to continue to get the word out on my mission to encourage prayer.

After the TV crew left, I said goodbye to my new friend Chad and hello to my hosts in Saint Louis. My sister-in-law Angela set me up with her friends, Jessica and Bob, for my time in the city. Jessica picked me up and took me back to their apartment where they immediately made me a home-cooked meal and put a Guinness in my hand. I had company, a good meal, a tasty beer, and a day off ahead of me. I could not be happier.

This was a great day, and once again, it was made by the people I met along my journey. Physically, I am very tired and exhausted. Mentally, I am so excited to be in St. Louis and keep going over in my head all the wonderful people I have met these past few days. I am going to go to bed and will certainly enjoy a night of sleep without having to set my alarm!

March 30—Day 70: Rest in Saint Louis, Missouri, 2,096.8 Total Miles.

The chance to sleep in this morning felt awesome. I was still incredibly sore from the previous few days, but it made a huge difference to my mental outlook, knowing that I did not have to put in another day of running on the roads. There was some down time in the morning, so I worked on logistics for the remainder of the run and attempted to predict my arrival date at Notre Dame.

I had spoken to Katie and William months earlier about my run through Saint Louis. They were a couple in medical school who asked me to speak to some students when I passed through their city. I could not believe the day finally arrived, and I was so happy to not only meet both of them but to also speak to a group of first and second year medical students at Saint Louis University. The group was so nice and had so many great questions. They asked about the physical aspects of the run, as they wanted to know about the number of shoes I wore and how much I ate. They also asked about the spiritual parts, since they were curious about my own spiritual growth and how prayer changed my view of the world. The hour I was with them felt more like ten minutes. I enjoyed their questions and interest in the various aspects of my journey. Katie gave me a quick introduction to some of the staff at the school before giving me a tour of the beautiful mosaic-filled basilica in Saint Louis. I said my goodbyes to William and Katie, which was surprisingly difficult to do given that I had only met them a few hours earlier. One thing I tried to start doing was to look for Christ in every person I met. In people like William and Katie, I did not have to look at all because they both so clearly emanated peace and love.

I was blessed to go from spending time with one great couple to another. I returned to where I was staying and met up again with my hosts, Bob and Jessica. They were kind enough to take me to a bike shop to see if I could get a new wheel since I noticed one of my wheels had signs of extreme wear. The store did not have it in stock, so I ordered a new wheel to be shipped to my next major stop at Notre Dame. We then made our way to dinner together at a local brewery before grabbing some custard for dessert. The chance to have some great conversation with both of them was very uplifting. We laughed together for most of the evening, and they nearly convinced me to take another day off in their great city. It was easily one of the best evenings of my entire run.

The time off served me well, and my spirits were rejuvenated by all of the amazing people I spent time with today. There is a big milestone ahead of me tomorrow as I will finally be crossing the Mississippi River. While I will not forget the people I have met so far, I am definitely looking forward to the road ahead.

FORWARD ON FAITH

The value of consistent prayer is not that He will hear us, but that we will hear Him.

William McGill

March 31—Day 71: Saint Louis, Missouri-Alton, Illinois, 28.2 Miles. 2,125 Total Miles.

After treating me to breakfast, Jessica dropped me off where I finished a couple of days earlier. It was a great way to start the day, and I felt ready to take on the miles that would lead me into Illinois over the following few hours.

Initially, the run went fantastic as I had many people stop and ask me if I was the person on the news who was running across the country. So many people honked, waved, and gave me a thumbs-up. A few people even yelled encouraging words out of their windows. My favorite person was the lady who tried to high five me as she passed by. The kindness and support of all these Saint Louis residents made me feel so happy and excited.

The excitement lasted less than thirty minutes as my unstable wheel started to noticeably wobble. I saw a couple of more spokes snap off, and then it completely gave way. There was no repairing the wheel, and it was impossible to move. The only way to fix the stroller was to get a new wheel. I was so frustrated, and I lost my cool. Out of annoyance, I kicked the already broken wheel. This was not productive to helping me fix the stroller, and it did not exactly help the overall health of my leg. After calming down, I said a quick prayer and devised a plan in my head. I then spent over an hour trying to figure out a solution. I made numerous phone calls to the manufacturer of the stroller, local bike shops, cab companies, and my motel.

Eventually, I had a cab pick up my stroller and drive it to my motel. The manufacturer of my stroller, BOB, was kind enough to send new wheels and tires to the motel at no cost to me besides the overnight shipping fee. I then started running toward my motel with a bottle of water in hand, my phone in one pocket, and a list of prayer intentions in the other.

My mind was jumping all over the place as I started to think of what time the supplies would arrive the next day and whether or not I would be able to make it over forty miles to my planned destination after a late start. Feelings of anxiety and frustration were teeming inside of me, and I could feel the tension throughout my body. I asked the Lord to help me relax and to focus on my mission. I believed the Lord set a record right then and there for answered prayers because no sooner was that prayer off my lips than the answer appeared directly in front of me.

Seconds after saying my desperate prayer, I spotted a young man wearing running gear a few yards ahead of me. I said hello to him, and he responded with the question, "Are you Jeff?" His name was JJ, and he was an easygoing college student who ran for Saint Louis University. JJ mentioned he had tracked me on my website via my GPS device and used it to find me on the road. It made my day when he found me because he wanted to join in for a few miles. We talked about running, my mission, and stories from my journey. He was with me for close to three miles before having to turn around, but by that time my mood was completely positive and optimistic.

Running with company forced me out of my slower stride and reminded me how much more quickly and easily I could move without having to push an oppressive stroller. There were a few times where I ran on overpasses and on sections of road that were extremely narrow. It would have been very dangerous if I had a stroller. In some sense, I started to think that the broken wheel was a blessing in disguise. I continued to put in an honest pace as I rode the high of passing the two-thousand-one-hundred-mile mark all the way to the Clark Bridge, which spanned more than three quarters of a mile across the Mississippi River.

I often stayed focused on the current day, if not the current mile. However, I could not help but think of hitting major milestones on this journey from time to time. One of the big milestones I had been thinking about for weeks was this crossing because it signified running into the eastern part of America. I definitely felt a little emotional as I ran over the bridge while looking off to my side at the Mississippi. I said a prayer of thanks among the whizzing sound of all the cars driving by me. There was a photographer at the far end of the bridge, waiting to capture a few shots of me crossing the river, which I thought was awesome. I was glad I was wearing sunglasses because my eyes started to tear up.

There was so much energy and attention at crossing the river that I almost forgot about arriving in a new state! Using my phone, I took a quick photo next to the Illinois sign and then made my way into the city of Alton. I finally arrived at my motel a few miles later and was thrilled to see that my stroller and supplies had made it there safely. After speaking over the phone to a very sweet reporter, I headed out to grab a quick bite to eat.

I am so thankful that everything worked out the way it did today. I felt some anxiety earlier in the day about my ability to get to my destination tomorrow given that I will not be able to leave at an early time. However, I now have an overwhelming sense of peace because I believe it is part of the Lord's plan, and all I need to do is trust in him. If nothing else, I now have the opportunity to meet with someone tomorrow morning who heard about my run and offered to take me out for breakfast. It is not something I would normally do, but since I will be waiting on the wheel anyway, I might as well meet someone and enjoy their company while I can.

April 1—Day 72: Alton-Litchfield, Illinois, 41.3 Miles. 2,166.3 Total Miles.

I went to bed at my motel in Alton thinking that my wheel breaking was part of the Lord's plan. By early morning, I was sure it was his plan to turn a frustrating situation into an awesome opportunity. If my wheel had not broken, then I would never have met Pat, who was the man who offered to take me to breakfast. Pat told me he was in the Air Force and also founded a group called the Life Runners. The runners raise funds to bring respect for all life and to end abortion. Pat met me in the early morning, and we ventured out to grab some food.

The initial diner we planned on going to was closed, so we stopped and asked a man who operated a local gas station where to get breakfast. He sent us in another direction. After getting lost again, we finally found the Sunrise Bakery. As soon as we entered and ordered our meal of biscuits and gravy, the day began to get awesome. There were a handful of kids in the bakery, and Pat told them about my run. The kids and their parents thought it was very cool, and we all took a picture together. It was a great chance to spread my mission of prayer. Then Karl, the owner of the bakery, gave me a tour of where they made all their food. We said a prayer together, along with Nicole, who worked at the bakery as well. We talked for some time before finally saying our goodbyes. Karl was too kind and gave me a dozen sweet baked goods and a loaf of bread for my journey.

On our way back to the motel, we stopped at the local church since Pat was friends with the priest. It turned out that the school was having Mass at the time, and Pat told the priest what I was doing there. The priest said that my mission fit perfectly into his homily, which was about making time for God each day. I was definitely humbled and slightly embarrassed, but I was thrilled that my mission helped to make a positive impact on the children and parishioners at Mass.

Finally, when Pat dropped me off at the motel, we had a woman who was walking by take a photo of us together. It turned out her name was Pat as well and she was having surgery soon. Right on the spot, we prayed together for her health and a successful surgery. I never imagined myself praying with a complete stranger in the parking lot of a motel, but it was where I needed to be and what I felt called to do. The entire morning reinforced my belief that I was following the Lord's will. I was as confident as ever that I was exactly where God wanted me. Knowing that I was on the path of the Lord was the greatest feeling I had ever experienced. It was certainly worth all the pain and discomfort it took to get there.

I said goodbye to Pat and headed back inside the motel, where my wheel had just arrived. It took me thirty minutes to assemble the new wheel on the jogger, but I was on my way by 11:00 a.m. My experience in the morning had me running strong. I started to put the miles behind me very quickly. At one point, a delivery driver stopped me and asked if I was the man running across the country. It turned out he was the person who dropped off my wheels at the motel. The front desk told him why the parts were sent to me overnight. We spoke for about ten minutes on the side of the road. He told me how he had found Christ again in his life and was encouraged by my journey. He gave me a few prayer requests, and I was off and running again.

There were a few dairy farms I had to run past, which made my stomach turn. Besides feeling nauseous, the only other obstacle of the day was running on roads with no shoulder. The events of the day helped my mood, which in turn helped me to continue running steadily. I was tired but surprisingly made my destination well before sunset. When I arrived, the only rooms they had remaining were on the third floor, and they had no elevators. I was not in the mood to carry all my things up a few flights of stairs, but fortunately a man sitting in the lobby saw my predicament and lent a helping hand.

I just finished reloading on calories at dinner before replenishing my food and drink supplies for tomorrow. As long of a day as it was, I would not change anything about it. The experiences I went through and the people I met have taught me to trust in the Lord even when things are not going my way. We may not see the reason for why things happen, but I believe good things can come out of difficult situations. I discovered this by the people that I came in contact with today, and I had no trouble seeing Jesus in each and every one of them.

April 2—Day 73. Litchfield-Pana, Illinois, 39.5 Miles. 2,205.8 Total Miles.

I awoke this morning to a very sore body. I was proud of myself for simply making it down to the lobby for breakfast. As I slowly ate a bowl of cereal, I contemplated how I was going to push my body through another long day on the roads. I tried not to think about it too much as I was very accustomed to having a difficult time getting out the door. This morning was slightly more problematic as I had to carry all my belongings down a few flights of stairs before I could even get out the door to start the day. It was not easy to do as I had to go down the stairs sideways to accommodate my aching muscles. Trying to do that while carrying my supplies made getting underway take all that much longer. Eventually, all my things were packed, and I was on the road once again.

After running in colder weather recently, I was pleasantly surprised by the warming temperature and happily ran in a T-shirt again. It felt great and my pace picked up slightly because of it. The miles were not easy to get through because of a fair amount of wind and very little shoulder to run on by the side of the road. For the first time on the run, I saw a large snake as I jumped off the road onto the grass to avoid a car. In the process, I almost ran directly into the dark-colored snake lying in the grass. I was very fortunate to see it at the last second and to stop just in time. Because of all the things that could go wrong, I learned that it was crucial to pay attention to my surroundings at all times. Avoiding the snake was just one instance of this, but I believed I had help from above in remaining safe.

I was working hard to put in long miles despite feeling excessively tired. As always, prayer helped me to make it through the miles. I received many more requests because of the exposure of my run when I passed through Saint Louis. One request that stuck out was from a woman who was praying for her sister to find a good husband. I felt bad for the woman I was praying for because it seemed that she was a great person with a heart for the Lord. However, because of a number of unfortunate circumstances, she had not met a good match for her. I felt as though I could relate to her in some sense. It had been five years since I was in any type of serious relationship. I had seen my dad, sister, and brother all get married and have great relationships in that time. I saw what they had and was torn because I would have loved to be in a relationship, but I also wondered if God was calling me to some type of religious life. This particular request had me in deep thought and prayer about the same topic in my own life. I also spent time praying for all those who were alone or trying to discern their path in life. My peace in the matter came with knowing I was where God wanted me to be at that moment. I believed that if I continued to follow his guidance, then things would come out according to his will. In my mind, being where the Lord wanted me was the best feeling I had experienced. I resolved to do everything in my power to ensure I remained on that path.

The miles went by at a consistent pace as I continued to push through the fatigue and pain. I guessed there were many people who saw the news because I received an incredible amount of fist pumps, waves, and honks. It was so encouraging and helped me get through the long day. My friend Pat from Alton put me in touch with his friend Kevin. I was in contact with Kevin throughout the day, and he offered to host me for the night. We finally decided to meet at the McDonald's in Pana. I ended up running slightly ahead of schedule and beat him there by a few minutes, which was long enough to order some food and scarf most of it down by the time he arrived. I was so glad to have company for the evening, and I knew the thought of it helped pull me through the final miles.

I had a fantastic time with both Kevin and his wife Kathy. They had so many good stories as well as a very nice family. I learned Kevin was an author, and I loved hearing about his books. His life story was very intriguing and he had so much wisdom to share. He was also a weightlifter for a long time and told me that he prayed as he worked out. It was heartening to hear someone else who understood the relationship between prayer and physical exertion. Kevin and Kathy were so nice as they treated me to some of the local fare. I had a good beer, a fantastic sandwich they called a horseshoe, and some ice cream to top off my caloric intake for the day.

I am very tired but so thankful for the opportunity to spend time with some great people. I do not think those who host me realize just how much they encourage me and lift my spirits. It is a true gift of charity. I pray I have the chance to pass on this gift to others in the future.

April 3—Day 74: Pana-Mount Zion, Illinois, 40.5 Miles. 2,246.3 Total Miles.

This Sunday morning began perfectly. I attended Mass with Kevin before he dropped me off at the McDonald's where we first met. Even with all the generosity Kevin and his family showed me, he insisted on giving me some funds to help me on the road. I felt as if I were part of his family while I stayed with them, so it was very difficult to leave.

The weather forecast called for strong winds out of the south, so I altered my original plan to run east for most of the day. Instead, I found a road that would take me north for a good section of the day since I was going in that general direction to get to Notre Dame. The gusts were so strong that I was almost knocked off my feet on a couple of occasions and had to do my best to ensure my stroller did not tip over. I was very happy to finally turn north and have the wind at my back. All was not easy as the constant howling of the wind in my ears gave me a terrible headache that made me feel sick.

I continued to battle the miles on a country road and barely saw any cars while I ran on it. There was a lot of open space, with only a few houses scattered along the lightly rolling terrain. I eventually came across a woman and her daughter playing in a yard with their dogs. When the mother asked what I was doing, I shared with her my mission, and she immediately asked me to pray for her father. I promised I would and continued on my way, thinking that if the weather had been different, I never would have run into this woman. This led me to believe that I was supposed to encounter them and to pray for their family. I knew in my heart I was meant to be on that road. The strong sense of purpose gave me courage to run through my own discomfort.

The back road I was on eventually ran into a main highway. It was exciting to be near civilization again, but the road had no shoulder and a lot of traffic. I found myself doing my best to push the stroller through the thick grass on the side of the road in order to move forward. I then weaved my way through a few side streets until I hit my motel. The feeling of stopping was nice, but it was much better to simply be inside and out of the intolerable wind. After taking medicine for my headache and eating two full meals plus dessert at a nearby restaurant, I felt much better.

I am icing my right leg tonight as it gave me problems for the second half of the day, but it does not feel as serious as some of the other issues I have experienced before. In addition to the prayer requests that continue to pour in, I also hear from people on occasion who I have not spoken to in a very long time. This is also encouraging to me because it shows me that the word on the run and its mission is spreading. I think this world needs God and needs prayer so much. This run is just a tool that is helping people recognize that need. It is my sincere hope that my mission will help people to not only make time for the Lord in their daily lives right now, but that it ignites their prayer lives in such a way that they will encourage people in their lives to pray as well. I will certainly never know the impact this run will have on those who follow it. However, I find comfort in knowing that I am doing what God wants me to do. I truly believe there will be a lot of good brought out of this journey of prayer.

April 4—Day 75: Mount Zion-Monticello, Illinois, 31 Miles. 2,277.3 Total Miles.

I woke up this morning to pouring rain and lightning. I planned to arrive at Notre Dame by a certain date, so the thought of taking a day off because of weather did not seem like a good idea. The last time I took a day off because of weather, I ended up having to make up the miles, and it wore heavily on both my body and my mind. I checked the weather forecast, and it appeared the worst of the storm would be moving out by late morning. The chance to have a few spare hours should have been used for sleep. However, I chose instead to do a much needed load of laundry.

After watching the radar for a couple of hours, I decided to finally get underway and start running behind the storm. The previous day hit eighty degrees, but there was no hope of getting out of the forties today. To make the situation more interesting, the cold front carried with it a strong wind out of the northwest. For part of the day, I was heading east and was doing just fine. I eventually got hit hard with the cold wind when I turned north. It felt like I was moving backward. I put my sunglasses on to keep my eyes from tearing up.

I was beginning to feel extremely worn down and was tired of the cold wind inhibiting my progress. It felt like all my energy was drained out of me, and I was moving forward on solely my will to get through the miles. I continued to run past open fields in the country, which did nothing to block the wind. A man stopped to ask if I was okay and if I needed a ride. It was not the first time I had been asked that question. I never considered taking someone up on their offer before, but I would be lying if I said I was not tempted. Before I could think it over in my head, I simply thanked him for the offer and told him I needed to run it on my own. Before his window rolled up, I heard him say, "Man, you must be freezing!" He was right.

I somehow continued to move my legs forward until my route turned in more of an eastern direction at nearly twenty-three miles into the day. The wind was therefore coming at me at more of an angle instead of in my face. While still a factor, it was much less burdensome and felt like a huge weight had been lifted off my shoulders. I instantaneously felt better and started speeding through the final eight miles. There were a few people that gave me strange looks as I made my way through the small town of my destination, but I was so used to it that I barely noticed them anymore.

The prayers continued to flow in one after another as I continued to have prayers submitted on my website and through e-mail. In addition to the requests sent to me, I prayed for my own growing list of intentions. Before the run started, I used to be much more concerned about mostly my own prayer requests. This journey opened my eyes to everything around me. Because of this awakening, I began to see opportunities to pray for everyone who passed me on the street, the people who had crosses in their memory on the side of the road, those buried in the cemeteries I passed, and the well-being of the people in the towns I ran through each day. I often got the impression that people were struggling in most of the small towns I passed. This taught me to be aware of both the people and the situations around me. The only way I could help at the time was to say a prayer for them. With each passing day, my belief in its power made me realize that prayer was a wonderful place to start.

I was so involved in prayer and thrilled to not be running against a headwind that I pulled up to the motel without even feeling tired. If there was another town nearby, I would have kept on running. I figured it was in my best interest to get some rest while I had the chance, so I checked into the motel and grabbed some food at the adjacent restaurant. I returned to the motel and had a couple of people come up to me asking if they could shake my hand because they heard I was the man running and praying across America. It was an honor to have people want to talk to me, and I was humbled by the experience. I prayed that my story brought hope to them and was in some way able to encourage them in their own prayer lives.

I am happy with progress on a day that I initially thought may be forfeited because of weather. However, my next week is going to be rough because I am now trying to arrive at Notre Dame by Saturday. This means an adjustment to my route and consequently some very long mileage days. I am hoping the thought of seeing my friends at Notre Dame and reaching campus will help pull me through those days. I am definitely going to go to bed early tonight because the adjustment to my route starts tomorrow with a day well over fifty miles.

April 5—Day 76: Monticello-Danville, Illinois, 54.2 Miles. 2,331.5 Total Miles.

I woke up early and grabbed a quick breakfast at the motel. I felt very encouraged when a few more people wanted to speak to me before I headed out the door. I was beyond humbled that complete strangers wanted to shake my hand and thank me for running across the country for prayer. In my mind, I knew it had nothing to do with me. Rather, it was through the grace of God that I was still making progress on the journey. We exchanged a few words after I had breakfast, but I needed to get back to my room to record an interview over the phone. I was psyched to start the day with such positive feelings all around me. These feeling helped me to move through the first fifteen minutes quite well. I decided to slow down and pace myself better because I still had the equivalent of more than two marathons to run before I finished.

The weather started out chilly but began to warm up into the fifties. The best thing about the day was that there was little wind, which was a huge improvement over the previous day. I was fortunate that the terrain was nearly flat because it helped me to run virtually the entire distance. Running on this new route meant I did not know how the roads would look, but it also meant I would be running through the campus of the University of Illinois. Looking at the sights in the town and on the campus itself helped the miles pass by quickly.

I stopped briefly to take some photos outside of the football stadium and received many inquisitive looks from students who were walking around campus. At one point, I passed two girls who were running. When I smiled and waved at them, I received only a disgusted look in return as they picked up their pace and ran away from me. A small smile spread on my face as I imagined what the girls said about me as they ran away. I was pushing a stroller through campus and looked extremely tired while sporting a straggly beard. I could not fault them for their reaction. It was a reminder to me that I should not judge anyone I come in contact with because I did not know their story or what they might be going through.

My pace remained steady as I exited Champaign and ran through Urbana, right back onto some country roads. It was a relief to have little traffic as I ran on a road that disappeared into the horizon with nothing but dirt fields around me. There were a few clouds sailing across the blue sky. It was beautiful and quite serene. The road eventually turned into an unpaved and rocky path, which did slow my progress slightly. I felt great besides some lingering soreness and a stomach issue for a few miles. I loved the quiet, and it was a perfect chance to get lost in prayer. There were so many requests for people's family members who were sick, going through difficult times, or who had lost their faith. While many of the specific situations were difficult to take in, I loved to see how concerned people were for members of their family. It was so encouraging to me that they were lifting up their needs to God. I was humbled and honored to play a role in that process.

Deep into the country road, I saw signs indicating that I was on the route Abraham Lincoln used to travel while riding on the judicial circuit back in the mid-1800s. I loved history, so it was an awesome feeling to travel on the same route as one of the most well-known figures of American history. This joy was short-lived as I entered a section of homes where there were dogs roaming the streets. I immediately sensed that the dogs did not like visitors. It did not take long to discover my instinct was correct. I picked up a large stick as I approached them and tucked it by my side as I slowed to a walk. There were about ten dogs, and most of them were very large and showing their teeth. I managed to get all of them to one side of me and walked backward against my stroller. When they started to approach, I yelled at them loudly to get back, and it seemed to work. After a few intense minutes, I was left with one very large dog barking and baring his teeth at me at the edge of the row of houses. He came toward me aggressively one final time, but I moved out of the way and yelled at him while getting my stick ready for action. It was his last maneuver against me as he then stood still and watched me until I was out of sight. Upon reaching that point, I turned around and started running again with an occasional glance over my shoulder to ensure I was still safe.

I felt mentally exhausted from the ordeal but still pushed on while trying to break up the remaining miles in my mind. My legs locked up around mile 45, but realizing that the end was near helped me to push my body through the final section. Ten miles used to be a very long ways, but I found it funny how it felt like I was in the home stretch once I was within ten miles of my destination. Despite that feeling, it did not necessarily mean those miles went by quickly. I was so close to reaching the motel when the road I was planning to take turned into a dead end. Being so close to the finish after running all day and having to add on even a small distance was a crushing blow to my mental state. I ended up backtracking then navigating through a park and up a steep embankment before finally reaching the motel. After being on the move all day long, I did not feel like going anywhere. I ordered a couple of pizzas to my motel room for the night and stared into space while eating my dinner.

I am psyched that my former college roommate, who is in the seminary at Notre Dame, was able to set up a prayer service for Sunday at the Grotto. I am looking forward to it so much. I am also praying that the desire to get there will help me get through another day of over fifty miles tomorrow. It will be the first time on this journey that I have back-to-back days over fifty miles. My body tells me that it is exhausted and cannot make it that far, but I have learned all things are possible with God. There is no way I am going to miss the prayer service on Sunday. I am in the mode now where I know the Lord is carrying me. He will not only deliver me safely to Notre Dame but will also ensure a safe arrival to New York. That confidence is something which gives me a level of peace I have never felt before.

April 6—Day 77: Danville, Illinois-West Lafayette, Indiana, 51.3 Miles. 2,382.8 Total Miles.

I awoke this morning very tired because I had a terrible time trying to sleep. I estimated I only slept for two hours because most of the night was spent trying to ignore the soreness that had set in throughout my entire body. After a quick breakfast and a prayer for protection on the roads, I was on the move once again through the sidewalks in town.

Two kids walking to school asked me where I was going in such a hurry. I told them I was running to New York, and one of them replied, "No, you're not." He simply did not believe me. When I stopped and started to explain what I was doing, he simply refused to believe me. For a brief second, I actually saw myself in the way he responded to me. I remembered times in my life when I felt the Lord calling me a certain direction, and I refused. My excuse was that I did not see how it was practical or even possible. I was not upset at the kid in any way and did not know why my thoughts took my mind in the direction it did, but I learned a lesson in that moment. Just because a task or situation may not seem possible or practical, I needed to have trust in the Lord if it was something I felt he called me to do. This run was in the smaller percentage of times where I felt I had obeyed God in that regard. I knew my life would have many more twists and turns in the future. I believed that the conversation this morning was to help me see how I acted when told something I could not comprehend. More importantly, it was meant to help me make better decisions in the future.

I thought deeply about listening to God for the first few miles until I hit the Indiana border and finally entered Eastern Standard Time. I was so excited to be in another state, especially since it meant I was within striking distance of Notre Dame! I took a few pictures before moving on since I still had a long day ahead of me. Even upon turning onto some back roads, there was quite a bit of traffic, and the terrain was rolling. I did not expect either of those things, and it took its toll on me. My legs already felt heavy, as though I were carrying a set of weights on them that rode all the way from my ankles to my thighs.

Forward motion was slow because it was also windy and the traffic never let up. At one section, there was a very long stretch of road that was under construction, and I constantly had to jump on and off the road to avoid the truck traffic. It did not help that the vehicles were producing so many fumes. It made me feel sick, and I was coughing for a long while.

I made decent time until I hit mile 30, where I suddenly hit a wall. My legs did not want to move any more, and my arms were equally as tired from pulling the stroller on and off the road all day long. I literally talked out loud to myself to win an argument against pulling out my sleeping bag and taking a nap on the side of the road. It was a grueling and tedious jog through about mile 47. Those miles seemed to take an eternity, and I was convinced it was solely the power of prayer that helped me make it through that arduous stretch. I was granted a new perspective by praying for a couple who was about to lose their home. I imagined they were feeling desperate and hopeless. Because of the economy, I knew there were many people in the same situation. I took the focus off my own exhaustion and placed it on those who were struggling to keep their homes. I felt frustrated that so many people were in a similar financial crisis, so I prayed for their peace and a positive outcome to all their situations.

The road finally opened up and created a shoulder for me to run on. As if taking off on a runway, I increased my pace and was soon running the fastest miles of the entire day. I was still sore and weary, but I wanted to be done so badly. I pushed it as hard as I could to ensure that my stopping point would arrive quickly.

Once again, I ran near a college campus; this time, it was Purdue University. As expected, I received many inquisitive looks. I did not care at all and finally made my way onto the steps of my motel. I was beyond thrilled to have a room on the first floor and even happier to have an Irish pub within walking distance. I had a well-deserved Guinness with my dinner before limping back to my room.

I am now about to fall asleep, which I am convinced will happen as soon as my head hits the pillow. One final note that has me excited to reach Notre Dame is that I received an invitation to speak at the Holy Half Marathon taking place Sunday on campus. I did not plan to arrive for the race, but it is not surprising that I am scheduled to arrive just in time to talk the day of the race. I believe it is one more example that I am exactly where God needs me.

April 7—Day 78: West Lafayette-Logansport, Indiana, 41.5 Miles. 2,424.3 Total Miles.

Trying to get my legs moving this morning was more difficult than any other time on the journey. I was literally shuffling out the door and did not know how I would manage to run for hours on end. My mind did its best to force my legs through the pain and soreness as I worked my stride into a run. As difficult as it was to get moving, I somehow got into a groove for the first part of the day and was making decent time.

I eventually hit Route 25, and my good progress was immediately halted. There was heavy traffic and almost no shoulder to run on. This part of my route was a recent change to my original plan and was devised on my cell phone. I was unfamiliar with the roads and did not have any other options, so my only choice was to bear the tough conditions for about thirty-three miles. The combination of the busy road, long miles, and exhausted muscles made the rest of the day absolutely brutal.

I did not have the energy to push my stroller through the grass on the side of the road when vehicles came by, so I ran when the cars were not passing me. As such, the majority of the day was spent in quick and short bursts. I would simply pull my jogger off to the side of the road when a vehicle approached. As soon as the vehicle was past me and I had a clear lane, I would pull it back onto the road and sprint as fast I could until pulling it back off to the side when the next vehicle came driving up. Since the road was incredibly busy, I was running in bursts of anywhere from five seconds to a minute at a time.

As long and tiresome as today was, it felt even longer when my tire went flat. I thought I fixed it, but a short time later it went flat again. It was so frustrating as I struggled to fix my tire and get back on the road. I could feel my head start to hang and my shoulders begin to fall. Not only did I feel completely drained, but for the first time in a while, I noticed just how weak my body felt. I realized how thin I was in comparison to when I started my run. My conclusion was that I was not eating as much as I needed to in order to replace the necessary calories. I simply felt incredibly weak and used the moment to ask the Lord for strength once again.

My legs continued churning through the heavy traffic and a brief conversation with a police officer who pulled me over. He was very nice, and I could tell he was genuinely concerned for me. I tried my best to smile when I talked to him, but I am sure he saw the exhaustion and weariness through my attempt at a disguise. He told me to be very careful and continued on his way. I felt bad because I was so focused on avoiding traffic that I did not get to pray too much for the intentions. I thought that days like today were when I was on the receiving end of prayers being answered. I believed it was a small miracle I was able to get through those dangerous roads unscathed.

Mercifully, the road finally gave me a place to run on as I neared the town of my destination. I arrived shortly before dark and almost considered going to bed without dinner because I was so tired. However, I knew I needed to maintain my weight, so I ate dinner and dessert at a restaurant attached to the motel before going across the street to get some fast food as well.

I have now finished all my food and am praying that it helps me sleep well. I am praying for the ability to stay healthy and to run through tomorrow's mileage as quickly as possible. Just like my body feels at the moment, I know I am weak. I need God in all things. It is only through his grace that I have been able to make it through both my difficulties in life and on this run. I will be praying for God's help because my body is telling me there is no way I can make it about fifty miles tomorrow. At this point, I know all I need to do is place my trust in the Lord.

April 8—Day 79: Logansport-Plymouth, Indiana, 51.2 Miles. 2,475.5 Total Miles.

I woke up early this morning in hopes of figuring out a way around the main road so I would not have to deal with heavy traffic again. I did not know what the roads would look like or what kind of conditions they would be in. The only thing I knew was that my day was going to be a long one. On a week where I was running so many miles, it was not easy making the distance of today even longer. My thought was that it would be better to add on miles than to fight traffic for the majority of the day.

It was once again very difficult getting started, especially given that it was raining on and off until about noon. My strategy was to run as fast as possible while I was fresh and bank all the miles I could before I started crashing. My pace stayed steady and strong for the entire morning. It was only broken up for a short while around 9:00 a.m. for a radio interview I gave over the phone.

As I continued on the country roads, I tried not to think of the overall mileage and instead enjoyed the quiet around me. The roads were empty, and the view consisted of open fields of dirt. The scenery was only broken up by the bare trees. I could not see very far because of the misty conditions. My bright reflective vest was the only splash of color in the entire landscape. It was a dreary day, but a perfect time to pray.

There were almost no people on the Indiana country roads, but I did have a dog follow me for a mile or two. Fortunately, he was a friendly dog. It was fine with me as I was happy to have company of any kind, and it helped my mood stay positive on a dreary day.

When I hit the thirty-five-mile mark, it might as well have been a physical wall. My body succumbed to the physical demands of the past week, and I found it extremely difficult to keep moving my legs. It was then that I prayed for a young man confined to a wheelchair because of a terrible disease. It was the thought of him that helped me to keep moving. I slowed down to a shuffle, but I kept pushing as hard as I could. It was in those miles that I ran for the man who could not walk. I found it amazing what my body could do when the pain and discomfort was offered up for someone else. There was something special in offering up my suffering, especially during the Lenten season. Through this experience, I developed a deeper relationship with God in that I was able to put aside the comforts of this world. In doing so, my focus was often on what was truly important in life. I believed life was about helping those around us by showing the people we encounter each day the love Christ showed us. My initial definition of success was a finish in New York. Although I still wanted to push myself to that point, I felt that my run would only be successful if I could point people—including myself—toward the Lord.

I smiled for the first time in miles as I entered the town of my destination. My body was screaming in pain. I had a difficult time locating what hurt the most. I simply continued moving as quickly as my body would allow until I finally rolled my jogger up to the motel. I had to sit down on the couch while the person in front of me checked in. I questioned my ability to stand back up.

There was a good chance I would have passed up dinner altogether if my stomach was not continually rumbling. I was glad I didn't because I not only had a great pizza, but I had a great conversation with my waitress. It started when she asked me if I was really going to eat the entire order myself. Her name was Samantha, and we talked about my physical challenge and its spiritual mission. She asked about the logistics of the run and some of my stories along the way. I was beyond happy to have a conversation with someone. As I finished my dinner, she told me not to worry about the bill because she already paid it for me. It was such an encouraging gesture and one that truly humbled me.

After running over three hundred nine miles this past week, my muscles feel like they are locked up in one gigantic knot. Thankfully, I will arrive at Notre Dame tomorrow. The thought of seeing my friends at one of my favorite places in this country brings me such great joy. Arriving at Notre Dame is something I have been looking forward to for a very long time. I remember planning my route, and I essentially added on five hundred miles to my route by coming to Notre Dame as opposed to running straight toward Washington DC on my way to New York. Like many things that are worth doing, there is a lot of work that must go into making it happen. I am sure the extra miles will be worth it.

April 9—Day 80: Plymouth-Notre Dame, Indiana, 27.3 Miles. 2,502.8 Total Miles.

I woke up with my muscles in knots, but the thought of a shorter mileage day combined with a destination where I had friends made it much easier getting out of bed. I was so excited to get to Notre Dame that I crushed the first four miles in about thirty minutes. My breathing was suddenly very heavy, and I had to remind myself that twenty-seven miles was still a long way to run. The day itself was dreary with a light breeze. I was fighting some stomach issues for the first half of the run, but it did not deter my positive attitude. Today was one day where I did not let any of the conditions around me affect my mood. A smile was on my face for the entire run as I closed in on campus.

My eyes continued to stay focused in the distance, hoping to catch a glimpse of the golden dome. Just as I neared campus, the sun broke through the clouds, and the temperature began to rise. It was awe-inspiring to see the dome shining in the sun as I approached Notre Dame. I got goose bumps all over. My memory flashed back to the first time I saw the dome, when I visited the university with my parents as a senior in high school. I started racing through everything that had happened in my life between that moment and my current situation. It was an emotional overload as I had a difficult time grasping onto the fact that I finally reached my alma mater.

As I did my best to take a deep breath, I was granted some comic relief by my friend Matt. He was always an athlete, but I had only seen him run once or twice. When I spotted Matt, he was running up to meet me in his street clothes with a huge grin on his face. He thought I was coming to campus by a different route, so he had sprinted over to me when he saw the updated location on my website. It was so good to see him, and he ran with me a short ways before peeling off because he did not want to be on camera when I reached Notre Dame Avenue, where a TV crew was waiting for me.

I reached the south entrance to campus and gave a quick interview with the TV station. Another one of my friends, Rob, met me with his wife Becca. Rob was always a great friend of mine, and I was honored to be the best man at his wedding. We were also roommates for all four years during college. He was always so kind and generous. He set up my website for the run and agreed to let me stay with him as I passed through town. Seeing Rob and Becca made me so happy. It was a constant battle to be on the road day after day without the physical support of friends and family. Upon seeing a few familiar faces, my spirits were lifted, and all my pain and frustrations melted away.

For about ten minutes following my arrival on campus, I literally did not know what to do with myself. I started running around in the street, lifting the wheels up on my stroller. Then I made my way toward the dome and took some photos there before heading over to the empty reflecting pool in front of the image known as Touchdown Jesus. I ran laps around the reflecting pool and then went to the parking lot where Rob was waiting for me. Of course, I continued to run laps around his car. For the first time in a long while, I felt pure joy.

After finally settling my emotions down, I showered and spent time with my friends at a barbecue Rob hosted. I did step out briefly for another TV interview. I never liked being on television, but I knew it was a chance to reach out and encourage people to make time in their lives for God. After the interview was done, I let myself relax and enjoy the moment since I planned on taking the next day or two off.

As nice as it is to have a physical break, I feel even more excited to take a mental break from the high intensity of my journey. The chance to spend the break with friends is priceless. I truly believe my arrival at Notre Dame at this time is in God's will. I did not plan it this way, but it works out perfectly because I will be able to speak before the Holy Half Marathon on campus tomorrow morning.

April 10—Day 81: Rest at Notre Dame. 2,502.8 Total Miles.

I slept in a little before heading over to speak before the race on Notre Dame's campus this morning. I encouraged people to take time for the Lord in their daily lives and to pray as often as possible. After talking with a few of the runners before the race, I made my way to the basilica on campus in time for Mass. It was amazing to be back at such a beautiful and familiar place. I found myself feeling like I was more in the presence of the Lord than ever before. I was able to follow up my time in church with prayers at the Grotto.

On my arrival the previous day, I saw a couple, who were just married, taking photos. While at the grotto today, I witnessed a couple get engaged. It was such a great feeling to be surrounded by such positive emotions. Notre Dame was a special place for me not only because of the time I spent there in college but also for all the time I spent in prayer at the grotto. As a replica of the grotto in France where Mary appeared to St. Bernadette, it was a beautiful place where I had spent many hours in prayer during my time in college. I also had countless memories at different spots all over the university with my family. Notre Dame campus was the last place my family was all together while my mom was still healthy enough to walk around, just two weeks before she passed away. There were so many emotions tied to my surroundings, and I was thrilled to add another memory to all those that came before it.

I lit two candles while at the grotto. One was for my niece, Valerie. The other was meant for myself and all the intentions on my run. I could not wait to meet my niece. I knew the thought of meeting her was going to help me get through many of the miles until I hit Alexandria, Virginia. Also, as much goodness as I felt surrounding my journey, I also sensed that there were forces that did not want me to succeed. That is one reason why I always said a prayer to Saint Michael the Archangel to begin each day. I felt beyond grateful for the prayers and Masses offered up by others for my run. I had lit candles for certain intentions at the grotto while I was a student, and I felt completely at peace continuing that practice while on my journey.

I believed with my whole heart I would complete the run safely. I also knew the only way I would succeed was if I had the Lord's help.

Praying at the grotto was such a peaceful experience. It was followed by a rosary and brief talk about my run. One of my other roommates from college, Matt, was at the Holy Cross Seminary. He brought a group of seminarians with him to the prayer service, and a few other people came as well. I knew I had been joined by others in praying the rosary in spirit over the past twelve weeks, but the chance to pray it with a group of people in person was so peaceful and encouraging. My spirit rose with each prayer and every conversation I had with those who showed up to pray. I walked away from the prayer service feeling blessed in countless ways.

I spent a number of hours today resting and catching up with my friends. I am so far behind on both rest and the logistics of the run. Therefore, I am looking forward to sleeping in tomorrow and taking one more day off before getting underway again. I feel unbelievably blessed to be surrounded by so many great friends as well as a familiar environment.

April 11—Day 82: Rest at Notre Dame. 2,502.8 Total Miles.

I was so glad I took another day off because my body was still very sore when I got out of bed this morning. The chance to nap during the day was much appreciated! I also worked on some logistics of the run on Rob's computer, which was so much easier to use than my phone. The open hours of the day allowed me to speak to my family on the phone, give another radio interview, and even get a much needed haircut. The gentleman who cut my hair, Andy, was so nice and said he would not charge me if I gave him an autograph. It was a generous act, and I made sure to sign it with my favorite Bible verse, 1 Corinthians 9:24. It says, "Do you not know that in a race all the runners run, but only one gets the prize? Run in such a way as to get the prize." This passage talks about a runner in a race who runs for victory, and it tells us to live in the same way. The passage always encouraged me to stay focused on the Lord even when things were difficult because the only thing I truly desired was eternal life in heaven.

Rob bought me lunch on campus, and I enjoyed eating while reading a story the school paper wrote on my run. I loved the ability to take unlimited trips to the food stations. I made trip after trip as I loaded up on sandwiches, pizza, pasta, and ice cream. It was phenomenal.

I have lost twenty pounds since I started running almost three months ago, so I have a renewed focus to eat as much as I possibly can to ensure I do not drop any lower. I have thoroughly enjoyed my time here and am hoping the morning does not come too soon. It is going to be very difficult to get going again after these two wonderful days with my friends at this very special place. I feel so blessed for this opportunity to see my friends and to have my spirits renewed.

PUSHING THE LIMIT

Only those who will risk going too far can possibly find out how far one can go.

T. S. Eliot

April 12—Day 83: Notre Dame-Shipshewana, Indiana, 41.8 Miles. 2,544.6 Total Miles.

Hitting the road again after a couple of great days at Notre Dame was very tough. As much as I struggled with it physically, the mental part was the true battle. I said goodbye to Rob and Becca before running with my jogger toward my next destination. My legs were feeling stiff, but I eventually found a level of comfort and remained at that pace for most of the day. I did my best to focus on the road ahead as well as all the additional prayer intentions I received over the past number of days.

The first part of the day was spent on sidewalks as I ran through a few sizable towns. Those busy streets eventually gave way to country roads once again. I really enjoyed running on the country roads because they were so peaceful. Because of the open road, I could concentrate on prayer much more than when I was trying to dodge vehicles. As I ran, I prayed for all those I spent time with at Notre Dame. I also prayed for all the new friends I made during my brief stay there. It almost made me want to turn around and take another couple days off. My next major stop was scheduled to be just outside of Washington DC. I could not wait to see my brother Dave and sister Kristina, along with their spouses and my niece. I estimated it would take three weeks to get there, so I started to use the motivation of seeing them to get me going on the long stretch of road in front of me.

In the midst of my prayers and thoughts about my family, I became very sad. I missed them all very much. I was reminded of how I depended on the support of others during my most recent stop. The worst of the loneliness I felt on my run always occurred after leaving places where I spent time with family or friends. I felt this way after I left Phoenix, Oklahoma, and Saint Louis. Each time, the feeling of loneliness sank a little deeper. I knew the only way I could get past it was through prayer and sensing that Jesus was with me each step of the way. I did not believe I could continue if I failed to sense his presence.

My legs continued to churn out mile after mile while I dealt with all these emotions. I prayed for all the people who had no family or friends to help them in their times of loneliness. My thoughts were lost in prayer when I suddenly found myself closing in on my destination. I was feeling a little more down than usual, but my spirits were picked up by the humor I found in all the strange looks I received. The area I ran into was in the middle of Amish country. I had to pull off the road often to avoid the frequent horse and carriage. When I did, I always smiled or waved at the folks in the carriages. The looks I received were priceless as I could tell they were trying to figure me out but did not have a clue as to why I was running with a packed jogger.

I helped to improve my mood by finding more humor in how I refused to care what I stepped in while running. Over the previous few months, I had run over some very disgusting things, some of which really turned my stomach. Most of them happened because I saw the roadkill too late or simply did not have a choice because of the traffic. Today, the road opened up to a wide shoulder as I approached town because it needed to accommodate the carriages. While it was great to have a shoulder to run on, it also meant the road was covered in horse droppings. Initially, I tried to avoid them as much as possible. However, after nearly forty miles, I did not have the energy to run around everything. I gave up and just ran straight ahead. I hit everything in my path, but at that point I did not care. That strategy definitely accounted for additional strange looks in my direction.

After many difficult miles on the day, I finally rolled up to my motel. I cleaned off my tires and scraped off my shoes before entering the building and taking a much-needed shower. The long day had my appetite raging, so I walked a ways to grab dinner. On the way, I confirmed plans with my hosts a couple of days away.

I am thrilled with my progress and am excited to be moving well this deep into the run. I can sense I am beginning to close in on the end. Tonight, I will be saying an extra prayer that my body remains intact over the final one thousand two hundred miles. I have a feeling it will hold up—but just barely.

April 13—Day 84: Shipshewana-Angola, Indiana, 31 Miles. 2,575.6 Total Miles.

I got started this morning without too much soreness and had a shoulder to run on for most of the day. I received a few more odd looks as I ran out of town and settled into a fairly quick pace.

The sun came out and was shining bright, warming the temperature up to a perfect sixty-five degrees. It was so great to run comfortably in good weather while not having to worry about jumping on and off the road to avoid traffic. This was one of the few days I had since the start where I was able to pray and spend time talking to the Lord for nearly the entire day.

My course kept me on Route 20 all the way to Angola. I had a shoulder to run on and nothing to distract me from my time in prayer. The terrain was flat, and I had nothing but fields outlined by trees to admire. I continued down my list of prayer intentions, praying for a broken family. The dad was struggling with some of his own issues that hindered him from being the kind of father his kids needed. I often found it difficult to read over intentions where kids were either sick or in some type of difficult situation. This particular intention was no different. I was blessed with a great childhood and could not imagine the types of circumstances the kids on my list of intentions had to face. I prayed intently for the children in that family to know the love and peace only our Heavenly Father could offer. The miles rolled by quickly when I focused on the intentions as opposed to the distance I had yet to run.

By the time I rolled into the parking lot at the motel, I was not even tired, and it was still early in the afternoon. I did not run into anyone on the roads today, so I took the time to have a nice conversation about families and faith with the woman who owned the hotel. After I got settled and cleaned up, I walked over to a nearby restaurant. I had a nice beer with my dinner while talking to some of the locals. Simply being in the presence of others was such a blessing. I knew I took things for granted before, but I hoped to never again look past the opportunity to talk to those around me. My life was so blessed to have such wonderful people surrounding me, but I had not always appreciated them. This run shed light on that area of my life. By doing so, it encouraged me to pray for those who did not have friends and family to lean on for support. I went through a brief period of loneliness today, but part of the lesson I learned was that I should keep in my prayers those who live every day in loneliness. One goal of mine was to not only pray for people who live in loneliness but also to reach out to everyone I could because even the smallest gestures could mean so much to a lonely person.

I just returned from stocking up on supplies. I am very excited as I will be crossing into Ohio during the early part of tomorrow's run. If more days were like today, then this run would be much easier. It feels great to be healthy and well-rested. I really hope I will feel this way for the remainder of the journey, but there is likely a fair amount of pain to be endured before I reach my finish line. As such, I am enjoying this feeling while it lasts, and I am looking forward to crossing another state off my list tomorrow!

April 14—Day 85: Angola, Indiana-Archbold, Ohio, 41.2 Miles. 2,616.8 Total Miles.

In the planning stages of the run, I mapped out each and every mile of the nearly four-thousand-mile trek. However, a lesson I learned was to be flexible as not everything would always go according to plan. My route, places to stay at night, and supplies had all been changed at some point because of unforeseen circumstances. Today was another instance in how it was a good idea to be flexible. My original plan was to run around twenty-six miles, but the weather forecast indicated a headwind that was supposed to only get stronger as the day wore on.

I decided to make today a little longer. The alternative would mean the next day would be a forty-seven-mile day into a stronger thirty miles per hour wind. It seemed like a good idea to go longer today given how great my body felt. After looking at the map and searching for motels, I located a perfect place to stay about forty-one miles away. Because of the weather forecast, I really pushed myself hard for the first part of the day in an attempt to get as many miles in while the weather cooperated. My spirits were lifted as I crossed into Ohio about eleven miles into the morning, but I was a little upset there was no "Welcome to Ohio" sign to mark the state line.

The wonderful things about the first part of the day were the open roads, the flat terrain, and the light traffic. The cars that did pass me by seemed curious as they slowed down to get a good look at me. I always smiled and waved. I was thrilled to get the same response from nearly all the drivers. My back road eventually ran into a main highway again, so I was stuck dodging traffic just as the wind began to pick up. I could feel myself tiring quickly and thought that I may not get going again if I stopped. When I ran through the small town of Montpelier, I had a quick conversation without stopping. Two men asked me where I was going, and when I told them New York, one of them replied, "You know that is a long ways from here, right?" I tried to think of something funny to say, but I just nodded and smiled as my legs continued to churn. I did feel bad for not stopping, but I simply felt a strong pull to keep moving. I took comfort in the fact that I would be praying for those two men since I had decided to pray for everyone I encountered.

The endless miles on the road took a toll on me mentally. It was so tiring to never get a break, knowing that a loss of concentration could mean a terrible disaster or even death. Many of the drivers were usually courteous and moved over for me, but quite a few were not paying attention or did not see me until the last moment. While I was always extremely careful, I came far too close to being hit by a vehicle on a number of occasions. Those kinds of experiences had me very vigilant and careful during those times I shared the road with cars and trucks. I was looking forward to a mental break because of a trail that paralleled my route. I figured I would be able to move quicker and easier since I would not have to worry about vehicles on the path. I was crushed when I reached the trail. It was covered in thick grass and had small trees lying across the path at a few locations. I did my best to tough it out for a few miles before finally giving up on it and heading back to the main highway.

I could feel my body sink into a familiar deep soreness as I hit the thirty-mile mark. Once again, it was in prayer as well as the requests themselves that helped me to keep running. For whatever reason, many of the requests I received the previous week were ones I could relate to directly. There were people asking me to pray for family members stricken with cancer. I had a request from a woman who asked me to pray for her husband. He had left her, even though she did not want a divorce. I had an intention for a family who recently lost a parent to cancer. A fear of mine when I began the run was that I might become numb to the pain people were going through because of the volume of requests. Rather, I felt a very real sense of pain that only deepened the compassion I felt for the people involved in my prayers with every intention. I almost felt that I could sense the pain they were in, especially those experiencing conditions I had been through personally.

Instead of letting the requests roll off my back, I embraced them, allowing the pain and sadness to sink in. It was through the requests that I found myself inspired to keep running. It was through the prayers for those intentions in which I found a sense of peace. I truly felt a heavier burden on my shoulders with each request I read. There is no way I was going to stop with so many people asking me to pray to them. I promised myself to do everything I could to endure the discomfort since they were counting on my prayers. The only time this burden felt lighter was when I brought the concerns and requests to the Lord. He continually granted me peace and strength whenever I asked for them. I hoped those I prayed for were experiencing some level of that peace as well.

The wind was a big factor by the end of the day, and my energy was completely sapped. Upon rolling into the small lobby at the motel, the woman behind the counter told me I looked as if I had a rough day. She suggested I order pizza in, and I was not about to argue with her. I had a sub, a large pizza, and a large soda delivered to my room. It was great, but after I finished eating, my first thought was that I should have ordered more.

It does feel good to stay put after running all day because normally I have to walk around to reload on supplies and purchase dinner. The wind today has me so worn out that I can almost guarantee I will be out all night until it is time to get up early in the morning. I hope I wake up with far more energy than I have now because tomorrow is going to be a rough one. I'll simply take comfort in knowing tomorrow's mileage is fifteen miles less than I originally planned. This sounds great because I realized that despite taking a few rest days so far, I have run the equivalent of approximately one hundred marathons over the past eighty-five days. While I am very pleased with my progress, that thought is making my soreness feel slightly heavier than before.

April 15—Day 86: Archbold-Maumee, Ohio, 33.6 Miles. 2,650.4 Total Miles.

When I woke up this morning, I did not have to check the weather report because I heard the wind whipping around outside my room. I knew things were going to be difficult, and the thought of going outside made me want to do nothing but stay inside and sleep. However, I did not undertake the journey to back off when things got tough. I took the challenge on to bring people, including myself, closer to the Lord. I told myself that it was not a time to slink away just because things were not easy. I thought of the saying that described how the road worth taking was often a difficult path. I was faced with a very literal road today that I knew would bring physical and mental discomfort. It was one of those moments where I needed to merely take the first steps and pray for the strength to keep going.

It did not take long for my energy to feel completely drained as the stroller felt like someone had packed it with lead weights. The wind pushed strongly against the jogger to the point where it felt like it was pushing back at me. My only break came when I gave an interview over the phone for about thirty minutes. It was so windy that I had to turn my cart sideways in front of me and duck behind it in order to hear the radio host on the other end of the line. It was encouraging to hear how people were interested in my mission, which helped my attitude remain positive. I talked about how the run was about pointing people toward God and how my hope was that through this run, we would all make more time for the Lord in our lives. Speaking my goals aloud over the radio waves made me feel even more motivated to continue running to the best of my ability.

I pushed myself as hard as I possibly could over the course of the day. I could not stomach the traffic on the roads any longer, so I made my way back to the trail. It was not easy pushing the heavy stroller on the grass for miles, but it mercifully changed to a paved path for the final stretch of miles. After what felt like an eternity, I finally reached the end of the path and was happy to give a quick interview to Karen, a very nice woman who wrote for the local paper. Her young son was with her, and he said I was very nice. My day up to that point was a complete struggle, but with those simple words, my concerns and pains almost vanished.

At the end of the tough day, I was blessed to be picked up and hosted by Tim and Kathy. I met them through a Notre Dame connection, and it could not have worked out any better. Tim picked me up and drove me to their home. Kathy was cooking dinner in addition to an array of chocolate chip cookies she had baked. I did my best to control my appetite, but I still did a number on those cookies! Dinner was awesome as well, and I absolutely loved feeling like part of their family as we exchanged all kinds of stories throughout the evening.

As awesome as everything was, I did feel a little sad. Before my mom passed away, I would often help her cook in the kitchen or sit at the table while she cooked. It was a great opportunity to talk and catch up on everything that was going on in our lives. I never realized how much I missed that until tonight, when I was sitting at the counter and talking with Kathy. It brought back so many memories, and I recalled how great my life was growing up. I had a blessed upbringing, and I always loved going back home and being surrounded by family. Tim and Kathy really made me feel like family, and it was the first time I felt even the slightest bit of that same serenity I had before my mother passed away.

I am going through so many emotions on a daily basis. It is very difficult to process them all. I can only imagine that it will take some time for all of these feelings to be sorted out and that it will have to wait until I finish the run. For the moment, my focus is on both the road ahead of me and on the intentions written down on the pieces of paper I carry with me every day. This run is certainly helping me learn more about myself. However, I am not running for myself, but rather for the people I am praying for and those I have met along the way.

April 16—Day 87: Maumee-Fremont, Ohio, 36 Miles. 2,686.4 Total Miles.

As Tim was driving me back to where I finished yesterday, I tried to fight off a sinking feeling in my stomach. My body was also aching. Despite sleeping well, I felt completely exhausted. The thought of running well over thirty miles was the last thing I wanted to do. I felt so welcome at Tim and Kathy's home that I knew I could have asked to stay another day or two to rest up. Even so, I made a commitment to the run, and I could not stand to slow down. I still wanted to finish the journey with my whole heart, but it was difficult when I sensed that my body had reached its limit. Tim was so generous and gave me some money to help with my next motel stay. He assisted me in loading my stroller, and then I said goodbye as I hit the road once again. I did my best to smile, but inside I felt like crying.

The difficulty of the run definitely caught up to me physically during that first mile this morning. As always, I turned to God in prayer and called to mind how my guardian angel was watching over me. Just as I began each day, I started praying the St. Michael the Archangel prayer and asked Saint Sebastian to pray for me. Then I said a decade for my niece, my family, the souls in purgatory, the unborn, those in the military, a couple who was having a difficult time getting pregnant, a little girl in a custody battle, and a friend's child who was battling cancer. Once I made it through my morning prayers, I felt stronger mentally. It was not as though the run became easy, but I felt like I was given just enough strength to fight through the miles. I was able to keep running somehow. I believed that as long as I gave everything I had, then God would meet me wherever I was at and carry me to my destination.

I was deep into the prayer intentions early on this morning. It became effortless to forget my own troubles when I was focused on an intention a mother had written. She asked me to pray for her young boy who was in pain because of his battle with cancer. The compassion I felt was so strong as I concentrated on his suffering. Before I knew it, I was ten miles into the day and had tears in the corner of my eyes. I had a decent shoulder to run on most of the morning and was only pulled out of my prayers because it began to rain fairly hard. The wind also picked up, which made the conditions quite unfavorable for running. I put on my rain poncho, but the wind was blowing it with such ferocity that it almost hurt me more than it helped. I finally took it off when the rain started to dissipate. At one point, a nice police officer stopped me just to see if I was okay and told me that I did not look very good. I thanked him for his concern but assured him I was fine and continued pushing on to the best of my ability.

I did my best to make it to the twenty-six-mile mark. At that point, I planned to pick up a paved trail. It seemed like forever, but the weather eventually improved, and I made it to the trail. Once again, I was reminded of how much easier it was to run when I did not have to dodge vehicles. I started moving fairly quickly and felt much better. Those last ten miles flew by, and I was suddenly at a small motel in Fremont. I checked in and took a quick nap in some dry clothes before ordering pizza. Despite the positive way in which I finished my run, I still felt like I was dragging and could not fathom having to walk into town to find food. I was proud of myself for simply making it across the street to restock my supplies.

As I sit in my motel room looking at the weather forecast, I am continuing to pray for strength. It appears the next week is going to be windy and rainy. I am doing my best to not worry about it because I have no control over the situation. Rather, I am trying to stay focused on the reason I am running and those who have asked me to pray for them. Whenever I am feeling weak, it is my mission of prayer that helps give me the desire to continue on this difficult journey.

April 17—Day 88: Fremont-Willard, Ohio, 38.3 Miles. 2,724.7 Total Miles.

I awoke this morning with the understanding I was going to get destroyed by the wind. Thankfully, it was coming from the general direction of the west, so I did not have to battle it head on. The wind was already fairly strong when I took my first steps out the door this morning. It was supposed to get more intense as they day carried on.

Even though the wind made progress difficult, I found encouragement through an analogy that came to me during the run. I was praying for a thirteen-year-old girl who was diagnosed with cancer. It was very difficult to read her story. I hoped my prayers would help her find peace and healing. There were seemingly countless stories I heard of people who were thrown into difficult times in their lives. I wanted to share my thoughts with these people. I believed that when we encountered those storms, we needed a strong foundation so we could persevere through them. I believed that base was a faith in Christ. Likewise, it was at that time in the run where I was completely worn down and fighting tough weather conditions. I relied on my foundation of faith to carry me through those tough situations day after day. I understood what my body was capable of doing. I also knew I passed that limitation weeks ago. Since that point in my run, I became entirely dependent on God to carry me. I truly felt as though I had run as far as I possibly could. It was my faith that carried me through the real storms as well as the proverbial ones on my run—and in my life.

As I continued running and praying, I found myself back on the main highway after enjoying a quiet path for the first few miles of the day. I had little road to run on for most of the day and again had to use my upper body to push my jogger on and off the road more times than I could count. The wind was very strong, and I had to do everything in my power to simply hold my balance. The wind was sustained at over thirty-five miles per hour and had gusts of over forty-five miles per hour. As tough as it was for the first twenty-two miles, it became much worse once I turned south and had the wind coming at my side. I felt so weak that whenever the wind blew strongly, I nearly fell over.

I really struggled the final sixteen miles as I felt I was dragging both physically and mentally. There was not a lot to look at other than some green grass, bare trees, and scattered houses. I had a small dog come out and chase me, followed by his owner trying to catch up to the dog. It was definitely comical, and I paused so that the owner would not have to continue chasing both me and the dog all the way to Willard.

I did my best to take encouragement from passing the two-thousand-seven-hundred-mile marker, which meant I had less than one thousand miles to go until the finish. While it was a great milestone to reach, one thousand miles seemed incredibly far given the condition of my body. Any thoughts regarding distance were washed away as the howling wind gave me a terrible headache. I tried to look at it as a motivating factor to help me finish as quickly as possible. Upon reaching my motel in the afternoon, I felt even more hungry than I did tired. As such, I made a beeline for the diner attached to my motel and ate a hearty meal. My stomach was not satisfied, so I walked into town and ate again at a fast food restaurant.

Now that I have replenished my calories for the day, I am very much ready to go to bed and hope tonight feels long because I need my rest. Everything hurts. I cannot fathom running another day, let alone one thousand more miles. I can feel my faith being tested with each mile and with every ache. It feels like my resolve is tested every time the wind gusts. A part of me wants to give in, but a bigger part knows I have more work to do. The only thing I can do is trust in the Lord. I know that it will be enough.

April 18—Day 89: Willard-Mansfield, Ohio, 30.3 Miles. 2,755 Total Miles.

The first thing I did upon waking up this morning was look at the weather forecast. I was pleased that the wind had died down, but I had to psyche myself up mentally to face another day of running in the rain. I bundled up to face the cool weather and had my rain poncho all ready to go. Before hitting the pavement, I ate a great breakfast at the diner to help give me some much-needed energy. I then paused before stepping outside, saying the St. Michael prayer for protection.

I only made it a couple of hours into the day when my stroller started to roll very heavily, and I noticed a tire was flat. I spent a long time fixing it in somebody's driveway because my hands were a little numb. It was very frustrating because running a long distance was difficult enough, but doing it while getting rained on and having to stop for equipment problems made it feel exponentially worse. I was thankful to get underway again as I chased down my goal of thirty miles on the day. I initially had planned to run over forty miles by taking a detour involving a bike path. However, I changed my route at the last minute to make it more direct. In order to make that possible, I had to give up the luxury of running on an unpaved path in favor of a shorter route involving heavy traffic. The focus it required to run on roads with a lot of traffic made for some very intense miles. That intensity was only amplified in the wet weather. The conditions made it more difficult to see the vehicles and to make sure they saw me as well. These factors made a good portion of today feel overwhelming from a mental perspective.

The rain poncho helped, but it did not keep me completely dry. It also offered no protection for my feet, so I had to do my best to ignore the squishing sounds my feet made for mile after wet mile. I was very frustrated because I wanted to read more prayer requests but was instead forced to focus on my well-being. Therefore, I only prayed for my daily requests and said a few quick prayers for my own health and safety.

My clothes were damp and heavy when I finally arrived at my motel in Mansfield. While I was waiting for my pizza to be delivered to my room, I turned on the weather. It only brought more bad news. The rain did not appear to be letting up, and there was a strong thunderstorm warning for the next afternoon.

It feels like such a long time ago that I saw the sun. My attitude is starting to be affected by the wind, rain, and cold weather. I have never felt so completely drained in my life. I almost passed on walking down to the ice machine earlier because of how tired and sore I felt. It made me ask myself how I could expect to make it through even one more long day if a trip down the hallway seemed too far. I do not know the answer to that question. I am going to bed tonight asking God to give me the strength to continue running with courage.

April 19—Day 90: Mansfield-Loudonville, Ohio, 29.7 Miles. 2,784.7 Total Miles.

I hobbled out of bed this morning and rubbed my eyes in an attempt to wake myself up. I looked at the clock just in time to see it change to 4:30 a.m. Ouch. I tried not to think about my lack of sleep. Instead, my focus was turned toward my stroller. Even in the dimly lit room, I saw the tire I had fixed the previous day was flat again. I took my time to put a new tube in and get it pumped up. I initially hoped to begin early so I could finish ahead of the storms scheduled for later in the day. I did not like the way things were starting out.

After a quick trip to the small continental breakfast, I hurried back to my room to finish loading up my stroller. Just as I finished packing, I saw the same tire was flat again. I pulled the wheel apart one more time. In replacing the damaged part, I used my final spare tube. My frustrations were mounting and I said out loud, "Well, I better not get a flat today."

Once I finally made it outside and started running, there was a light rain beginning to fall. The clouds in the sky were dark and menacing. I immediately said the St. Michael the Archangel prayer, sensing that I would need his help. I started to pick up my pace and wondered if I would be able to outrun the approaching storm. The terrain did not help my cause of trying to run quickly. The land was very rough as I ran through a number of hilly country roads, passing farms and isolated houses along the way. Having very little traffic on the road was a big help, but getting rained on and dealing with massive hills did not help my situation. I was exhausted and felt like calling it a day just a couple of hours after leaving my motel.

I continued to push my legs through the miles as I weaved my way toward my destination in every which way but a straight line. I passed a small town around noon before disappearing again into the back country. While going down one of the roads, I felt the all too familiar feeling of a dragging stroller. I did not want to look down, but when I did, my fear of another flat tire was confirmed. I put air in the tire and ran with it until it went flat again—which was about thirty seconds. I hung my head and let out a deep sigh. I was tired, wet, and seemingly out of options. I simply stood there too exhausted to show any emotion. My body felt nothing but soreness. My mind and emotions were entirely numb. The vast majority of the miles of my journey were spent praying for others. This time, I prayed from my bottom of my heart for myself. I took off my hat and placed it over my heart. I prayed earnestly to God for help because I was out of solutions. I was completely spent. I needed the Lord's help. I was not doing anything or going anywhere until He answered my prayer.

I thought about how pathetic I must have looked—standing on a country road next to a stroller on its side. I was soaked from the rain and dirty from running through mud and wet grass. Suddenly, a man in a truck pulled up and asked if I was okay. I couldn't answer. He continued to ask if there was anything he could do to help me. I searched for words to explain my situation but simply said, "I don't know." I was at a complete loss for words as I tried to explain how my tire was flat and I did not know what to do. He pointed toward what looked like a large garage near a house that was only about a quarter mile up the road. He told me the garage was a body shop and that they would help me.

I had no alternatives at that point, so I dragged the stroller up the road to the garage. The place was called Precision Collision, and the only person there was a mechanic named Dave. I initially told him I was done with the stroller and asked if they had a dumpster where I could toss it. In my supplies was a backpack, so I thought I could put my essentials in it and continue on my way. My body was too exhausted to push the jogger any longer. Dave obviously saw I was not thinking clearly, so he told me he would put some slime into my tires to keep them from going flat. I let him work on the tires and gave him the few dollars I had on me for his help.

The flat tires delayed me so long that I did not see how I was going to get all the way to town before the thunderstorms arrived. As I left the body shop, the rain was starting to fall harder, and the skies were growing very dark. Dave gave me directions to a place to stay for the night, and I started to make my way there. I began to move quickly as the rain became steadier. When I was still about a mile away from the motel, the rain turned into a downpour, and thunder cracked viciously all around me. It was enough to startle me, and I frantically looked for my rain pouch. I could not find it. Within seconds, I was completely soaked.

Amidst the downpour, I passed a campground on the way to the motel. After running by it, I saw some cabins and thought that perhaps they had one available. I turned around and ran to the office. When I reached it, nobody was around, and the doors were locked. I debated looking around for someone, but a flash of lightning served as enough motivation to keep running up the road and find the motel. I hurried back onto the road a soaking mess. By that point, my legs were locking up in pain. It was a grueling battle to run to the motel through increasingly adverse conditions and on a dangerous road with traffic. I tried to imagine what types of thoughts the people in the cars had as they saw me running with a baby jogger through a violent storm. After rounding a bend, I saw a sign for the motel—pointing up a very large hill. There was no way I could run up the hill, but I used everything I had to push the stroller up the steep incline to get to the motel. I just needed to get out of the weather and into some form of shelter.

The winding road finally opened up as I reached its summit. I smiled to myself, thinking of everything I had just gone through to get there. The smile was quickly wiped off my face when I saw a note stuck on the door of the office. I called the phone number on the note and reached a woman who told me they had decided to close for the day. My spirit sank, and I felt like breaking down. I put my back against the wall and sank down to the ground. If I had more energy, I would have let myself cry. However, I could not even manage to muster up the energy to shed some tears. I sat there silently in complete disbelief. The closest motel was back in the small town I had passed around noon. I could not fathom going back even further, but I could not take the chance of getting seriously sick as I was drenched and it was cold. I thought of pitching my tent, but with a defective rain fly, I knew that it would not be much help in the violent weather.

As I sat there praying, a deafening clap of thunder came from the sky directly overhead. It was almost as if my legs took it as a sign to get going. I started moving as quickly as my battered body allowed me to run as I went back down the hill and started backtracking. I got lost three times on my return to town and had to ask directions at a fast food restaurant near town. I took off one last time for the motel and was thankful that the rain had finally let up. When I saw the motel on the horizon, I breathed out a huge sigh of relief and prayed that it was open and had rooms available. I was thrilled to stop running and to hear they had a room I could stay at for the night. I showered and put on dry clothes before walking down the road to pick up a pizza and restock my supplies.

Today was extremely frustrating, and I have to admit that while I did not consider quitting, a big part of me felt like breaking down and allowing the situations to get the better of me. While getting a flat on the road was a disaster, I am so thankful it happened close to someone who could help me. I know my angels helped me find my way back to a safe place for the night. This run is so much like life in how we can get caught in storms that come through our own lives. However, I learned through my experience today to always remain focused on the Lord because he is with us through it all. I know it is only through the grace of God that I was able to endure all the frustrations and make it to safety at the end of the day. I pray I can treat the problems I face in life in the same manner. I believe that as long as I stay focused on the Lord, he will always deliver me to where I need to be—even if it is not exactly where I had in mind.

April 20—Day 91: Loudonville-Millersburg, Ohio, 25.3 Miles. 2,810 Total Miles.

I started out this morning with the intent to simply make it to Millersburg, which was my planned destination the prior day. Instead of piling on a very long day, I decided to wind my way through a shorter mileage day on some back roads. While the miles on the day did not seem overwhelming, I knew better than to assume it would be an easy day.

Once again, I was greeted by showers as I hit the road. I found my poncho while unpacking, so at least I was able to stay mostly dry. In addition to the showers, I was in for a rude awakening of nasty hills for the better part of the day. A number of them were unpaved, and the wet dirt became caked onto my tires. This made running with the jogger virtually impossible at times because of the inability to get any traction. It was a brutal battle pushing a stroller that continued to sink deep into the mud. The mud got so thick on my tires that the accumulation got knocked off when it hit the metal frame of the jogger. It was a huge mess and turned an already difficult situation into a nearly insurmountable task. I simply took things one muddy step at a time and cleaned the muck off my tires when I finally made it back onto paved roads.

My body was still holding up somehow, but my mind was starting to show signs of extreme fatigue. I rarely made mistakes on which roads I took, but I made a wrong turn today. I was not pleased to have the error unnecessarily increase my distance. Part of me wanted to blame it on the splitting headache I had all day. I was taking in so many fluids that I doubted it was dehydration, but I guessed anything was possible.

The good thing about going slower than I anticipated was that I had a long time to pray. I prayed for the intentions of a mother who was battling cancer. I prayed for a young man who was fighting through a recent spinal injury. When I reflected and prayed on their situations, I immediately ceased feeling any sort of pity for myself. Instead, I realized how blessed I was to be able to even attempt a run across America. Despite all the frustrations and pain, there was nowhere else I wanted to be than where I was at.

My day improved when I hit the nineteen-mile mark. A postal office worker named Darlene was delivering mail in the area and stopped to make sure I was doing okay. I let her know I was fine and explained why I was out on the roads with a jogger. We had a nice conversation, and she was very impressed I had made it through the hilly terrain while pushing the stroller. Darlene told me the best news I had heard in a long time, which was that the hilly terrain would be coming to an end as I ran to the edge of the county. She was so sweet and took a photo of me because she wanted to tell her family about my journey. Darlene also seemed excited to explain why I was running across the country. We said goodbye, but she drove by me a second time on her route and stopped to give me a few dollars before continuing on. I finally emerged onto a main route and ran hard to the finish, praying for Darlene and her family in the process.

I arrived at the hotel in Millersburg, which was one of the nicer places I stayed at on my journey. The people at the desk were very helpful because they directed me toward a store that carried replacement tubes for my tires. I ate dinner before loading up on supplies and purchasing a couple of extra tire tubes. On my walk back to the motel, a car full of girls slowed down and waved to me. I smiled and waved back because I was accustomed to doing that since I began running. I then realized I did not have my jogger with me and laughed to myself that they were not waving at me because I was running.

I was happy to see humor in things despite my constant exhaustion. Before settling in for the night, I was still hungry, so I went out to Dairy Queen and purchased a large ice cream shake. It was so good. It was also strange looking at it as not only a dessert but also as a vehicle carrying calories into my body.

After taking some time tonight to plan logistics, I am forecasting my arrival in Alexandria to be within the first few days of May. I really do not want to take any days off before I get there, so I plan on pushing as hard as I can to reach my family as soon as possible. I am focusing on pushing myself to get there as soon as I can because I know the loneliness is taking its toll. I received another picture of my beautiful niece today. Baby Val is adorable and has the cutest cheeks underneath her beautiful eyes. I feel terrible that I have not even met her yet. I miss seeing my family and cannot wait to hold my niece for the first time. The thought of seeing them is all the motivation I need to push through this next section of miles.

April 21—Day 92: Millersburg-Uhrichsville, Ohio, 38 Miles. 2,848 Total Miles.

The first couple months of this run were all about the sun as I did not see any rain until day 48. I became accustomed to the nice weather and took it for granted. When I hit the road this morning to a bright sun and blue skies, I could not be happier. I took the opportunity to thank God for a nice day to run. My legs were sore, and the terrain started out hilly. I was so thrilled to run without my rain poncho that I barely noticed the discomfort.

The terrain remained hilly for about the first fifteen miles as I weaved my way through back roads in order to avoid the main street. I stopped to take a photo of a sign that read "SLOW" placed just before a hill that went straight up for a half mile. I laughed to myself, thinking, *Going slow is not going to be a problem up that monster!* I tried to see humor when I could, and that sign had me laughing for the next few miles. I climbed the hill and looked back at the rolling hills of green, underneath a blue sky dotted with only a handful of puffy clouds. I was relieved to have that hill behind me and prayed the road ahead would not be as difficult.

The miles were taxing as my legs were still beaten from the previous few days of rolling hills. The road finally started to flatten out. I was so excited that I started running way too fast because of how much easier it felt. I reminded myself that I still had a long ways to run and I should take it easy to ensure I would arrive in one piece. It was another lonely day as I did not encounter anyone to talk to, but I was able to use that time to talk to God. I felt his presence with me more today than I ever had experienced before in my life. It was such a great feeling to sense that he was right there with me every step of the way. I hoped the feeling would remain with me long after my run was complete. More than ever, I offered up my pain for those I was praying for. I believed it was one reason why I felt so close to the Lord.

I continued to receive more intentions. Also, there were a few new posts by people who asked me to stop and rest before moving on again. I knew the advice sounded logical. However, I had an unexplainable drive to keep pushing forward. I felt in my gut that I needed to keep moving and keep praying until I reached Alexandria. I had complete faith I would be given the graces to help me push through any walls I hit along the way.

My mind was put at ease as I passed the thirty-mile mark because I still had eight miles to go and was still feeling quite strong. The route did present a problem as I came within a few miles of Uhrichsville. The road became narrow as it ran along a river, and there were barriers along the side of the road. I got pinned down a few times against the side of the road because traffic was heavy, and there was no place to go. I leaned over as far as I could and was nearly clipped by a few vehicles during that stretch of road. While it was an intense couple of miles, I did not have any sense of fear. I was not sure if that was a good thing or not, but I felt an overwhelming sense of safety. My belief was that my guardian angel was taking very good care of me. I knew Saint Michael the Archangel heard the prayers I offered up first thing every morning. I believed he was listening to those prayers. My legs continued their relentless push forward all the way to Uhrichsville.

Given the beating my body has taken on the hills these past few days, I am very happy with thirty-eight miles. I just returned from my glorious meal consisting of pizza and ice cream. I am enjoying a chance to relax today because the weather is calling for more bad conditions over the next few days. While I am not looking forward to getting rained on again, I can look forward to meeting up with a host family tomorrow afternoon. It will be great to be surrounded by a family on Good Friday.

April 22—Day 93: Uhrichsville-Cadiz, 26.5 Miles. 2,874.5 Total Miles.

Once again, I woke up to less-than-ideal conditions. The sky was very cloudy, and it was cool out as I started running this morning. It did not take long for the sky to open up and the rain to come pouring down. Even though I had my rain poncho on as I ran, I was still getting very wet. My attitude was taking a beating, even though I tried to stay focused on prayer, especially since today was Good Friday. The season of Lent brought me much closer to the Lord because of how much I denied myself and focused on him. I considered it a true blessing and was so happy to feel as close to the Lord as I did today. Despite that feeling, the discomforts and frustrations still got to me every once in a while.

Just a few miles into the day, I was already exhausted and soaked. To make matters worse, I pulled my left quad, and it only added to the pain. I tried to compensate, but nothing I did helped my leg feel any better. Additionally, I misplaced my water-repellent gloves, so I spent a good portion of the day running with numb fingers. These conditions made it difficult to stay positive on a day where I also continued to get sprayed by the traffic driving by me as they hit large puddles on the road. As frustrating as things were, I found myself laughing pretty hard after getting completely drenched when a truck drove through a pool of water. In my mind, I imagined how it looked to anybody who saw me get soaked by the spray. It made think that they would probably be laughing. This thought caused me to laugh very hard. I learned that even in our frustrations, seeing humor in them can go a long way in helping our attitude.

Much of the day was spent running on a road that weaved its way alongside a large lake. At fifteen miles into the day, I actually had to pause and sit down. Stopping was not usually something I did, but my body needed a rest. I grabbed a snack and sat down on a flat post while watching the lake. I was exhausted, but I was still able to appreciate the beauty of God's creation. Even in the wet and misty conditions, the lake was beautiful. There were small hills filled with both bare and green-colored trees rising above the edges of the lake. I wished I could see it in the sunshine, but there was no hope of that today.

After my short rest, I hit the road with a renewed purpose and fought through my latest injury. I offered the pain up to the Lord and focused my attention on what Jesus endured on Good Friday. While prayer intentions and kind words from others inspired me, the thought that Jesus willingly died for us all was incredibly powerful and helped me to endure some very uncomfortable miles.

My original plan today was to run about thirty-five miles, but I was really struggling and dragging at the halfway point. I continued to fight through the distance until I hit the town of Cadiz, nearly twenty-six miles into the day. My leg had me in tears by this time, and even though I wanted to get in more miles on the day, my better sense knew I would only do more damage if I kept running. I stopped outside of a hospital and called my friend Ron, my host for the night. This was the first time I was meeting Ron, but he interviewed me on his radio program earlier in the month. He was kind enough to offer to host me when I ran through his part of Ohio. Ron told me he could come pick me up at the hospital and drive me to his house. I was so thankful to hear that I could end my day a little early. Ron and his family were so kind. They cooked pasta for me, and we all prayed together. I loved the company, the fellowship, and the conversation. We talked about faith as it related to sports for hours. I felt appreciated for my efforts, and it was refreshing to talk to another athlete who saw how God fit perfectly into athletic pursuits.

I wish I had more energy to talk with Ron's family tonight, but I think they understand how tired I am at the moment. It was a rough day and one that showed me this run is going to be a fight to the finish. I am not looking forward to the remaining struggles but have full confidence that the Lord will help me through them all. As such, I know I will sleep in peace tonight.

April 23—Day 94: Cadiz, Ohio-Elm Grove, West Virginia, 28.1 Miles. 2,902.6 Total Miles.

Ron drove me back to the hospital and helped me load up my running stroller. Again, it was tough to say goodbye and hit the road after making such great friends. Because of the amount of difficulties I had experienced in Ohio, I was anxious to put the state behind me. I thanked Ron for his hospitality and starting running under the cloudy sky, praying that I could get through the day without being rained on again.

The road did not have a shoulder to run on, so I was again hopping on and off the highway for a good portion of the day. At one section, I jumped off the main road for two miles and wished I had not because I ran directly into a very hilly section. The last hill I hit before reaching the next town was so steep that I actually thought I would not be able to reach the top. After a brutal battle with that long hill, I emerged completely exhausted back onto the main road in a small town. I felt like calling it a day and finding a place to rest, but I needed to get out of Ohio for the sake of my mental health. I grabbed my list of prayer intentions from my pocket and forced myself to continue running.

The past few days had brought in a few requests for two specific young men who were suffering with extremely difficult physical problems. One was recently paralyzed, and the other was on a ventilator as a result of some type of heart failure. It tore at me to hear of the circumstances some people had to endure. The only thing I could do was pray for them, asking the Lord to bestow upon them both strength and courage. Although I did not know the plan God had for them, I prayed that they would be healed. More than anything, I prayed they would find peace and comfort in the Lord.

After a flat tire and lots of jumping on and off the street to avoid vehicles, I finally arrived at the West Virginia border. Shortly before hitting the state line, the sun came out, and it warmed the temperature up to nearly seventy degrees. My attitude was improving, even though my body felt like it was falling apart. I first ran over an awesome bridge. After that, I tried to find the Greater Wheeling Trail. In the process, I ended up lost in a neighborhood where I did not feel safe. As strange as it was, I almost felt invisible because nobody paid any attention to me as I pushed my cart through the streets. I eventually found a street that led to the trail and bounced my stroller down a high section of stairs to the path.

Once I hit the trail, it was like I flipped a switch. I suddenly felt so much better, and I was running at a much faster pace. Sometimes I forgot how difficult it was running on busy roads. As soon as I was on the path, running seemed exponentially easier. After flying through the final miles of the day, I reached my motel with my stroller and legs still intact. It was not a very long day, but I felt great finishing in West Virginia.

One reason for finishing earlier in the day was to ensure I could make it to church for the Easter Vigil Mass. I took about fifteen minutes to walk over to the church of St. Vincent de Paul. I read the time incorrectly and showed up more than an hour early. It was perfect because I had plenty of time to sit and pray in total silence. I reflected on the Lenten season and on everything I had experienced the previous three months. As sore as I felt and as much as I missed my family, I could honestly say I was at complete peace sitting in the church. The Vigil Mass was great and was helpful in getting my heart and mind in the right place for the final section of the run. I was reminded of how much the Lord loves us. He sent Jesus to die for our sins. The ensuing resurrection of Christ brought with it great hope and wonderful joy. I felt both supreme joy and hope as I walked back to my motel. I prayed those gifts would radiate in my life so others could feel the same way and be led to Christ.

It is my hope that this run will point everyone to Christ so that they may experience the same joy I am feeling tonight. It is a remarkable feeling, and I could not be happier knowing I am where God wants me to be at this moment. I will always have improvements to make in my own spiritual life, but it is a great reminder to know Jesus is by my side as I travel in that journey. I am feeling incredibly tired after a tough run and a late night, so it is off to bed with the hope I can get a few hours of restful sleep before running into Pennsylvania tomorrow.

April 24—Day 95: Elm Grove, West Virginia-Washington, Pennsylvania, 30 Miles. 2,932.6 Total Miles.

I knew today was going to be difficult from the moment I woke up this morning. I did not sleep well because of the deep soreness that remained in my left quad. While it was still dark outside, I got out of bed on only three hours of sleep and started fixing my stroller. After a quick breakfast, I jumped onto the quiet streets. Since today was Easter, there was almost no traffic on the roads early in the day. It was so desolate that I ran in the middle of the street for part of the morning.

My family used to have a tradition of watching the sun rise on Easter morning. I remembered being on the beach with my family on cold Easter mornings. We would always read the story of the resurrection from the Bible while sitting on the shore. It was never easy waking up so early, but being with my family while watching the sun come up over the ocean was one of my favorite things to do. I wished I could go back in time for just five minutes to be with my entire family once again. These thoughts had me feeling sad because it only accentuated my loneliness.

The weather did not help my mood as watching the sun come up was impossible given the dark clouds in the sky. Within about an hour after setting off, the rain started coming down in spurts, and I was caught in some terrible downpours. One of the downpours was so heavy that I stopped underneath a tree in someone's front yard to help shield me from the rain. I could not remember ever being rained on that hard before. As I stood partially covered and already drenched underneath the tree, my head hung down, and a few tears of desperation managed to escape. My body was beyond exhausted, and my left ankle suddenly screamed in pain as if I had just sprained it. I was drenched and sleep-deprived while standing under a tree in a stranger's front yard with still about twenty-five miles to run on the day. I missed my family and felt completely beaten.

I prayed for strength to fight through my battle. I also offered multiple prayers of gratitude to Jesus for dying for us and then rising from the dead. Somewhere in the midst of those prayers, I must have started running again. It was slow and painful, but my feet were moving. The terrain was brutal, as it seemed I was always pushing the stroller either up a hill or attempting to control it on a descent. The best part of my run came when I passed the Pennsylvania state line. It was great to cross into a state that was so close to my destination, but the physical pain I was in negated any positive mental boost.

I ran on the best I could, but my ankle was in severe pain every time I put weight on it. Once I reached the town of Washington, I was reduced to an odd combination of a shuffle and a hobble. I passed people who were either coming from or going to church. It made me miss my family even more. I wanted to get to my destination as quickly as possible but was reduced to a walk for the final mile. It felt like I was never going to get there as each step was more painful than the previous one. However, those steps eventually led to the front door of my hosts for the evening.

Joe and his family were so kind to host me. I never met them before but was introduced to Joe through a friend of a friend. He was tall and strong with a powerful voice. Joe wore a smile on his face and made sure I had everything I needed. He let me shower immediately. It felt awesome to get into some dry clothes.

Upon entering the kitchen area, there were people everywhere, and conversations had the noise level out of control—in a good way. It was a stark contrast to my lifestyle of quietness and solitude. It was just what I needed to take my mind off my own issues. There were family members from all over and a table full of food. We prayed before digging in to the wonderful meal. I then enjoyed a couple of hours of conversation, great food, and wonderful company. The time I spent with Joe's family only enhanced my belief that there was no greater feeling than being surrounded by family. I truly felt like I was adopted for the day. As nice as it was to have shelter for the night, the true gift they gave me was taking me in like family. One of Joe's sons was kind enough to give me his room for the night. I was beyond grateful for the generous hospitality. I got ready for bed extremely early because I was starting to fall asleep in my chair.

I am so exhausted from my run and the little sleep I got last night. This run has also left me feeling emotionally raw. I do not think I have the capability to shield my emotions at the moment because I do not have the energy to put up any walls. As such, I feel guilty about not talking to my family today, but I know that if I got them on the phone I would have broken down in tears. I know they are worried about me, and I do not want to worry them any more. There is no doubt in my mind I will be okay, but I am in the midst of a rough patch from both a physical and mental standpoint.

April 25—Day 96: Washington-Smithton, Pennsylvania, 29.8 Miles. 2,962.4 Total Miles.

Once again, the day started out with rain as I hit the road early in the morning. Fortunately, Joe joined me through the first four miles of the day. The miles seemed to go by so much faster and easier with the company. The road we ran on was fairly narrow and had a few dangerous curves, but we made it through just fine. I was so happy when the rain cleared up and the temperature started to rise. It made running so much better, and my ankle was not in as much pain as it was the previous day. After rolling steadily to the four-mile marker, I said goodbye to Joe as he headed back to his home. I then paused at a gas station to give a scheduled interview over the phone.

Upon starting again, the road gradually became more narrow and extremely treacherous. There was a lot of traffic on the road this morning. Many of the vehicles were large, and a number of trucks displayed the bright yellow "Oversize Load" signs. My heart sank every time I saw them coming around a corner or down the road because I did not have much room to step aside. At one point, I had to flatten myself against a guardrail while the truck went around me to the best of its ability. It cleared me by a couple of feet, but it was still too close for comfort.

I had to laugh at the conversation I had with a woman who was holding a stop sign for a road construction crew. I told her what I was doing on the streets with the jogger. She told me I was either incredibly brave or incredibly stupid to be running on the roads. I ran away hoping that it was the former.

My legs continued to drive forward until I came to a bridge I needed to cross. I stopped when I got there because it had barriers and signs around the bridge indicating it was closed. I pulled up a map on my phone, and it looked like a detour around this bridge would cost me an extra three to four miles. That kind of detour would have destroyed my mental state.

Instead, I found a spot where my stroller could fit and jumped onto the bridge and ran across it as fast as I could. I made it to the other side without incident and caught my breath while turning onto a new road.

On a dangerous and difficult day, the final few miles were forgiving and ended on an unpaved path. I was so excited to pick up the Great Allegheny Passage because I did not have to deal with any traffic. After being so tense for the better part of the day, I was finally able to relax and enjoy the scenic path while breezing along in a short-sleeved shirt. Despite the troubles, pains, and dangers of the day, I reached my stopping point in a great mood. My host for the evening was a woman named Maryann, who wrote an article on my run earlier in the journey. Maryann and her daughter, Sarah, picked me up from the trail and brought me back to their home. We stopped at a grocery store where Maryann purchased supplies for me. It was very generous, and I was so happy to have some company for the evening. Maryann's husband, Mark, joined us for a very delicious dinner. I found myself relaxing and did my best to push aside the pain and soreness I still felt throughout my body.

Sarah had to go back to college, but before leaving for the night, she took me on a tour of the basilica at St. Vincent's. It was so beautiful. We sat and talked about our concerns in life in a small chapel there. I felt so peaceful in that moment, and it was just another example of how I knew I was on God's path. It was such a blessing to be surrounded by people who were so caring. It meant a lot to me that they understood and appreciated the meaning behind my journey. I thanked God for allowing me to meet such wonderful people.

The last couple of weeks have been very difficult. After my time today with my host family and a chance to pray in a basilica, I feel both mentally and spiritually refreshed. Physically, I am still in a great deal of discomfort, but I am ready to make a big push to my next major destination where my family is waiting for me.

April 26—Day 97: Smithton-Confluence, Pennsylvania, 48.3 Miles. 3,010.7 Total Miles.

My plan of running nearly fifty miles today got off to a great start when Maryann bought me breakfast on the way to dropping me off at the point where I stopped the previous evening. I felt ready to tackle the long day and was looking forward to running on the beautiful Great Allegheny

Passage. We said our farewells, and I started running on the trail, which paralleled the Youghiogheny River.

Running on a trail was such a luxury not only because of safety reasons but also because it allowed me to focus entirely on my list of prayer requests. I went through numerous intentions today, including many requests for family members. So many people seemed to be struggling financially. Others were battling eating disorders, fighting addictions, or struggling with illnesses. It was extremely tough to read heartbreaking stories mile after mile. However, it gave me great hope knowing that they were bringing their concerns to the Lord. The requests people sent me helped me to realize all the blessings in my own life. It served as a constant reminder to take nothing for granted and to turn to the Lord for everything. I was also encouraged by how many people were sending me notes simply to wish me well and to explain how my run had encouraged them in all aspects of their lives.

Based on the weather forecast, I kept an eye out for severe thunderstorms. It was certainly warm and humid as the temperature climbed to eighty degrees. The humidity really wore on me, and as a result, I went through my fluids very quickly. I ran by a number of short waterfalls on the side of the path. I would take a quick snack break next to them because it felt much cooler by the water. In addition to the waterfalls, I was also taking in the sights of the beautiful hills and great looks over the Youghiogheny River when I passed over bridges on the trail. My body was holding up well as I continued to make good progress. Before I knew it, I was running past the thirty mile marker.

As I continued on, a passing rainstorm hit me for a few minutes. I was thankful for it because it felt so refreshing. I did not see many people on the trail today, but during the downpour, a guy on a bike rode by and yelled exactly what I was thinking, "Isn't this awesome?" It was. The rain cooled me off, and I felt ready to get after the final stretch of miles. Nearly five miles later, I hit the three-thousand-mile mark of my run. It was a great mental boost because it signified the final thousand mile marker of the journey. It was a huge number, which made me feel like I had truly made significant progress. The thought of physical progress had me thinking about what kind of impact my run was having on people. I had received messages from people letting me know that my run encouraged them to pray, given them hope, inspired them, and increased their devotion to the rosary. While I knew I would never realize the full impact of my run on others, I trusted that I was where God wanted me to be. For the moment, I was simply thankful for the effect it was having on my own prayer life.

I was lost in these thoughts when I was suddenly jarred back into the moment by a huge clap of thunder. There were dark clouds developing overhead, and the sky looked very ominous. Even though I knew there would be no outrunning the storm, I kicked it into a higher gear and started moving as fast as my body would allow me to run. I had never seen a tornado in person and did not know if they were in the forecast at all, but the conditions reminded me of what I had seen on television immediately before tornadoes appeared. The rain started coming down steadily, and I began to hear loud cracks of thunder more frequently. I literally jumped when a booming crack of thunder sounded directly overhead. It was the loudest roar of thunder I had ever heard in my life. I typically enjoyed a good thunderstorm, but that was when I was in the safety of shelter. At that moment, I was not enjoying it at all. I prayed for safety as I saw numerous lightning strikes near me. One bolt of lighting struck within a hundred feet my location. My eyes became wide as I felt a surge of adrenaline sweep through my body. I felt the hair on the back of my neck stand up, and my eyes became very wide as I took a deep breath. I was definitely out of my comfort zone as I could feel myself trembling.

I continued to push forward with everything I had, which was not much after well over forty miles on my legs. My thoughts were so much in prayer for my safety that I almost failed to notice the rain begin to dissipate and the dark clouds move onward. Momentarily, I paused and took a deep breath while saying a prayer of gratitude. In the interest of finishing as soon as possible, I continued my relentless push forward all the way into town. When I arrived, I could not find a motel or bed and breakfast that was open. I must have run over a mile around town while looking for a place to stay as I did not want to camp out with the chance of more thunderstorms. Finally, I saw a man working in his backyard and he was kind enough to let me borrow his phone since mine had no signal. I called the number of a local bed and breakfast. The owner was nearby and came into town to open up the house for me.

As exhausted as I was, I knew I needed to reload on calories and supplies for another long day. I ate a quick dinner in town and went to a small convenience store to purchase additional food and drink supplies. Another heavy rainstorm came through, and I was completely drenched as I made the ten-minute walk back to where I was staying for the night.

My energy reserves feel absolutely depleted, and I need a good night of sleep if I am going to be able to put in nearly fifty miles again tomorrow. I am praying for good weather and renewed strength come morning. I know I will make it to Maryland tomorrow, but I am not looking forward to the pain I will have to endure to get there.

April 27—Day 98: Confluence, Pennsylvania-Frostburg, Maryland, 48.4 Miles. 3,059.1 Total Miles.

There have been too many mornings where I have woken up to find that a tire on the jogger had gone flat during the course of the night, and today was another instance of this frustrating scenario. The circumstances surrounding this morning's case is what made it worse: I used my final spare tube to fix the tire. I kept a close eye on the jogger during the first few miles of the run because I knew I would be in trouble if one of the tires went flat.

The beginning of the run was absolutely gorgeous. Even though the rain finally let up, the conditions created a heavy mist on the wet trail. I felt the moisture cling to my skin as I ran through the heavy air. The mist was so thick that upon entering a river crossing, I could only see a vague outline of trees at the end of the bridge. It was so picturesque, and I was thankful for the opportunity to experience such beauty.

The mist soon lifted, and the only noise I heard on the quiet trail was the occasional bird chirping and the constant sound of the wheels on my jogger rolling over the soft terrain. My thoughts turned to all the people I had met on my journey. I made sure to include them in my prayers. It was so relaxing being able to simply run and pray. I did not worry about cars at all and enjoyed the comfortable and dry weather as I put the miles behind me one at a time.

The only thing that broke my concentration was the one thing I was hoping to avoid—a popping sound that came from the front of my jogger. My front tire had been fine the entire trip, but it finally gave way when I rolled over something sharp. I tried to inflate it again, but the air seeped out of it quickly. It was clear that making repeated stops to reinflate the tire was not an option. My next move was to push down on the back of the stroller and roll it on the back wheels, but this was far too exhausting. I just ran the best I could given that the jogger seemed to drag more than it rolled. I was only at the twelve-mile marker at that point. I kept up this tiring act until I ran through a small town with a bike store at mile 20. I stopped for about fifteen minutes to purchase a few tubes and to fix the busted tire.

I knew I was in for a long day and wanted to make sure I finished before dark, so I picked up the intensity once the tire was replaced. After hitting the trail, two women immediately passed me while riding bikes. When they passed me on their return trip a couple of hours later, one of the women told me, "Wow, you must be strong!" I was definitely exhausted because that comment had me smiling for at least the next five miles. Although I knew she was referring to my ability to push a stroller on the trail for hours on end, it made me laugh because I was always a thin runner. I could not remember anybody ever calling me strong. I thought it was simply the case of having zero emotional barriers because of the intense physical and mental wear. Anytime something was sad, I found it incredibly sorrowful. Anytime something was interesting, I thought it was the best thing ever. And like today, if something was the least bit funny to me, I found it hilarious and could not control my laughter. I was thankful it was something good because my mood was great today despite the ever-present physical discomfort.

I almost forgot I would be passing the Eastern Continental Divide until I was right up on it at two thousand four hundred feet above sea level. After running through the mountains in the western part of the country, the elevation did not seem so high. However, I was encouraged knowing that I would be running downhill over the following few days.

Rain began to fall shortly after passing the landmark. I stayed dry because my route took me through a nearly three-quarter-mile-long passage called the Big Savage Tunnel. I did not have the energy to dig through my supplies for a flashlight, so I ran straight into the darkness. It was extremely eerie as the dim overhead lights spaced along the tunnel did little to alter the pitch-black conditions. The only light I could see was at the end of the tunnel, so I kept running forward through the chilly tunnel. When I finally emerged on the other end, I was treated to an awesome view of the country landscape. The sky was gray, but the phenomenal view allowed me to see rolling hills covered in greenery as far as I could see. As I took in the scenery, a beautiful rainbow formed over the land. Even though I was extremely exhausted, it was one of the most peaceful moments of my life.

I called Kevin, a man involved in the running scene in the Maryland area and my host for the night. Unfortunately, he was sick and did not want to risk getting me sick as I approached the end of my run. He did call a motel in town that otherwise would be closed. Kevin said the owner would wait at its doorstep for me to arrive so that I would have a place to sleep for the night. I was so thankful he was able to set me up with a place because I would have been in trouble given the dangerous weather system descending on the area.

Once I got off the phone with Kevin, I started pushing the pace down the slight decline to town. I passed the Maryland state line and stopped briefly to take a quick photo. I finally rolled up to the motel after another forty-eight-mile day and was given a room just as Kevin promised. I made my way to dinner where I pounded a large pizza in a matter of minutes. The meal seemed like an appetizer for my huge appetite. I was the only person eating in the restaurant, and the owners could not believe how fast I had eaten the pizza. It naturally developed into a conversation about what I was doing. They were so nice and took a photo with me to put on their wall. After dinner, I quickly restocked my supplies at a gas station before heading back to my room. The wind really picked up, and the air gave the distinct impression we were about to be hit with a nasty storm.

The news tonight indicates that the entire area is under a tornado and severe storm watch. While I do not mind camping out, I am very thankful that I have a place to stay indoors tonight. My legs are spent, but somehow I continue putting in these high-mileage days. I am sending up another request tonight for strength to get through a long day tomorrow. If God is getting tired of hearing my same prayer every night, it is not stopping him from answering them time and time again. God is definitely patient and is so good!

April 28—Day 99: Frostburg, Maryland-Paw Paw, West Virginia, 45.8 Miles. 3,104.9 Total Miles.

I managed to hobble around my motel this morning while packing my supplies in the jogger. My body was in pain simply walking, so I was not expecting much comfort on the trails. The thought of putting over forty miles on my legs wore down my positive attitude.

There was a fair amount of debris on the trail given the windy weather that had passed through the previous twelve hours. Even though there were tornadoes reported on the news, nothing had touched down too close to Frostburg. It reminded me of how blessed my run had been since the beginning. I had come close to disaster and nearly ran out of options on many occasions but had remained safe through it all. As I took those first steps of the day, my spirit found immediate peace through prayer. There was no better way to begin each day.

Once again, I felt a sense of protection after beginning with a prayer to St. Michael the Archangel. I then went on praying decade after decade for my personal intentions, which always began with a prayer for my niece. I thought of how close I was to Alexandria and felt so excited to see her for the first time. It was a great motivating factor to help me make it through the day. I thought about the day when I could tell Val how much she inspired me to run. I thought it would also be a great time to discuss the importance of prayer and to tell her just how much I prayed for her during my journey.

I prayed for my family and friends for a good portion of the first fifteen miles. The section was relatively uneventful, with only a brief stop to snack on some pastries for breakfast. After I passed the fifteen-mile mark, I entered the town of Cumberland, where the Great Allegheny Passage Trail ended and the C & O Trail began. I stopped at a bike shop to load up on cold drinks and a few snacks. My plans were flexible for the night, so I did not know if I would be stopping at a motel or camping out. I wanted to be prepared for anything, so I also picked up a map of the trail along with its camping locations and mileage markers. I was anxious to get going again, so after a brief conversation with the employees at the shop, I was back on the road.

When I lived in Alexandria, I ran on the C & O Trail frequently. Even though those miles in training were nearly two hundred miles east of Cumberland, it felt great to be approaching familiar territory. I hit the trail and was running on a soft dirt path in no time, trying to skirt around some puddles to ensure I kept my feet dry. The sun was shining down on me quite intensely, so I fashioned a bandana to my baseball cap in order to protect my neck from sunburn. It was warm out, but I did not let it bother me as I continued to pound out the miles along the path.

Within thirty minutes of leaving Cumberland, the trail became very desolate, and I went an hour or more at a time without seeing anyone. It was very serene and a perfect place to pray as the partially covered trail paralleled the canal. I often found myself simply talking to God, telling him my concerns and giving thanks for all the graces he had bestowed on me during my journey.

There was an occasional animal that crossed my path. There were turtles everywhere, and I would stop to move them off the path to ensure that they would not be hit by an unsuspecting bike. I also saw snakes, some of which were very large. One animal scared me as I saw a beige-colored figure about the size of a large dog jump into the water as I approached it. Since it jumped into the water from behind a bush, I only saw the size of it and its color. I never saw it resurface, even though I stood there and waited for a minute. I had no idea what it was and did not feel like taking the time to figure it out.

My body began to really fight me about thirty-five miles into the day. I did my best to continue my solid pace, but it was not easy given how many miles I had recently put on my legs. They were weighing me down, and every muscle was aching. They were also visibly bruised. There were so many sticks on the ground, and it was impossible to avoid them. I would often catch one of them on a wheel, and it would be shot back directly into my legs. As if my legs had not taken enough of a beating already, they had to also endure miles of getting slammed by sticks. I made up my mind to make it into the next town instead of camping for the night because I needed to load up on calories.

The final ten miles were exciting, which helped the time pass quickly. At about the forty-one-mile marker, I had to stop short and slide my cart off to the side. On the right side of the path was what looked like a stick but was actually a snake. I did not believe it was dangerous but had no desire to anger it and possibly find out otherwise. I made some lame joke in my head about making a bad first impression on the snake. For some reason, it seemed hilarious to me at the time and had me laughing pretty hard for the next mile. It must have taken my mind off the pain and soreness because I was running along at a solid pace. As I was nearing town, two men passed me on bikes, and we exchanged stories while on the move. They said they were impressed by how quickly I was moving, and I noticed that I was not going much slower than they were traveling—and they had bikes! They were not riding hard, but knowing I was still running strong really lifted my spirits. Before I knew it, I was off the trail and crossing a bridge to the small West Virginia town of Paw Paw. I found a motel to stay in and went across the street to load up on pizza and groceries.

The pizza tasted so good, and I am happy I made the choice to come into town for the night. I think I would have slept fine wherever I decided to stop given my level of exhaustion. However, having a shower and a big dinner makes a big difference in my mental attitude. Because of the intake of calories, I feel physically prepared to go after another long day tomorrow.

April 29—Day 100: Paw Paw, West Virginia-Clear Spring, Maryland, 48.7 Miles. 3,153.6 Total Miles.

There were two things that went through my mind when I woke up this morning. First, I remembered that today would have been my mother's fifty-fifth birthday. Second, the new day marked one hundred days on the road since I started my journey in California.

In many ways, it felt like much longer than one hundred days since I began running from the shores of the Pacific Ocean. I was physically and mentally drained from the constant pounding each day. The thought of running even one more mile often seemed impossible. However, I somehow managed to put them behind me one at a time. With nearly six hundred miles yet to run, I did not feel like I was near the end. Many people were telling me how close I was to the finish, but I never thought six hundred miles was a short distance. The best thing I could do was to stay focused, stay positive, and remain steadfast in prayer.

Just as I began the run in prayer, I continued it completely fueled by prayer. As I went through my daily intentions, I stopped after the decade I prayed for my mom. Because of how tired I was, I did not think I could both run and handle my emotions simultaneously.

I missed her. I missed my family being together. I missed the sense of pure happiness I felt before she was diagnosed with cancer. It was difficult to think of how things used to be and all the great times we had together. Tears started to flow, and I had no power to stop them. My mind flashed back to how she used to bring me to the track with her, take me to Mass, come to my games or races, and simply sit with me to ask me about my day. Everything she did, she did for our family out of love.

I recognized how much effort she put into her family, and I only wished I saw it years ago so I could have thanked her for it. Before she passed away, she changed from her nursing career to work for a congressman. My mom did this to help people solve problems. She worked there as long as she was physically able to work. Her life was spent serving others and showing God's love to every person she met. Each person she came in contact with was changed in a positive way. It hurt me to think just how much I took what she did for granted.

My thoughts took me back to the final, painful days we spent together as a family. My mom lay in bed at home and was simply waiting to die. I had barely started my run today, and I was already a mess as these memories came storming back. As much as I would have liked to change things, I was ultimately grateful for the time I was blessed to spend with my mom. I was also so blessed for the positive difference she made in my life. I knew that if it was not for her, there was no way I would have ever considered running across America. Even though she was not physically with me, I knew she continued to watch over me and lived on through myself and all who knew her.

Once I made it through my emotions, I felt better and continued running hard. I had a lot of miles to get through and wanted to complete them as quickly as possible. The trail was beautiful as it continued to wind along the Potomac River. I went through a tunnel and saw small waterfalls all around me. The recent rain the area received made the path very wet. I stepped in a few deep puddles early on that made my feet very uncomfortable. After slogging through a few miles with wet feet, they finally dried out, and I prayed the conditions would not result in blisters.

I took a break today from all the intentions that people sent to me and instead used to the time for pure prayer and reflection. It was such a fantastic opportunity to spend the day with the Lord. I had a long conversation with him, simply saying what was on my mind. I asked for direction in not only the remaining miles, but also for the next steps I would take in my life after the run was over. While I was not looking ahead too far, I thought it could only help to start praying for what my life would bring after the run was completed.

I loved the feeling of being on the Lord's path and wanted to do everything I could to ensure I did not stray from the course the Lord laid out for me. I was at absolute peace speaking to God for the majority of the day. I believed I would miss the opportunity to do this once the journey came to an end. There was truly nothing so spectacular as spending all day in conversation with the Lord.

These thoughts and prayers occupied most of my time on the trail. I did not have an exact stopping point mapped out but was trying to get as far as I could comfortably run to make the next day manageable. As I ran on the C & O Trail, there were campgrounds every few miles. I continued to pass one after another all day long and finally started feeling tired around the thirty-mile marker. I pressed on and was fortunate to run by the town on Hancock. Because of the limited food I had on me, I decided to run into town and loaded a small pizza and a sub into my jogger. The thought of having a good meal once I finished for the day had me looking forward to setting up camp for the night.

I considered stopping a little past forty miles but decided to push myself a little bit more. Eventually, I made it to a small campground over forty-eight miles into the day. My body was so sore that it took me about thirty minutes to get my tent set up because I needed to take breaks to sit down. I finally pitched my tent next to the Potomac River and sat down to enjoy my meal. I loved looking through the thin, green trees to the gently flowing river. It was so peaceful and it gave me the rare opportunity to simply relax and reflect on everything I had experienced on my journey.

After reflecting on everything for a few minutes, I now find myself thinking about my purpose on this run. My goal was never to set any records, gain fame, or become a super athlete. All I want to do is to bring myself and others closer to the Lord through the power of prayer. I consider myself so blessed to be where I am. I could not be happier with the opportunity I have been given to use the gifts God gave me to help others.

April 30—Day 101: Clear Spring, Maryland-Shepherdstown, West Virginia, 39.2 Miles. 3,192.8 Total Miles.

After a restless night of sleep, I struggled to get everything packed up. The additional miles I ran the prior day were a huge help because it meant I did not have to run quite as far today. As sleep-deprived and exhausted as I felt, I knew not having to run those extra miles would make a huge difference in my day.

My pace started slow but picked up quickly. None of the miles were easy or went by quickly, but I was making progress and only thought about a single mile at a time. The path was surrounded by greenery and was absolutely peaceful and quiet as I said my prayers. When I prayed the first decade of the day for my niece, it hit me that I would get to meet her in just a few days. It made me anxious to reach Alexandria, and it definitely put an extra kick into my step.

My attitude was encouraged by the people I met along the scenic towpath. I was thankful for the conversation and looked at it as an indication I was approaching more populated areas. I met a very nice woman named Tonya who owned a Bed & Breakfast in the town of Williamsport. She was so generous and gave me water and food to take with me for the journey. We had a great conversation about faith. My spirits were lifted as we said goodbye, and I continued onward. I ran into a female cyclist as I tried to figure out a detour from the trail. We both complained about how we had to get off the peaceful trail and onto traffic-filled roads. After so many miles on my own, it was a relief to have someone understand some of the frustrations I ran into on a daily basis. She wished me luck on the remainder of my trek as we crossed paths again on her way back. As I had done for months, I prayed a decade of the rosary for those I ran into on the road. Today, that included these two women among a few others I encountered on the trail.

The plan for this evening was to stop near Shepherdstown, but a family who had followed my journey from the start called me while I was out on the detour. Maria and Terry offered to host me for the night since they lived close to Shepherdstown. I had forgotten about their offer and was so glad they saw where I was and extended a helping hand. Maria told me when Mass was that evening, and after a quick calculation in my head, I realized I could make it if I ran hard for the final miles of the day. I kicked it into high gear and made unbelievable progress over the final sixteen miles. I really wanted to get to church, and despite my extreme fatigue, I made it to town in time to be picked up and taken back to their house to shower. I knew I did not have the strength in me to get to the town as quickly as I did. I could only explain it as a gift bestowed on me from God.

Terry and Maria treated me so nicely. Maria spoke Spanish, so she was kindly translated all my Spanish prayer requests that were posted on my website during my trip. It saved me time and was a huge help in understanding all the intentions written in Spanish. After helping me with the intentions, they were now giving me a great place to sleep, taking me to church, and cooking me a great meal. As if that were not enough, it was all done with their seven wonderful kids running around. The kids had followed my journey and knew all my stats and where I had run. It was so humbling to have the children be interested in my run. One of them came with Terry to pick me up in town and told me he prayed for me as he watched me run across a bridge. After meeting me, another one of the children told his parents, "He is nice to me!" Comments like that were absolutely priceless and were one aspect that made the journey so rewarding.

I wish I could stay awake and talk with the family more, but I am so exhausted and need my sleep. Tomorrow is going to be another long day, but I am encouraged because it will bring me into Virginia and even closer to seeing my family!

May 1—Day 102: Shepherdstown, West Virginia-Ashburn, Virginia, 53 Miles. 3,245.8 Total Miles.

Terry dropped me off this morning back on the C & O Trail. I had such a great time with his family and was already looking forward to seeing them sometime in the future. It took a couple of miles to get into some kind of rhythm again, but my body finally responded, and I was well on my way to putting the towpath behind me.

As I ran into more populated areas, I also started to meet more people along the way. Just a couple of miles into the day, I struck up a conversation with a man who was biking from Cumberland to Washington DC over the course of a couple of days. We encouraged each other on our respective journeys before he rode off. While I wished I could have kept up, I knew I was doing well at my current pace and was keeping it steady. My path eventually led me to a section on the Appalachian Trail, where I ran across a few people who recognized me. The interesting part was that they were nearing the end of a one-hundred-mile race. One of the pacers knew what I was doing, and we struck up a conversation. It turned out that I knew one of the runners I spoke to through a mutual friend. It was a case of it being a "small world" but was uplifting to both of us who were struggling to continue on in our individual battles.

I stopped to say hello to some people at an aid station a couple of miles down the path. Upon leaving the station, I ran into a woman I had seen earlier. Her name was Shelley, and she stopped to tell me how inspiring I was to her. She told me she was having a tough time with her run but received strength from watching me run with a jogger full of supplies. I filled her in on my journey and how it was part of a much larger run. Shelly was so nice and her reaction was priceless. Additionally, I told her why I was running and how it was all about prayer. When I asked her if she had any prayer intentions, her eyes immediately filled with tears. She told me about a young boy who was battling a life-threatening issue at a children's hospital. Shelly explained how the boy loved a medal she had given him from a race she ran. I asked if I could give her something to pass onto him. I brought two rosary rings with me at the start of my run, and I knew I needed to send one of them along to that child. I took the rosary ring and put it in her hands. With tears now slowly streaming down her face and my own eyes becoming misty, Shelley promised to deliver my gift. We hugged each other goodbye, and I continued on, more determined than ever before to make it to the finish.

The exchange with Shelly was a powerful one. It certainly affirmed that I was exactly where God needed me to be. I pushed out of my mind any complaints as I prayed for all the people I ran across today as well as their prayer intentions. It gave me great strength to have such compelling reminders as to why I undertook my mission in the first place.

Before I knew it, I reached the point where I jumped off the trail and crossed a bridge into Virginia. I was a little wet from some scattered showers but was psyched to get into a familiar state. I was on a mission and my legs churned away, determined to run strong all the way to the finish. It was truly a case of being fueled by prayer.

I continued to meet great people as I ran on the roads toward a bike path. Two men who were walking their dogs stopped to ask me what I was doing. Once again, I was able to share my mission and took more prayer intentions for their families and a baby on the way. One of them took a photo of me and my jogger so he could tell his friends about my run and the mission of prayer. I never envisioned myself as a missionary, but this run allowed me to spread the love of God. The beautiful thing was that it was done through the medium of running, which was something I felt extremely comfortable doing. God truly blessed me with the chance to spread his love through the sport I loved.

I finally made my way through some dangerous and narrow roads onto a paved bike path called the Washington and Old Dominion Trail. I took a brief rest to grab a snack at the start of the trail before pushing the jogger onto the path and hammering away once again. Running on a path I knew well with a whole new set of prayer intentions inspired me to run hard. I spoke to a few people on the trail and also called my previous employer, Ray. He was my boss while I worked at Potomac River Running and had helped me out with supplies throughout the run. Ray had arranged a place for me to stay in Ashburn, which was six miles further than I originally planned. However, I knew my hosts and I was extremely anxious to make it there. I figured I had to run those miles eventually, so I might as well get them behind me as soon as possible.

The remaining miles were plagued by rainstorms, but it did not discourage my positive attitude. My legs locked up once I hit fifty miles, but I continued to run through the pain. After speaking to Adam and Alicia, my hosts for the night, I learned where I had to turn off the trail to get to their home. Adam was a great runner and met me after I departed from the trail. He took my burden of pushing the stroller as we finished up the run to their place. Adam had run with baby joggers before, so I felt validated when he expressed just how surprised he was at its heavy weight. It took a little while for Adam to get used to it, and he could simply not believe I had run the previous three thousand two hundred miles while pushing such a burdensome load. I was glad he appreciated the added level of difficulty because it truly made running long distances every day exponentially more challenging. I felt beyond exhausted for so long, but by the grace of God, I managed to put in my longest week of the run at over three hundred fifteen miles. It proved anything was possible with God.

After speaking with Adam and his wife Alicia, I showered and put on some dry clothes. Ray organized a small gathering at a burger joint to celebrate my arrival. Seeing some of my old coworkers made my day, as did the large meal! It was so great seeing the excitement on their faces and their interest in everything I had experienced. I loved sharing my stories and being in the company of friends. We talked until the restaurant closed. After dinner, we headed back to Adam and Alicia's place to crash for the night.

Today was truly remarkable, and I cannot wait to see my family and meet my niece tomorrow! I find it amazing at how much my outlook is improving the closer I get to my family and familiar surroundings. I am just hoping I have a good night of sleep with all of the excitement.

May 2—Day 103: Ashburn-Alexandria, Virginia, 31.9 Miles. 3,277.7 Total Miles.

I awoke this morning feeling incredibly sore from the high-mileage week. I knew I would be seeing my family at the end of the day, so I could not get to Alexandria fast enough. Once my supplies were in the jogger, I hit the road pretty darn fast.

My friends from Potomac River Running were beyond helpful. Adam started out the day with me, and he was pushing the jogger for me. We talked the entire way, and despite feeling physically exhausted, I was in great spirits and running exceedingly well. The miles sped by, and pretty soon my former coworker Brian showed up on the side of the trail. He was also a great runner and perhaps an even better conversationalist, which was what I needed at the moment. We continued talking as we put the miles behind us at a quick pace. As with Adam, most of the miles were right around eight minutes. It was a terrific pace and one helped by my friends pushing the jogger for me. Brian also had a difficult time believing how I had pushed the heavy jogger all the way across the country. We joked that I should have looked a lot stronger given how much energy it took to push the jogger.

At the end of Brian's shift, Ray met up with us on the trail. Ray pushed the stroller for me and was shocked at how much it weighed. I was happy that all three of my talented friends had a strong sense of appreciation for the overwhelming physical challenge of not only running across America but also doing it while pushing a heavy load. Ray loved hearing stories from the run and what I had learned from my experiences on the road. I could not have asked for a more supportive boss. From the moment I left the job, he had been nothing but 100 percent in my corner. He never doubted in my ability to be successful and believed in me without any reservations. It was remarkably encouraging to have that kind of support. By the time he had to leave at the eighteen-mile mark, I was feeling great and was on an awesome pace.

Many of my long training runs were done on the W & OD Trail while I lived in Alexandria, so I was very comfortable in my environment. My pace slowed just a little because I was pushing the stroller again and did not have anyone to run with me. It was a great chance to spend time with God. I prayed many intentions of thanksgiving for all the great people God had placed in my life. I considered myself so blessed to be surrounded by such extraordinary friends.

The trail eventually ended, and I jumped onto the familiar streets near my sister's condo. These particular streets were where I got back into running just four years earlier. I remembered how much of a struggle it was to get through a four-mile loop. I considered it a miracle how I went from a person who felt defeated a few years prior to a person who was so confident in everything I did. It was only through the grace of God and being steadfast in prayer that this change was able to take place.

I knew my sister was tracking me via the GPS feature on my website. Sure enough, as I rolled down a small hill, I saw her holding my niece, Valerie. I stopped quickly and let go of the jogger so I could hold Baby Val immediately. She was such an adorable baby with the cutest cheeks I had ever seen. She had plenty of dark hair that stuck up in the air and was dressed in a cute blue outfit with a picture of a bunny on it. I took a good look at her and then pulled her in to give her as big of a hug as I could while still being gentle. I did not want to let her go. Since day 1, I had said my first prayer of each day for her. To finally get to meet Val was an indescribable experience, and I was so thankful she was in my life. I had thought about that moment for so long. To finally arrive there brought me great joy. Not only did I get to see my niece, but it was also the first time since Christmas I was able to see my sister Kristina and her husband Roberto.

My dad flew in for a quick twenty-four-hour trip, so we picked him up from the airport. My brother Dave and his wife Angela came over, and we had a fantastic dinner together. It was everything I had thought about for the previous few months. I loved my family before I started, but after being on the road by myself for so long, I appreciated them more than ever before. Their support throughout my journey was priceless. To have us all in one place was my definition of a perfect day.

Today was definitely the best day of the entire run. It is an amazing feeling to have all the loneliness from the past few months completely disappear. I am tired but thrilled to be around my family. I know I still have a long ways to go until reaching the finish, but for the moment, I am allowing myself to enjoy the accomplishment of making it this far. I am anxiously awaiting a day off with my family tomorrow before taking off for the final stretch to New York.

May 3—Day 104: Rest in Alexandria, Virginia, 3,277.7 Total Miles.

Not having to worry about getting up at some crazy early hour made this morning so peaceful. At the same time, I was happy to get up to spend more time with my niece. I then gave an interview over the phone before meeting a local reporter in person. My dad accompanied me on a couple of errands, and we were able to catch up on life. It seemed like so long ago when we saw each other back in Arizona. I had so much to tell him. I was often too exhausted at the end of the day to talk, so this gave us a great chance to relax and spend time together. We also grabbed a beer at one of my favorite places—it was incredibly peaceful, and I was in my own little heaven.

Ray called me and explained that he had arranged a sports massage for me with a very good massage therapist in town. It was so great and relaxing that I nearly fell asleep because of the rare opportunity to lie down during the day. The massage was refreshing, and it helped my spirits, which were already sky high.

I was sad to see my dad head back to Florida, but I was hoping he would be able to make it to see my finish in New York. After he went to the airport, I drove out to Reston for some food, drink, and conversation at one of the Potomac River Running locations. I saw many coworkers I had not seen in a long time. It was great to spend time with my old friends and to share my experiences with them all. I probably stayed out a little too late, but it was worth every minute.

The support and encouragement from friends and strangers alike means a great deal to. It inspires me to finish this run strong. For now, I am ready to go to bed so I am rested enough to begin my final push to the finish. Only four hundred more miles to go.

May 4—Day 105: Rest in Alexandria, Virginia, 3,277.7 Total Miles.

My plan for the short-mileage day was to simply run up to Washington DC. However, things did not go as planned this morning. I set out with my jogger in the late morning because my legs were feeling very sore, and I sensed a fair amount of pain in my inner thighs. I made it about a minute into the run before my legs seized up in an incredibly painful manner. I could barely walk. There was no question I would not be making it to DC. In fact, it took me nearly ten minutes to walk back the distance I traveled in the first minute out the door. My legs were completely locked, and the pain was very severe. I tried to look at the bright side in that I was able to spend some extra time with my family and have fun playing with my niece for most of the day.

After returning to my sister's place, I was so upset that I almost canceled my talk at the DC Potomac River Running location. However, I decided to drive up to the store in the evening for the talk and make an appointment with a chiropractor for the following day. I was so glad I followed through on the talk because the store was packed. It was the store I used to manage, so many people who knew me came out to wish me well. There were many people who were group runners, some old coworkers, a boss from a previous job, customers I had helped in the past, strangers, and even a former high school cross-country teammate who I had not seen in a decade. A few of them had sent me intentions, so it was especially great to see them.

I wished I had more time to talk to everyone, but it was not possible to spend the amount of time I wanted to with each person individually. I gave a brief talk about the run, including stories from the road and the lessons I had learned. After the store closed, we went out for wings and beer. The chance to see the faces of my friends and the many people following my journey was far better than I ever imagined. People were telling me how encouraged and inspired they were because of the run. They told me how much it meant to them and how it gave them hope. It was a truly humbling experience and one that I was sure would help carry me to the finish.

I would be lying if I said I am not frustrated with the current situation. The finish line is within reach and I am stuck here in Alexandria without a clear idea of when I will be able to run again. While I want to get going again as soon as possible, I have to take care of my body. This is frustrating and scary, but I still have faith God will deliver me to the finish. One thing is for sure: it will be in the Lord's time and not mine.

May 5—Day 106: Rest in Alexandria, Virginia, 3,277.7 Total Miles.

There was not much I could do about my injury, so I took the attitude that these days off were providing me with a chance to catch up on much needed sleep. I slept for a good portion of the day and played with my niece for the majority of the remaining hours. She was so adorable, and I absolutely loved every minute we got to spend together. My family thought it was funny how Val and I shared the same napping schedule today!

The pain on the drive to the chiropractor this morning was so severe that I actual had tears streaming down my face from its intensity. On a couple of occasions, I yelled out in an attempt to release some of the anguish. I finally made it to Capitol Rehab. They had helped me a couple of years earlier and were known for being a phenomenal practice. Although I was frustrated with the situation, I realized how blessed I was to have the problem happen in an area where I had family and could get the treatment I needed.

I received some therapy on my legs. It appeared I had some type of issue with a muscle at the back of my hip. There was also a chance I was dealing with a case of sciatica, which explained the shooting pain going down my legs. It was not something expected to heal overnight, but Dr. Beck understood my situation. He promised to do everything in his power to help get me back on the road as soon as possible. I scheduled another appointment, so the best case scenario was that I could have another two days of rest before hitting the road again.

I wanted to dwell on the frustrations of the injury, but I tried to keep my mind off it as much as possible. One of my friends in the area, CD, met me in Alexandria for lunch. He had run marathons and ultra marathons as well, so it was nice to talk to someone who had an understanding of what I had experienced. After lunch, we met up with one of his friends at a coffee shop before I made it back to Kristina's place. As tough as it was to battle an injury, I truly treasured the time with my family and friends.

This run has thrown so many situations at me, and my plans have changed so frequently. Even though I have encountered many difficulties, I have remained safe and experienced great things because of them. My trust is in God. I believe I am exactly where I need to be, even though it is not what I desire at the moment.

May 6—Day 107: Rest in Alexandria, Virginia, 3,277.7 Total Miles.

My test run this morning did not go well—at all. I planned a three-mile jog to see how my body responded. I got my answer, but it was not the one I was hoping to discover. The first mile went well. My legs were stiff, but I was able to move and put one foot in front of the other. Unfortunately, that is as far as I got. Both legs locked up, so I immediately turned back around. The mile "walking" back was the most painful mile I had ever completed on my feet. I had to stop numerous times for breaks as I did everything I could not to lie down on the ground. I was not audibly crying, but the pain caused tears to flow continuously from my eyes. In a moment of trying to see humor in the situation, I told myself to drink lots of water when I made it back because I was losing so much water through my tears. It brought a short-lived smile to my face before I clenched my teeth again, determined to make it back to the condo.

After what seemed like an eternity, I made it back to the front door of the building. I could not move my legs another step because they were completely tightened and caused excruciating pain. I was forced to lie down and use my arms to carry me through the door and up the stairs to my sister's place. Finally, I dragged my body inside. My poor brother-in-law was home and had to watch me pull myself in on the floor. It was beyond discouraging and was certainly a humbling experience. The rest of the day was spent lying in bed . . . and in prayer for healing.

Here I am, nearly three thousand three hundred miles into my run. I cannot even manage to walk up a few stairs. I have never been more agitated in my life. I am at a loss for why I am paused here and have a difficult time thinking about it because of how much pain I am feeling. The biggest motivation for me is to read over the list of prayer requests I have not made it to yet. I will make it because I have to pray for them. It is hard to believe right now that I could make it a mile under my own power, and I have over four hundred remaining. However, I know the Lord has worked bigger miracles. I am going to bed tonight, praying for a small miracle of my own.

May 7—Day 108: Rest in Alexandria, Virginia, 3,277.7 Total Miles.

After yesterday's disaster, I was intent on finding a way to make some kind of progress. I spent the early morning looking at how many miles the Atlantic Ocean was from Alexandria. I desperately wanted to finish at my planned finish line off the coast of Long Island, but I figured making it to the Atlantic would be better than not at all. I thought about using crutches to make my way to the finish. My mind was certainly in full panic mode, and I spent most of the day trying to calm it down by playing with my niece and taking naps. I felt as though I had made it to the home stretch in a long race only to take a break with the finish line in sight. I was so excited to get done and would have pushed on if it was physically possible. Since it was not, I could only remain patient and have faith.

After moving almost continuously for three and a half months, sitting still for five days had me feeling very restless. I was so thankful that Dr. Beck at Capitol Rehab saw me again early this Saturday morning. The work he did on my legs was painful at the time, but I knew it could only help my situation. I was still tight in both of my legs, but they certainly felt better than when they were locked up the previous morning. I scheduled an appointment with a pain specialist group for Monday morning to discuss possible steroid injections. I knew I would need treatment after the run was complete, but for the moment, I was completely focused on making it to the finish line.

While I am still very tired, I did not sleep as much as I should have given the many hours of free time I had today. I seem to toss and turn, thinking about how I am going to make it the final stretch to New York. In the end, I can control certain factors of this problem and will leave the rest up to the Lord. It has worked for everything else on this run, and I have no doubt I will be taken care of again. I said a prayer of thanksgiving, grateful that this injury occurred while I was near family. I have enjoyed the chance to see them all and spend time with my niece. If I have learned anything these past few months, it is to take nothing for granted, so I intend to make the most of this opportunity while I am here. I have a feeling this attitude is going to help me sleep well tonight.

THE HOME STRETCH

And I am sure that He who began a good work in you will complete it.
Philippians 1:6

May 8—Day 109: Alexandria, Virginia-Washington DC 12.2 Miles. 3,289.9 Total Miles.

For the prior three months, I had put my trust in the Lord. My attitude with the injury while in Alexandria had not always been the best. My frustrations affected my mood and my thoughts. It was not until the previous night that I turned it over completely to God. Instead of thinking how I was going to fix the problem, I simply placed it in the Lord's hands—and what better place to set all of my problems! I did not believe it was a coincidence that I felt called to get up and go around 11:00 a.m. this morning. The feeling of restlessness had taken over. I believed I should gather my things and start moving.

Two days earlier, I was crawling up the stairs because my legs had completely shut down. This morning, I was heading out the door to walk the twelve miles into DC. While I wanted to run, I knew that my body needed to gradually get back into it. I headed out the door determined to make it into DC. I was nervous I would get locked up again. I prayed I would be okay as I took step after painful step. I did have to stop a few times to stretch when the pain in my legs returned. It was enough to make my eyes water about seven miles into the walk. I almost called for a ride back home but decided to push on until I could no longer move—I never got to that point.

I steadily made my way through familiar training grounds all the way to the Washington Monument. I had so many memories of the historic place from my years in the DC area. Making a new memory of such great magnitude revealed to me just how perfectly everything lined up to make the run possible. Despite the physical pain and mental exhaustion, I felt so blessed to be standing there in that moment. My sister called to say that she decided to come up to DC with my niece to join me. I was so excited when she pulled up with Val in her stroller. We walked the final couple miles together before I decided to call it a day. I was thankful for their company but was even happier for their support.

Tomorrow morning is my appointment with a pain specialist, and we are going to discuss the possibility of steroid injections to help with my injury. For whatever reason, I am not feeling nervous. The only feeling I have is a powerful sense of urgency to get going again. I am looking forward to hearing what they have to say about my problem. At the same time, I believe there is nothing that will keep me from finishing this run. I cannot believe how peaceful I feel now despite the turmoil in my body. I simply feel that the Lord is in control. Because of that, I have nothing to worry about.

May 9—Day 110: Washington DC-Ashton, Maryland, 18.5 Miles. 3,308.4 Total Miles.

I had a long day before I even hit the road at about four this afternoon. It started out with a doctor's appointment at a pain specialist before going somewhere else to get an MRI. I returned to the pain specialist's office early in the afternoon with the results of the MRI for a final diagnosis. The doctor I saw was very understanding of my situation from our first conversation early in the morning. He confirmed that I had a bulged disc in the lower part of my spine. The disc was pressing on a nerve, which caused pain to shoot all the way from my back down to my calves.

I was faced with the decision to have a steroid injection or to take some anti-inflammatory medicine along with a strong painkiller. The injection seemed like the option that would give me the best chance of having the issue clear up. However, I felt in my heart that the injection would not be necessary. The pain the past few days had been severe and even debilitating at times, but I felt a deep peace about moving forward. I prayed about the decision all day long. When I was faced with it, a big part of me really wanted to take the shot. However, I felt led to opt for the oral medication. There were countless people praying for me, and I trusted the Lord would answer those prayers.

After picking up the prescriptions, I loaded up my CamelBak and took the metro to where I ended the previous afternoon. It was about 4:00 p.m.

when I finally hit the road. Progress was slow as the heavy bag weighed me down during my trek. However, I was moving forward. When my body was cooperating, I would run. When it wasn't, I would walk. The only time I stopped was for traffic signals and to take a photo when I crossed into Maryland. Was it painful? Absolutely. But was I able to move? Yes. I accepted the pain and offered it up for the remaining intentions people had sent me. The road ahead was assuredly long, but there was no doubt in my mind God would carry me to its end.

I finally finished up the eighteen miles shortly before dark. My friend CD met me at the finish and bought me a large pizza. My appetite was still ravenous, and I polished it off as if it were an appetizer at one of those fancy restaurants where everything was served in tiny portions. I was especially happy to see a friendly face. We discussed all things running and rehashed all things that did not have to deal with running. CD was a great friend who I first fit for shoes over a year earlier. I never could have imagined he would be helping me out on an epic journey. I considered myself so blessed to be surrounded with wonderful friends like CD. It meant a great deal to me that he and all my friends and family supported me from the beginning. I could not wait to make them proud when I crossed the finish line in New York.

For now, I cannot wait to fall asleep as I will need my rest for the remaining miles. The way my body feels right now is just a small indication of something I know is true: the final four hundred miles are going to be an all-out battle. It is a good thing I feel ready to fight for every remaining step, which will no doubt be accomplished not so much by the movement of my feet as the movement of my lips in constant prayer.

May 10—Day 111: Ashton-Owings Mills, Maryland, 31.3 Miles. 3,339.7 Total Miles.

As difficult as it was to make progress, I was blessed to simply possess the ability to move forward. After the walk and run combination of the day before, I was pleasantly surprised by my body's ability to run as I hit the road in the morning. A part of that success was because of the lightening of my CamelBak. The weight really dragged on me before but was much more bearable on my route today. I carried only the absolute essentials, including my list of prayer intentions and my rosary ring.

While I still had intentions to pray for, it seemed I received more and more messages of support. I had many people tell me they were praying for me and doing things like lighting candles for me in front of a statue of our Blessed Mother. I found it so incredibly helpful. I was aware God was carrying me on the final section of the journey. It was the only explanation I had for why I was able to continue moving on after all the issues I experienced and the thousands of miles on my legs.

I quickly realized the blessings of my rest period while in Virginia. If not for the time off, I would have continued pushing my stroller. The roads were dangerous as they often had no shoulder. Running on the roads with a stroller would have been extremely treacherous. The shrubbery came right up to the edge of the road, and I often had to jump into the bushes at the last second to avoid the approaching traffic.

Right now, I am concerned about the soreness in my back and legs along with the blisters that are forming all over my feet. I have not had anything more than a tiny blister the entire way, but I think the added weight of the CamelBak is causing extra pressure against the sides and bottom of my feet. As long as things do not get any worse, I can see myself being able to make it to the finish by the end of next week. For now, I am too tired to worry about it. I will be going to sleep knowing that everything will work out because it is in the Lord's hands. As much pain as I am in, this thought will enable me to sleep in complete peace tonight.

May 11—Day 112: Owings Mills, Maryland-Hanover Junction, Pennsylvania, 42.3 Miles. 3,382 Total Miles.

After dealing with dangerous roads my first full day out of DC, I searched out a different route this morning. I discovered a trail I could pick up about twelve miles into the day, so I mapped out a new course and hit the road just after the sun came up. I was still sore and was still feeling very tired. However, I had the goal of getting in at least forty miles, so I did not want to waste any time.

It was absolutely remarkable how I was able to run at a steady pace right away. The miles did not go by quickly, but I felt strong mentally. The scenery was beautiful as I passed by many open green fields and horse farms. I still had to be careful of traffic on the road, but I kept telling myself how much easier it was to run and avoid cars as opposed to running with the stroller. After pushing myself for nearly two hours, I picked up the trail and continued heading north.

I remained steadfast in prayer during the morning hours for my personal intentions—for my family, loved ones who had passed away, a little girl with cancer, a woman whose husband abandoned her, the unborn, the souls in purgatory, and a little boy battling a life-threatening illness. So many of the intentions I received since starting my journey captured my heart. I added them to my daily list of prayers, which typically consumed the first couple hours each day. I wanted all those I prayed for to experience the peace and love that only the Lord could provide. I not only prayed for outcomes I wanted to see, but I also prayed that the Lord's will would be done. I trusted in his plans, and I had faith that no matter the outcome, he would be with us through it all.

Within a couple of miles of picking up the trail, I was joined by my friend CD. He was battling a leg injury of his own but ran through it anyway for six miles. Having him keep me company for those miles helped the time to go by much faster than it did when I ran alone. I was sad when he had to leave, but I continued pushing on because I still had well over twenty miles to run.

I was happy to be on a path that had a fair amount of shade because the weather was warm and the sun was intense. My legs were generally heavy and sore, but I continued to run as hard as I prayed. Before too long, I found myself approaching the Pennsylvania state line. It was so uplifting to cross into Pennsylvania. It meant I was getting very close not only to the finish but also to my home state of New Jersey, where I had a lot of support waiting for me. I became more excited to arrive there with each step.

A couple of miles after running out of Maryland, I met up with a TV crew. After an interview, they drove up to intersections where the path crossed a road to grab some more footage of me running. I turned it into a game to see how fast I could get to the next intersection. It was not the smartest thing to do, but it helped me run faster and made those few miles fly by! Just after they finished shooting footage of me, I ran past a place that sold gelato. I decided to tack on a small amount of distance to my run and made a U-turn. I did not regret it as the gelato was incredibly refreshing. I often took for granted the small things in life. Something as simple as a cold and tasty treat on a hot day used to be something I would not even bother to appreciate. However, I learned through my experiences to treasure even the smallest treats—and the smallest blessings in life.

My body was tired upon reaching the end of my long route, but my confidence was riding high. My hosts for the evening, Ash and Vrush, were friends of CD. They were so kind to me and invited me to partake in their dinner with a group of friends at their house. I really enjoyed all the company and the encouragement of everyone who came to dinner. I was so exhausted that I immediately forgot each person's name, but I promised I'd pray for all of them during my remaining miles.

It seems each new day brings with it not only challenges but also new blessings. I have met so many great people and have heard from even more who I will never meet in person. I have received so many kind words and assistance from a multitude of individuals. The best part about this is that I have seen Jesus through the words and actions of these wonderful and kind people. In all I set out to accomplish on this journey, I never imagined receiving such a beautiful gift. It has only strengthened my faith, and it makes me more determined than ever to reach the finish line for them. I originally thought that reaching the end would bring with it a gift of great personal satisfaction. That thought has been completely transformed. It is now about making the finish a gift to others. This gift is for those who helped me in one way or another, for those who believed in me from the start, for those who prayed for me, and for all those who I prayed for on this journey. My vision now is that finishing this run will give all those people the gift of hope and a stronger faith. I pray they will feel part of my accomplishment. I hope their faith will be strengthened by seeing the wondrous work of the Lord present in my run across this great country.

May 12—Day 113: Hanover Junction-Lancaster, Pennsylvania, 36.6 Miles. 3,418.6 Total Miles.

I woke up this morning excited to go deeper into Pennsylvania and was treated with a run on the bike path for the initial ten miles of my route. For the first time in a long while, the miles passed by fairly quickly. In seemingly no time at all, I was already a few miles down the trail.

Leaving the jogger behind was a great move. My injury was improving, running on roads was much easier, and I did not have to worry about flat tires any longer. The tough part was that running with the CamelBak had its own problems. I did not weigh my supplies because I had no intention of knowing how much weight was on my back. It felt manageable for about thirty minutes, but it became more burdensome the deeper I ran into the day. I believed the blisters on my feet were because of the extra weight because they only showed up when I switched to carrying supplies on my back. The problems of the pack were not limited to my feet. My shoulders burned, and it hurt to merely touch them. My back had a constant deep ache in it that did not go away even when I put the pack down to take a rest.

My body was in disarray, but I was still running with a smile on my face because I was excited to be making progress. The days of counting miles until the finish were behind me. When I ran today, I was down to counting footsteps. I just told myself that with each one, I was bringing myself that much closer to the finish. It almost seemed to be within grasp as I approached the end of my time in Pennsylvania. In many ways, I felt like I was in a pit of quicksand. With each step, I was sinking deeper and deeper. I had the sense I was near the end, but I was also nearly buried. With outstretched arms, I was grasping for something to hold on to and pull me out. I was in a constant state of prayer, hoping I could grab hold of something before I sank completely.

The description of the pit of quicksand accurately described the final miles of my run today. I fought for every step but kept moving forward in prayer until I finally reached my destination. After showering and treating my blisters as best as I could, I hobbled on over to dinner. It felt so good to sit down as I enjoyed three pizzas and a tasty beer.

I stayed up late tonight to give an interview over the phone and to review my route for tomorrow. It is beginning to feel more like a battle plan than a running route, but I look forward to taking it on nonetheless. During my run today, I thought how the physical weight on my back was an appropriate metaphor for life. It made me think of all the invisible burdens we all carry around every day that wear us down. Just like I survived the run today through prayers to the Lord, I believe we can make it through anything in this life if we lean on God. We do not have to carry our burdens alone.

May 13—Day 114: Lancaster-Morgantown, Pennsylvania, 25 Miles. 3,443.6 Total Miles.

I could not believe it was time to get my things together when my alarm rang this morning. My eyes were heavy, and my body ached as I packed my things and put on the CamelBak for yet another day. Starting to run felt much more like trying to ride a bike up a steep mountain. My legs and back fought me more than ever before, but I managed to get into a decent run by the time I hit the second mile of the day. The prayers were well underway by then as I went through my list of ever-growing daily intentions. Additionally, I had another request to pray for my own health and safety as I neared the conclusion of the journey. I was more than happy to offer up that intention. Another request was sent my way to pray for a young girl who recently went missing. It became very easy to forget my own troubles when praying for the girl and her family in an unimaginable situation.

I continued my run until about the fifteen-mile mark. At that point, I had passed through small towns and some rolling hills. It was nice being able to run on sidewalks and shoulders while looking at both the towns and the open countryside. However, my feet were in such pain that I was unable to walk. I limped over to a stone ledge just off the highway in front of a house. I felt bad sitting on someone's property, but I did not have a choice. While cars and semitrucks drove by, I took off my socks and popped my blisters one by one. The biggest problem was a blister a couple of inches in diameter on the ball of my left foot. I also had a long blister on the side of my left foot that dug into my shoe with every step.

My attitude took a plunge as I started to become frustrated, realizing I would be unable to reach my planned destination at my hampered pace. I put my socks back on and tried my best to smile, but there were clenched teeth behind the forced grin. My move to pop the blisters helped in that I was able to put weight on my feet once again, but it also allowed moisture to penetrate each one. The result was an intense stinging sensation that sent waves of pain through my body. I did the only I thing I could do—offer it up to the Lord for each prayer request I was praying for at the time. I found a motel ten miles down the road and did the sensible thing by stopping for the day.

Once I checked in, I was able to finally sit down. I was thrilled to get off my feet. I removed my shoes to inspect my feet. They were a mess, and my left sock was soaked in blood. I felt frustrated with ending the day early, but I felt better knowing that I clearly made the right decision to stop short. After bandaging my feet up and taking a shower, I ordered pizza for dinner. Pizza always made me feel better, and this time was no different.

It is early, but I am going to bed to catch up on some much needed sleep. I will need it as I plan to catch up on the miles tomorrow that I missed running today. The weather does not look to cooperate as it has rain in the outlook for every day in the ten-day forecast. I certainly hope my feet hold up and that the weather forecast is incorrect. However, I know that at this point it can rain on me all it wants. I plan on pushing through whatever I encounter in the next two hundred sixty miles to finish at this time next week. This run is much like life in that the pain and suffering is something we must confront, but faith makes it possible to understand and ultimately make it through to the other side. Nothing is going to keep me from the finish. I have too many people counting on me, and I know God is with me.

May 14—Day 115: Morgantown-Montgomeryville, Pennsylvania, 39.5 Miles. 3,483.1 Total Miles.

I set out this rainy morning with the goal of making up some of the miles I fell short on when I called it a day in Morgantown. I was thankful for the rare sensation of feeling well-rested. I tried not to focus on my torn up feet as I hit the pavement. At places where there was not a shoulder, I had to jump off to the side of the road and run in the wet grass. My feet and body held together for the first few miles. Once my feet eventually got wet, the problems returned. The blister on the bottom of my left foot was huge and centered where I put all of my weight down, causing a sharp pain with every step. I did not help my cause by calculating how many times I landed today on that foot alone, which I estimated to be thirty-five thousand steps.

I did everything I could to stay positive, but it was getting difficult to remain optimistic. Besides prayer, I thought the only thing pulling me forward was a slight gravitational pull of the finish. In the back of my mind, I hoped the final week would be more of a long victory lap. Instead, every mile was a prayerful battle. As difficult and frustrating as it was, I felt like I witnessed a miracle every time I completed another mile. My body constantly told me to quit. It threatened me with breaking down completely if I dared to continue. However, prayers for myself, my family, and a multitude of my brothers and sisters in Christ pushed me on.

The only excitement to pull me out of my personal struggle was an interview I gave to a local reporter at mile 22. It was perfect timing as it gave me a chance to vocalize why I was putting my body through the tremendously long miles—I was doing it for everyone who needed prayers. I felt mentally refreshed after the interview was over. The interview was one more chance to spread my mission of prayer. I knew there will be more opportunities to talk about prayer and making time in our lives for the Lord. As long as I continued moving along, I would have that chance to be an instrument of God's peace. I owed everything to the Lord and wanted to make sure I gave my all for him today. In that thought, I knew there was no way I could stop. I continued my painful steps forward. I prayed for strength and for my message to reach as many people as possible.

I am exhausted. My back and feet are in so much pain that the painkiller I am taking seems to be of no help. However, I am psyched to run into New Jersey tomorrow, where I will see friends of mine. I have also thrown out some more supplies from my CamelBak to make my back feel better. It occurred to me as I was tossing out food and clothing from the pack that it was a great metaphor for life: we need to detach ourselves from things of this world that weigh us down if we are going to reach our spiritual finish line. I have realized through this run that I need God more than anything else. I firmly believe it is only because of his wondrous grace that I will be able to reach the end of this journey.

May 15—Day 116: Montgomeryville, Pennsylvania-Princeton, New Jersey, 36.4 Miles, 3,519.5 Total Miles.

I did not think anyone could tell how tired or sore I was feeling just by looking at me this morning. I felt all of those things, but I had a huge smile on my face because today was the day I planned to enter New Jersey!

The day brought with it even more rain. My feet were still a disaster, and I had to pull off the road at one point because of them. The sharp, shooting pains were beyond tolerable because of the moisture getting into the large blister on my left foot. I changed the bandage and put on a dry sock about twelve miles into the day. It got wet again soon, but at least I was able to move again and hold a decent pace.

Many of the roads were narrow, but I stayed focused and avoided any close calls with traffic. My lips moved in prayers of thanksgiving today for delivering me past the three-thousand-five-hundred-mile mark and to the state line. Just before crossing into New Jersey, I stopped for about twenty minutes to down some awesome pizza and a cold beverage. I felt energized and took off again, excited to put Pennsylvania behind me for good!

I approached the bridge that would carry me across the Delaware River and into New Jersey. I remembered how just a couple of years earlier I had driven on the same road with my brother Dave. I told Dave that if I ever ended up running across the country, I wanted to run across that same bridge into Jersey. We talked about how awesome it would be to have the rest of the country behind me and to run over the Delaware River. I brought myself back to the present moment, about to do exactly what we had talked about a couple of years before. I never talked about something I did not seriously consider taking on, but to actually be at that point in the run felt very surreal. I grinned from ear to ear as I took pictures on the bridge at Washington Crossing. I finally put Pennsylvania behind me and took a few photos next to the New Jersey sign on the other side of the river.

Once I made it into my home state, I ran onto a road with a shoulder and continued my trek eastbound. My legs and back were in rough shape, but I continued pressing on as fast as I could, which I knew was not very quick. By the time I made it to the outskirts of Princeton, my legs could barely move and my feet were in severe pain. I was forced to limp for the final mile of the day. My spirits were still high as my friend Bob picked me up in Princeton as I called it a day.

Bob and his wife Debbie took great care of me. They had a cold Guinness ready for me and fed me very well. In addition to being a fellow Notre Dame alum, Bob was an Ironman and a fellow ultrarunner. I really enjoyed talking with him about my journey because he had an appreciation of the physical challenges that went along with the athletic pursuits. He was supportive of how far I had run and grilled me about all my experiences on the run. I felt pumped up just listening to the excitement in his voice.

I am still hobbling around, but I am beginning to feel an uncontrollable exhilaration building inside me as I am set to run to my hometown of Holmdel tomorrow! Despite the excitement I feel, I am confident that my exhaustion will ensure I sleep very well tonight.

May 16—Day 117: Princeton-Holmdel, New Jersey, 35.5 Miles. 3,555 Total Miles.

I found myself having a difficult time coming to reality this morning. It was hard to believe I was actually about to run to Holmdel, the town I grew up in as a kid. While I had directions written out, I hardly glanced at them because of how well I remembered the area. It brought a sense of great excitement and peace to be running on streets I knew so well.

One thing that made the day so much easier was that Bob drove the CamelBak over to my destination, so I did not have to worry about running with a heavy burden on my back. I immediately noticed the difference when Bob dropped me off. My pace was quick, and while my feet hurt, it was not the intense pain that showed up every time I put on the CamelBak. After I said goodbye to Bob, I took off past Princeton's campus, but not without some looks from students. Even though I was carrying nothing but a water bottle, my demeanor of weariness was easily noticed. I believed it was clear that I was not out for a short jog.

I brought my list of prayer intentions, which was short, but still powerful. I continued praying for those on my list as well as for those I passed each day. Among my new requests was a baby who was having surgery to remove a tumor and for a man who was looking for work. At that point in my journey, I really felt as if I was with each person I prayed for as I said the Our Father and each Hail Mary. It was almost as if time and space no longer applied. I felt as if I was in the midst of the people I was praying for at the time. I had never experienced anything quite like it but felt blessed to sense such a deep connection with each intention.

The running itself went very smooth as I continued to make my way closer to my destination. I only took a short break to give an interview and film some footage for a local television station. As excited as I was to talk about my mission of prayer, I was even more anxious to get going again. I made sure my route went past my mother's final resting place. As I neared her grave, I stopped and bought a small pot of flowers. I carried it with me and placed it in front of the stone that bore her name. In many ways, I still could not believe she was gone.

I sat on the ground and talked to her just like I used to when she was alive. I poured out my heart, and tears poured out right along with it. I told her about all the challenges and blessings that came with my journey. Most of all, I thanked her for the wonderful influence she had on my life and for the beautiful example she set for me. I never expressed to her just how much I looked up to her when she was alive, but I had the strong sense that she knew how much I admired and loved her. I wished in that moment more than anything that I could spend just a few more minutes with her. I wanted to tell her I that I loved her. I wanted to hear everything she would have to say to me in return. I knew I would see her again one day, but it did not make things any easier in that moment. With tears still in my eyes, I stood up, said goodbye, and hit the pavement for the final miles of the day.

The weather was not pleasant for most of the day, so I was psyched to finally reach my destination and get inside around 4:00 p.m. I was even more thrilled to be staying with my hosts for the night, Mr. and Mrs. Vignone. I ran with their son, Leo, in high school. Our families had been friends for a very long time. Mr. and Mrs. Vignone cooked me a fantastic meal and two more of my high school running teammates came over for dinner. It was so invigorating to see my friends again. It felt in many ways like we turned back time for a couple of hours.

My spirits are riding high after seeing so many friendly faces, and I am encouraged by their support. It is a wonderful thing my mental state is in a good place now because my body is a mess. I am limping around, and it seems impossible that I could possibly run one hundred fifty more miles in the next four days, being in such a state of disrepair. I know I am completely in the Lord's hands, and I have faith that he will carry me through all the way to the end.

May 17—Day 118: Holmdel-Newark, New Jersey, 36.9 Miles. 3,591.9 Total Miles.

I woke up around 4:00 a.m. to get ready for the day. A news crew was scheduled to shoot footage of my morning start. The weather was so nasty, and I assumed it was the reason the news van left shortly after it arrived. Craig and Paul also showed up early, but I knew I could count on them to stick around despite the weather conditions. We stood around in the garage for a few minutes waiting to start the day as my hosts wished me well. The rain started to come down a little harder, but my friends needed to get to work, and I needed to get done as soon as possible, so we began our run in the wet weather.

Running with Craig and Paul was so cool because it felt like we were back in high school. We talked and joked as if we were on one of the hundreds of training runs we had done together. A good benefit to this was that my mind was taken off all my aches and pains. While I was sure they felt like we were moving slowly, I was thrilled to be running consistently at eight minutes per mile. The only problem was that the rain became very steady, then it quickly became an absolute downpour. We were not yet a mile into the run when I realized that I could not get any more wet. As uncomfortable as it was, we were having fun splashing along the side of the road, and I was happy to have my two friends out there with me in the pouring rain.

As much as I wished they could have stayed longer, I was thrilled for the company. They veered off after four miles to head back and get ready for work. One of the biggest challenges of my journey was trying to cope with the extreme loneliness. Not only was it tough to run hundreds of miles on my own, but I also had to describe my experiences to others when I felt that words would not suffice. I was extremely thankful to have friends with me for the early miles. They definitely got a taste of what it was like to face the road in all kinds of weather conditions.

I thanked God for great friends and prayed for them as I continued onward. I also thanked him for sticking with me through everything on the run. Even though I could not see him, I knew He was with me. I could not ask for anything more in the course of my journey as well as in the course of my life.

I forced myself to move on at a decent pace through the miserable conditions. My feet occasionally stung badly, and I would pause briefly while taking a deep breath before continuing on my way. The highway was completely full of deep puddles, and I had to laugh when I got completely soaked from a truck that splashed through a large puddle. The tall wave of water landed a direct hit on me. I was sure anyone who saw it happen probably had a chuckle to themselves in the sense that they felt bad for me but could not contain their laughter. Since I was already drenched, I did not really mind and figured I might as well laugh along since there was nothing I could do about the situation.

Mercifully, the heavy rain turned into more of a drizzle after about five miles. The weather was still miserable, but at least I did not have to run through a downpour any longer. I thought back to all the times I drove on the highway I was running on. There were memories of meeting up with friends at fast food restaurants, going shopping at the grocery store, and running errands at the bank. It was so surreal passing those places on foot, about to finish a literal cross-country run.

I was so far into New Jersey that I could not go much further east and was finally heading north toward New York. As I crossed a tall bridge, I looked off to my right and could actually see the Atlantic Ocean! My body was telling me that I should save myself some miles and make my way over to the ocean. However, I made a commitment to finish at the southern coast of Long Island. That is exactly what I was going to do. I still had to get through New York City and see so many of my friends and supporters at the end. It was a huge landmark of the run, and there was no way I was going to pass on that opportunity after running so far already.

My feet continued to slosh though puddles one foot in front of the other all the way into Newark. I was soaked, in pain, and exhausted when I met my uncle and cousin at my finishing location. It was so great to see them in person, and we talked nonstop as they drove me back to their house. It felt so great to get a shower and put on dry clothes.

I ate so much pizza tonight and also met a reporter at a local ice cream place, which was chosen by no small accident! I am in such a good mood and loved seeing my aunt, uncle, and cousins. We caught up as much as we could before my body let me know it was time to call it a night. I am not looking forward to running in the rain yet again tomorrow, but I cannot express how excited I am to make it into New York City. For perhaps the first time on the entire run, I am just fine if the morning comes quickly!

May 18—Day 119: Newark, New Jersey-New York City, New York, 34.9 Miles. 3,626.8 Total Miles.

I slept very well at my aunt and uncle's house, but I felt an incredibly deep soreness throughout my body when my I was dropped off again in the morning. The weather was still cloudy with periods of rain. It was difficult making progress because of all the people on the streets. To make things more interesting, most of them were carrying large umbrellas. I did my best to weave in and out of them but turned my ankle on the curb when a woman stopped abruptly directly in front of me. I stepped to the side to avoid her, and my ankle turned hard. It immediately swelled up, and I was forced to walk on it for ten minutes. After realizing that I did not do it any serious harm, I decided to deal with the pain and continue running in the rain.

The weather and my new ankle problem did not make things easy, but I had firmly resolved to power through any obstacles I encountered. My mind was kept busy as I wound my way through the streets of northern New Jersey. I had to go the opposite way of traffic on ramps, run over bridges, and take shortcuts behind buildings. I finally made it to the west side of the George Washington Bridge where Mr. Barrett met up with me. He was so excited to see me, but I guaranteed him I was the one who was happier at that moment. We had lots to talk about because of our common interest in sports and our conversations about my experiences on the road. I called him Mr. Barrett because he was the father of my college roommate Brendan, who owned the running store on Long Island.

If I had the energy, I would have jumped for joy as I ran across the bridge that carried me into New York—my final state. I could not have been happier to share the experience with Mr. Barrett. I considered myself so blessed to have company for the huge milestone. Once we ran across the bridge, we picked up a trail on the west side of the city and continued running at a solid pace heading south. The weather momentarily improved as there was a break in the clouds, and the sun emerged for the first time in days. We took a brief rest to snack on some fruit before continuing our run into the city.

My body was dragging, but somehow we ran strong and weaved around people all the way into Times Square. I had the biggest smile on my face as we took some photos at the landmark. I remembered seeing a shot of Times Square on the news when I was in Arizona. I felt like I was dreaming, but it was no dream. I was actually in New York City! Mr. Barrett helped me celebrate by buying me some delicious New York pizza. He had to get back to Long Island, so we said our goodbyes as we parted ways at Penn Station. I ran the final miles to my hotel in a downpour, but I did not care.

After showering, I finally put on some dry clothes. I met my friends Dave and Anand for dinner, who were both friends and cross-country teammates from high school. They took great care of me as we went to a fantastic steakhouse for dinner. I ate so much at what was definitely the best meal I had eaten in the previous four months. As great as the food was, my night was made much more by the company. I loved being able to catch up with my friends and to step out of my routine for a night. I knew I was beyond blessed to have such great friends.

I cannot describe how excited I feel to be just seventy-five miles away from the finish. I am so blessed to be here, and I am giving God all the credit for allowing me to make it this far. There is still a lot of work to do over the next two days, but I am willing to put in whatever is required of me to complete those miles. I am looking forward to a good night of sleep. At this point, I have no problem allowing myself to start dreaming about the finish.

May 19—Day 120: New York City-West Babylon, New York, 41.6 Miles. 3,668.4 Total Miles.

I was so psyched to get started this morning because my route was going to take me out of New York City and into Long Island. I moved well through the fairly empty streets early in the morning. Just before I hit the Brooklyn Bridge, I stopped for a very tasty bagel and a glass of juice. It brought a smile to my face and energy to my body.

The backpack was feeling extraordinarily heavy today, but it was in large part because of how beat up my body felt. I paid no attention to it as I ran over the Brooklyn Bridge. It was a beautiful sight because of the foggy conditions. When I was planning the route over the bridge, it seemed like it would be such a cool experience. I was not disappointed. I spent many of the morning miles reminiscing on the run and everything that had transpired since I first decided to undertake my journey of faith.

It would have been nice to spend my day thinking over everything I had experienced on the run, but I needed to stay focused on both my run and my prayers. While I ran through Brooklyn, my prayers were said for a priest with cancer, a woman searching for a job, and two different women who were pregnant. I was reminded through these intentions that while my journey was coming to a conclusion, many others were in the midst of their own situations requiring prayer. It inspired me to remain steadfast in prayer through my final miles.

My left ankle was still in a lot of pain and quite swollen. The additional weight of the CamelBak did not help the situation. Fortunately, that situation improved when a friend of Sayville Running Company named Bill tracked me down and took a few items from me that I no longer needed. It helped out tremendously as I picked up the pace quite a bit with the lighter load. As if that were not enough, I was caught off guard when I heard my name from the side of the road. A fellow Notre Dame graduate, Brian, tracked me down via my GPS tracker. Brian told me he came out to run a few miles with me as I headed toward the finish. I was so psyched! We moved well on the side of the busy highway as we spoke for what seemed like five or six miles. We passed a sign for the beach, but I was not tempted in the least to change course and finish my run early. I had such a great excitement building inside of me. I could not wait to see my friends and family. I could not wait to finish what I had set out to accomplish.

Brian eventually turned back, but his company was so appreciated . Running with him helped my pace to shift into another gear. Shortly after he left, my host for the night met me at a gas station to see how I was holding up. I told Tommy I was doing fine and that I was good for running the final eight miles to his place. He kindly took my bag, which helped my pace speed up even more as I relished in being able to run without a weight on my back. I thought it was so cool how my load continually became lighter as I progressed throughout the day.

I finally made it to Tommy's house and enjoyed spending some time with his family. I also gave another interview over the phone and spoke with my family and friends. I could not wait to see many of them at the finish.

I cannot wait for tomorrow! My friends, my dad and his wife, and my brother and his wife will all be at the finish to see me complete the journey. As I am getting ready to go to bed tonight, my heart is beating out of my chest! For one of only a few times in the entire run, I am hoping that the night passes quickly so I can start running as soon as possible! One thing I have not lost sight of is the importance of prayer. It is how I got here. It is how I will finish tomorrow. It is how I am going to take the next steps in my life. I am intent on continuing my prayer life long after the run is complete. I hope to still have the opportunity to lift up the requests and needs of others in addition to my own. It is a powerful experience, and I feel so humbled to be involved in the prayer lives of so many people from all over the world. I hope they have experienced the same joy and peace that God has brought to my life through this journey.

May 20—Day 121: West Babylon-Smith Point, New York, 33.4 Miles. Final Total Mileage: 3,701.8 Miles.

I woke up this morning at 3:30 a.m. and could not go back to sleep because of the excitement pumping through my veins. Once the time closed in on sunrise, I got packed up in no time at all and laced up my twelfth pair shoes. They were in tough shape, but I knew they would hold up for the final miles. Tommy was kind enough to join me for the start, and we were running steadily at eight minutes per mile. The company was a huge boost, and I was so thankful for all of his help. He turned back after five miles, and I was left alone for the remaining distance to Sayville Running Company.

There were a few people scheduled to run the final eighteen miles from the store to the ocean. It hit me that I was on the last section where I would be running on my own. I prayed through all the adrenaline. After four months filled with intentions, I only had a few remaining miles to pray in solitude. I looked forward to continuing my prayers for others as it had become part of me. While I lifted up intentions for a few others today, I made sure to take the time to pray straight from my heart as well. Prayers of thanksgiving continued to rise up from my innermost spirit for the countless blessings I had received every step of the journey.

I spent a few minutes thinking about the phrase I had heard about walking with the Lord. Through my experience, I truly felt I had run with God over each one of the three thousand seven hundred miles. The run was amazing, but the true accomplishment was how much closer I felt to the Lord for everything I had gone through. I felt his presence in my life more than ever. It was a priceless gift and one that was certainly worth all the pain and suffering I experienced on the road.

My conversation with God was only interrupted a few times as a number of people stopped to congratulate me or to take a photo with me on the side of the road. It was such a great feeling to see the excitement on their faces. I was so honored they were happy because of my journey and the prayers I had offered. Witnessing the positive effects of my run brought an indescribable joy to my heart. I felt so inspired that I flew down the streets and arrived at the store an hour ahead of schedule.

During my run across America, I talked to Brendan many times over the phone. It was always nice to hear a friendly voice, but it did not compare to see his great excitement in person. He was bouncing off the walls and must have said the word "epic" about fifty times. I had also become great friends with the employees of the store over the years. They were as excited to see me as I was to see them. I gave a few interviews to some of the local media before stepping outside the store to face the final eighteen miles. We took some photos and then hit the road for the final stretch.

There were five of us running together toward the Atlantic. I loved running with my friends, especially at that point in my journey. To make things even better, Mr. Barrett and my brother Dave showed up on the road to finish with me as well. My dad, his wife Jennifer, Mrs. Barrett, and my sister-in-law Angela periodically stopped along the side of the road to cheer for our group as we ran by. I did not have words powerful enough to describe how amazing it was to be surrounded by such outstanding people. My sister had to stay in Virginia to take care of my niece, but I had no doubt that she and many others were following my GPS tracker online as I steadily closed in on the Atlantic.

I made the final turn south with just a few miles to go and ran past the three-thousand-seven-hundred-mile mark. If my body was tired, I did not notice. The endorphins were flowing freely at that point. We crossed a small bridge and veered into a parking lot. After running through an underpass, our group of seven emerged onto the sand and up a small hill. Upon reaching the summit, we started running down the sand on the beach toward the ocean. My dad and my friend Mike were holding the ends of a makeshift finish line. Raising my hands, I ran through the tape with a huge smile on my face. I immediately felt a rush of relief come upon me as if a burden was lifted off my shoulders.

I started my run touching the Pacific, so I continued running toward the water of the Atlantic after breaking the tape. As I did so, I could not help but take a look at the sand I was making footprints in. It made me think of the picture of footprints in the sand involved with the poem bearing the same name. The lesson of the poem was that the Lord carried us when we were unable to walk on our own. I momentarily felt overwhelmed because I knew the Lord had carried me through so many miles of the journey. Without God's help, there was no way I would have finished. I quickly high-fived my brother before I ran into the water.

I immediately took a knee and bowed my head in prayer. I thanked the Lord for giving me more than I deserved and for carrying me across America. I thought of my mom and felt certain she was watching proudly over me at that moment. After praying, I stood up and ran into the cold waters of the ocean. I dipped underneath the water before wading back to shore to see all of my supporters. It felt like a second baptism as I sensed a different man emerge from the shores of the Atlantic than the man who had left the Pacific four months earlier. I felt so much closer not only to God but also to those around me. My desire to do his will in my life was so much stronger because of my experience. My heart overflowed with joy.

I was handed a "3,700" sign to hold for some pictures once I made it out of the water. Holding that sign and standing at the shores of the Atlantic after such a long battle was beyond overwhelming. Memories from the journey flooded my mind, and I leaned over for a few moments. My emotions took over briefly as I allowed a few tears to pour out. I felt so much joy for making it through all the times I wanted to give up. Standing at the finish and looking back on the run made me realize that each painful mile was more than worth the effort in order to help bring the prayers of the world to the Lord. I knew completing the journey would have been impossible without the help of friends, strangers, family, and my faith. I could not describe how humbled I felt knowing that God stuck by me through the entire journey despite my mistakes in the past and my wavering attitude. I experienced a very real sense of God's love, perhaps more in that single moment than at any other time in my life.

I regained my composure and stood up wearing an ear-to-ear smile. Kevin, one of the guys who ran the final eighteen miles with me, offered up a prayer. I started the run in prayer and continued running in prayer, so it was only appropriate that the run ended in prayer as well.

It was so great having a group of supporters at the end. I told everyone at the finish that the run was all about helping others and pointing them—as well as myself—toward the Lord. I ran in prayer and relied on God for everything during the journey. I said that while the run was a success, I would consider my life a success if I could live it in the same manner as I did on the run.

My run has ended, but my goal is to live in the same way moving forward—as a light of the Lord and to help those around me. If I can do that, and inspire others to do the same, then I will consider that the greatest blessing to come out of my run. At first glance, this journey may appear to simply be a completion of a difficult physical challenge. However, it is much more than that. To me, it will always be a very blessed time in my life where I went running with God across America.

EPILOGUE

I am the vine; you are the branches. If you remain in me and I in you, you will bear much fruit; apart from me you can do nothing.

John 5:15

Even months after my run's completion, I often find myself reminiscing on some aspect of the journey. The reality has finally set in that I ran across America, but I know I did not do it alone. I was blessed with the support and prayers of those who followed my journey. I was inspired through the prayer requests I received. Above all, I was blessed by the many graces God so generously bestowed upon me.

I was worried about a letdown after completing such a monumental run. However, I have only experienced more joy in my life since its finish. I see the world through a new outlook on life. As opposed to before the run, I now make an effort to recognize all the wonderful blessings in my life. I am able to look at people with a greater sense of compassion. I try my best to understand others rather than judge them. I am far from perfect, but I am making an effort. If nothing else, this run changed me as a person. I believe that is a great place to start in changing the world.

The run itself was extremely difficult, so I do not miss the long miles. However, I do miss spending so much time in prayer each day. I experienced a deeper devotion to Mary because of my time in prayer. I strongly believe it was through the intercession of the Blessed Mother that I remained safe on my run. Mary helped draw me closer to Christ than I could ever experience on my own. While I can no longer spend seven hours a day in prayer, I do make time for him every day. It is my greatest hope that those around me see Christ in the way I live my life. I desire nothing more than to draw closer to Jesus and point others to him as well. While I am far from perfect, I know God will meet me wherever I am at and carry me the rest of the way.

Physically, I felt worn down for a long time. The journey was brutal, and my body took a beating. While I still run a little, my motivation to run is very low, and I am not sure if I will ever be at the same level of fitness again. My joy and passion for the sport is not lost but has simply been redirected toward life. I love helping others reach their goals. After the summer, I found work at a Catholic school. Eventually, I moved to Virginia to be near my family and to work in a running specialty store in addition to being a coach. I love hearing people's stories and it gives me great joy to help them in any way I can. Often, I find the best way to help them is through prayer.

Prayer is a wonderful thing. It enables us to connect with God. After this run, I am even more convinced of the power of prayer. I believe God wants a personal relationship with each one of us. He can perform wondrous works in our lives if we only let him in. There are so many difficulties and struggles in this life. If we make the time for God, then he will carry us through our tough times. I've learned that God's ways are so much better than our own ways. As I battle my own desires and disappointments, I pray daily for the wisdom to follow his call. I believe prayer helps us to place ourselves in God's will, and there is no better place to be.

I set out on my journey to help bring our world closer to God. I wanted people to trust in the Lord. While I prayed for healing, I often hoped in my heart that those I prayed for would develop a stronger relationship with the Lord. I wanted everyone to know the love, hope, and peace that only he could provide. I believe the world needs God more than anything. I think this is evident by the prayer requests I continue to receive, even though the run has ended.

While I did not follow up on the thousands of intentions I received, I did hear back from a few of the people who sent me requests. One person let me know that their child with cancer went into remission. Two couples who had trouble conceiving became pregnant—both gave birth to healthy baby boys. An elderly woman who was very sick returned to good health. The boy I sent one of my rosary rings to made amazing progress and is now doing great! A child who doctors believed would have brain damage turned out just fine. These were great to hear, but I also heard from people saying they started praying the rosary or that hearing of my journey reminded them to pray. I may never know the true effects of my run, but I do not need to. I know the journey brought me closer to the Lord, and I pray it did the same for others.

There were so many occasions on my run where I felt helpless. I also felt helpless many times in my personal life. The solution to both of these situations was the same: prayer. In both life and on my run, I did not know what I should do. I prayed that the Lord would give me strength and lead me to the right path. I continued to trust God and followed where I felt led. I believe I have followed the path I was meant to be on and because of it have been blessed in so many ways. I believe his plan for us is one we may not always be able to see or understand, but our lives are truly remarkable when we trust in God. He will be with us every step of our journey on the path to heaven. This is the only journey that truly matters.

Edwards Brothers Malloy
Thorofare, NJ USA
August 26, 2013